1982

DARYL G. MITTON
is an experienced corporate executive
and university professor
whose career spans more than thirty years.

BETTY LILLIGREN-MITTON
has built a reputation as
an effective coordinator
of educational, corporate, and community programs.

DARYL G. MITTON & BETTY LILLIGREN-MITTON

MANAGERIAL

TAKE ACTION, GET RESULTS, INFLUENCE PEOPLE & EVENTS

A SPECTRUM BOOK

PRENTICE-HALL, INC., *Englewood Cliffs, New Jersey 07632*

Library of Congress Cataloging in Publication Data

MITTON, DARYL G
   Managerial clout.

   (A Spectrum Book)
   Includes bibliographical references and index.
   1. Management. I. Lilligren-Mitton, Betty, joint
author. II. Title.
HD31.M53   658.4   80–11768
ISBN 0–13–549816–3
ISBN 0–13–549808–2 (pbk.)

Editorial/production supervision and
   interior design by Carol Smith
Cover design by Dean Morris
Manufacturing Buyer: Barbara A. Frick

A SPECTRUM BOOK

Printed in the United States of America

10 9 8 7 6 5 4 3 2 1

PRENTICE-HALL INTERNATIONAL, INC., *London*

PRENTICE-HALL OF AUSTRALIA PTY. LIMITED, *Sydney*

PRENTICE-HALL OF CANADA, LTD., *Toronto*

PRENTICE-HALL OF INDIA PRIVATE LIMITED, *New Delhi*

PRENTICE-HALL OF JAPAN, INC., *Tokyo*

PRENTICE-HALL OF SOUTHEAST ASIA PTE. LTD., *Singapore*

WHITEHALL BOOKS LIMITED, *Wellington, New Zealand*

CONTENTS

PREFACE

When you have CLOUT you can get things done. You can take action, get results, and look good in the process. You can take charge of your own life and influence other people and events.

You can have CLOUT if you want it—personally, socially, and professionally. This book shows you how.

It's a self-help book with a difference. Most such books are a little like *Playboy*—or *Playgirl*. They excite—but they don't really satisfy. Unlike such other books, the self-development program we offer here lives up to its promise. You can actually *do* what's suggested, not merely *wish* you could. You *can* change!

The program consists of ten stages or Rounds of a Bout for CLOUT. As you progress gradually from Round to Round you accumulate a broad repertoire of viable action skills to draw from in dealing with all kinds of peo-

ple and situations. Using the book as a guide and wherever you are now as a starting point, you begin to expand experience. Under your own direction and at your own speed, you initiate and carry out actions in the real world of your everyday living.

The first tasks are so easy that you can't help but succeed. This encourages you to continue—and to gradually increase the challenge of your experiential exercises. Because you always keep within the breadth and context of your past successful experiences, you continue to succeed. As you accumulate a succession of satisfying, real experiences, you build self-dependence, self-confidence, and self-esteem that improve your effectiveness in every area of your life.

You can choose to go the whole ten Rounds or stop any time. If you decide to go the distance, you'll learn how to gain and keep the advantage over top contenders in tough transactions wherever you encounter them.

But even though the program teaches you to be tough, you seldom have to act tough, and you never have to ride roughshod over others. At all levels the emphasis is on maintaining a climate of mutual respect in transactions. The aim of CLOUT is to accomplish goals of your choosing. The ultimate accomplishment is to do so with the willing cooperation or approval of those you deal with.

We know this program works. It works for women as well as for men; for students of management or managers at any level or with any degree of training or experience; for people in general who want to improve their personal, social, or professional impact.

The book developed from a method for training managers that originated in the classroom—both on the university campus and in industrial training sessions. Hundreds of people have been tested before and after our training and against control groups using conventional experiential classroom methods. The changes we predict have been verified statistically.

More convincing yet, we've seen people change dramatically before our eyes. They become more imaginative and mobile. They're more willing to initiate action and take charge. They're eager to do new and unique things. They enjoy a new, confident self-image. They report keen satisfactions in the actions they take and the results they get. The progression is virtually never-ending; as their skills increase they seek ever-increasing challenges and enjoy ever-greater success.

We believe this program can give you CLOUT. You can be a winner. From here on, it's up to you!

WHAT CLOUT'S ABOUT

A few years ago, in the motion picture *Hombre,* Paul Newman played a resourceful character who saved the stagecoach passengers and a large amount of money from enterprising, murderous bandits. In the midst of suffering the ordeal of rescue—and it was a prolonged ordeal—one of the women passengers questioned Newman, "Can you tell me why we keep trotting after you?"

Newman's reply was simple: "I can cut it, lady!"[1]

That's what CLOUT is all about. When you've got it, you can deliver. You can get things done, do them uniquely, and leave a subtle impression of unquestioned competence. You can shape people and events.

When you've got CLOUT you look good to others. They seek your attention, your presence, and your counsel. They yield to your influence and endorse your suggestions. They also see you as a formidable contender—and give you room.

When you've got CLOUT you have the edge in dealing with others, especially the prestigious, the bold and the clever. You can make and use contacts and connections to get results. You can reach your own greatest potential and also bring out the best in those around you. You can get what you want and make things go your way.

CLOUT AND THE FOUR C'S

Mastery like this is the product of the Four C's: *Competence, Commitment, Credibility,* and *Contribution.*

The *competence* has to be unique. It involves conceiving strategies that are unpredictable and unexpected; initiating action that gets results; employing resources and time to gain and keep the advantage.

The *commitment* has to be central. It must aim toward a comprehensive, long-range goal; motivate a driving devotion to cause; serve a need to achieve.

The *credibility* has to be total. It must reflect unquestioned integrity with those who count as well as with those who observe.

The *contribution* has to be significant. It must lead to determining outcome, influencing people, and controlling events.

WHAT *CLOUT* IS NOT

In contrast, CLOUT is *not* embodied in the consensus seeker who floats in a sea of agreeable but apathetic constituents—free of storms, perhaps, but with a low head of steam and no port.

Neither is CLOUT found in the consenting responder who relays directions from some perceived higher authority, whether that authority is an individual or social force. These kinds of people, who run the gamut from quiet milquetoast types to blustering authoritarians, are devoid of real personal strength.

Nor is CLOUT manifest in the person who derives authority exclusively from the many props which only give the illusion of leadership—emblems on the shoulders for military officers, carpets on the floor for executives, a whole hierarchical system of proper titles for pecking order in organizations. Such props conveniently tell others that they should behave as subordinates and will get their rewards for doing so. But as with crutches, the leader often can't stand alone when they're removed.

THE TEST OF *CLOUT*

The real test of CLOUT is being able to assume leadership over people who don't yet know that they're subordinate. The challenge is to take charge, keep power, and accomplish what you believe needs doing when the job is *not*

THE TEST OF CLOUT

"I don't understand . . . at the office when I say 'Jump!' they ask, 'How high?'"

assigned and when the resources and methods are not at all evident.

Those who have CLOUT know what needs to be done. They can muster and activate the necessary resources to do it. They can subordinate everything else to get results. They can rationalize or legitimize—and even popularize—the resulting actions. They can continually adapt to the realities of the situation. They can conceptualize and adjust ends, means, values, and circumstance. In short, people who have CLOUT can cut it!

If this sounds like a big order, don't despair. The unique personal and managerial development program that follows cuts it down to a size you can handle.

The kinds of things you do and how the training program works are explained in the next chapter.

OUTLINE
OF THE CLOUT LINE

Cutting it in any endeavor requires work—systematic training and conditioning—to make you better than those you go up against.

Training for CLOUT is not unlike training for prizefighting. Boxers train to put CLOUT in their punches. They hit the bags and spar with partners to put power in their fists and improve their timing. They skip rope and do roadwork to toughen their legs to launch their blows and to maneuver freely. They toughen their bodies to give and take and go the distance. They fight contenders to know the ropes and learn the tricks of the trade. They feint to distract attention and increase their opponents' vulnerability.

Managers—or anyone who wants to be a winner—need similar (though less physical) skills: strength, timing, maneuverability, toughness, even cunning. They need to condition themselves alone and with others, taking on a succession of increasingly tougher con-

tenders, to learn the skills they need and gain the insight and stamina to use their skills effectively.

A BOUT FOR *CLOUT*

Based on the analogy between boxing and managerial effectiveness—or success in any undertaking, for that matter—we labeled our development program "A Bout for CLOUT." It consists of ten Rounds which proceed incrementally from easier to more difficult.

The order is based on several generally accepted observations:

▶ The familiar is easier to handle than the unfamiliar.

▶ Trivia is easier to handle than matters of importance.

A BOUT FOR CLOUT

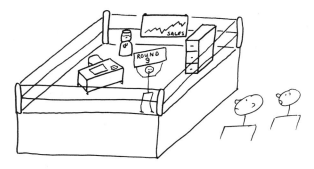

"The boss says it's the latest thing in managerial training."

● New ways of dealing with people are easier to handle when emotional involvement is low than when it is high.

● Interactions with one other person are easier to handle than those involving groups of two or more.

● Interactions with people we see as subordinates are easier to handle than those with people we see as prestigious or superior.

The suggested exercises or training Workouts within each Round are also arranged in order of increasing difficulty. Each Workout builds competence and confidence that prepare you to tackle the next, more difficult skills. Each Round provides you with skills you can use immediately as it also conditions you for the following, more difficult Round.

It's a learn-as-you-do and do-as-you-learn approach that works because of the following unique features:

● Your learning is enjoyable and easy.

● You learn and change gradually.

● You learn as a part of your everyday life.

● Your skills accumulate and last.

● You see immediately that action pays off.

● Your present abilities don't matter.

● You're the boss.

● You keep what you're doing to yourself.

● Your rewards are intrinsic, resulting from your own actions and internal satisfactions.

In the early Rounds you train in your non-work world. You build a personal maturity and dexterity that prepares you for whatever your social or professional demands are. For this reason anyone can benefit from the program, regardless of his or her personal or professional goals.

PREVIEW OF THE TEN ROUNDS

Following is a brief synopsis of each of the ten Rounds, along with a typical experience for each level of training.

ROUND 1: MANAGING SIMPLE CHANGE

The training program begins with exercises in breaking trivial personal routines and habits that affect only yourself. You can change your routines for getting up in the morning, going to bed, eating, traveling. You vary grooming, buying, and leisure patterns. These are simple, low-risk changes that make starting easy and virtually guarantee success.

They're obviously not the "high-priority" items that managers are usually taught to concentrate on. But these changes are not ends in themselves. They serve to show you, first of all, the extent to which trivial routines rule your life, sometimes literally making you a slave to habit.

Secondly, at the easiest possible level, you see that you can make things happen your way. You enjoy the feeling of being in control. And you find that you can live with the consequences of actions you've freely chosen.

Finally, mastering trivia conditions you for more difficult "encounters" later. Success, even though you're shadowboxing at this level, builds confidence and makes you want to try again.

The overall effect is to discover that you can discard your security blanket of sameness and live more comfortably with change.

Got up at eight on Sunday morning—an unheard of hour for me on weekends. Instead of sitting with the Sunday paper and coffee, I drove to the beach and took a long walk. Then I sat on a rock and just watched the surf and listened to it pound into the shore. Had brunch in a seaside restaurant. The food and service were great. I was apprehensive about eating alone at first, but I enjoyed it.

ROUND 2: MANAGING PERSONAL MOBILITY

In this Round you take habit breaking a step further. You explore your surroundings and observe the people and things around you. You go places that are new to *you*, to fill in gaps in your previous experience and to make more of the strange familiar.

You explore new geographic areas, including parks, residential, commercial, and industrial districts. You visit museums, libraries, churches, schools, auditoriums, depots, hotels, and hospitals, for example. You attend lectures, concerts, auctions, swap meets—whatever the community offers that's a new experience for you.

Again the purpose of the Workouts is twofold—to enrich your everyday life and to condition you for dealing directly with people in the Round that follows.

As you expand your physical horizon you see more and are seen more, even though you still avoid deliberately initiating contacts with people. You discover new interests and practice covertly expressing positive feelings about your surroundings. You see what works or doesn't work for others as you observe their interactions with each other. You become aware of alternatives and broaden your outlook. In short, you increase both your physical and intellectual mobility—and you have fun doing it.

Coming home from work I noticed the sky turning a bright pink-orange color. I cut off the freeway and looked for a high spot where I could watch the sunset. I found myself at the city dump. I could see all the way past the city buildings to the bay and the ocean beyond. I stayed and watched until the sun sank out of sight. I was awed and thrilled by the beauty. I felt amused by the irony—the city dump was the best place for me to find beauty at that moment! I think I enjoyed it more because of that.

ROUND 3: MANAGING SIMPLE SOCIAL RELATIONSHIPS (TRANSIENT STRANGERS)

Your first Workouts with other people take place in this Round in one-on-one contacts with transient strangers.

For our purposes, transient strangers are people you don't know and with whom you have only passing contact. They may actually be temporary "captives" of circumstance as they wait in lines or reception rooms or ride on public transportation.

You greet them and carry on conversations. You ask questions designed to get the answers you want. You search for commonality to cement a passing friendship. You practice making favorable comments to put others at ease and make them like you. Your practice ring includes stores and restaurants as well as all the new places you visit in continuing your mobility Workouts.

Dealing with people is more difficult than dealing merely with events as you did in the first two Rounds. The fact that your first personal encounters are with people you probably won't ever see again makes it easy to get started, because you don't need to worry about "what other people think." By choosing your partners carefully and planning out what you want to do in advance, you regulate risk and guarantee the greatest possible control over the interactions.

The emphasis is on understanding the social interaction process and getting along with strangers on your own terms rather than on trying to accomplish specific ends. The ability to manage contacts with strangers is a useful skill in itself, but the confidence and expertise you build up by succeeding here also prepare you for dealing with people you know.

While in Santa Barbara on business I stopped at a coffee shop for breakfast. It was surprisingly crowded and I was in a hurry. The hostess had nothing but large tables available, at which she was only seating parties of two or more. I had a sudden inspiration: I turned to a pleasant looking elderly man next to me who also was alone and asked him if he'd like to share a table. He agreed and the hostess seated us immediately.

After we introduced ourselves I asked him if he was from out of town. He said he had moved to Santa Barbara from Indiana when he retired two years ago. I told him my parents were from Indiana and asked him where he lived and what he used to do. It turned out to be a bigger coincidence than I expected. He was an engineering professor from Purdue at the same time my dad was a student there. We had a pleasant meal and conversation—mostly about Purdue. When I told my dad about it later, he said he remembered the prof well. He got a real kick out of hearing all about his alma mater and former professors.

ROUND 4: MANAGING SIMPLE SOCIAL RELATIONSHIPS (PEOPLE YOU KNOW)

In your second Round of managing one-on-one contacts with others, you work out with people you know—friends, relatives, and people you see regularly in personal business transactions.

The emphasis is still on improving the process of interaction, not on getting specific results as such.

You practice personalizing greetings and giving positive verbal strokes. You learn to listen for both facts and feelings and reflect back understanding. You try to make others understand how you feel without putting them off or putting them down.

Dealing with people you know is a bigger challenge than dealing with strangers. Not only is there more emotional involvement with them, but people who know you also have certain role expectations concerning you. They see you as friend or adversary, lover, brother, sister, parent, son or daughter, neighbor, or customer. More often than not it's harder to change such relationships than it is to start with a clean slate as you do in contacts with strangers. For this reason you design your workouts with people you know to *improve* relationships. Your attempts to be spontaneous, cordial, likable, credible, and energetic are the kind of positive changes which are most likely to succeed with people who know you.

The increased compatibility will improve the quality of life for everyone concerned, and the skills you learn will prepare you to achieve specific goals in the next Round.

To practice with someone who's really accepting of me I went to visit my parents. I hadn't seen them in several months. I gave my mom an extra big hug and kiss, my dad a handshake and a hug. When my wife went to help my mother get dinner, I asked my dad if he'd like to go for a walk. (We usually share joint silence watching TV.) As we walked I asked him about his work and listened with follow-up questions. He obviously enjoys his work and he enjoyed talking about it. I enjoyed listening and let it show.

Dad was more talkative at dinner than usual. I could see it pleased Mom that he was. When he left, he held my hand with both of his as we shook. I didn't recall his ever doing that before. I hugged him and brushed his cheek with mine—gave Mom a big goodbye hug and kiss. I knew they felt good about my visit. I felt terrific. As we drove off, my wife put her arm around mine and kissed my shoulder. This stuff is catching!

ROUND 5: MANAGING
THE BALANCE OF SOCIAL EXCHANGE
(GETTING YOUR FAIR SHARE)

Although you still try to keep relationships with others cordial, now you try to even the score in interactions.

Your Workouts make you gradually self-dependent and assertive. You make your wants known and try to get others to comply with your wishes. At the same time, you practice resisting or refusing requests from others. You contribute more to conversations, offer more suggestions, and make more decisions.

You begin to use the telephone to advantage.

You only push far enough to get what's rightfully yours. You change only those relationships where you feel that you're not getting your fair share of the respect, action, or winnings. If you have a good thing going, you leave it alone.

As you even the balance of social exchange, your self-esteem rises and your life becomes more satisfying. You also build the strengths you need for the tougher contacts ahead where you try to tip the scales in your favor.

My brother asked me if he could borrow some money. I usually give him a long speech about his making more than I do and that he should budget his money more carefully. I also always end up giving him whatever he needs even if it puts a nick in my own spending ability. This time I said, "Gee, Cad, I'm a little close myself this month so I can't afford to help you. If you do come up with any money, though, I could use some of what you still owe me from last month." Later that day he brought me twenty dollars he'd borrowed from our older sister.

ROUND 6: MANAGING
THE BALANCE OF SOCIAL EXCHANGE
(TESTING LIMITS)

In this Round you try to get more than your fair share of the action. You test how far you're willing to go to get what you want as well as how far others will let you go before putting up resistance.

You intrude on the rituals of others, break in on conversations, and try to take over. You delegate tasks to others, try to change other people's minds, and test the limits of propriety. You use the phone assertively and try to get special treatment and service in personal business transactions.

You learn firsthand that CLOUT implies results, not equity, and you find out how much mastery you can handle with comfort and pleasure. At the same time, by learning to impose on others in ways that leave them feeling good about the interaction, you discover that you can often satisfy the needs of others as you satisfy your own.

Even so, these Workouts with both strangers and people you know pose more potential risk to relationships than any you've tried previously. By designing tasks incrementally and choosing practice arenas carefully, you minimize the risk.

Finally, even if you decide that you can't handle being "more than equal" to others, you find that the Round helps you to avoid being imposed on by others.

My husband invariably watches TV on Sunday nights. This is after watching sports events all Sunday afternoon. Last Sunday I decided we'd do something different. I told him I'd made reservations at an Italian restaurant and told him I wanted to go bowling afterward. He bought it. He likes lasagne and bowling.

When we were returning the shoes after bowling, there was a backed-up crowd waiting to be served at the counter—no line, just people waiting patiently while the attendant sprayed shoes with disinfectant. I told my husband to bring the car around in front while I paid the bill. I knifed through the waiting people, plunked the shoes on the counter, called out my lane number, and said, "How much?" The attendant stopped and looked at me, then rang up the tag. I paid and left a whole crowd of people wondering what happened. But it did stir them to start asking for service. I was waiting at the door when my husband drove up. "How did you get out of there so fast?" he asked. "Pure feminine charm," I answered.

ROUND 7: MANAGING COMPLEX SOCIAL RELATIONSHIPS (DEALING WITH GROUPS)

Here you begin deliberately to deal with groups for the first time. You repeat many of the exercises you did earlier in your one-on-one contacts—now with two or more other people. In addition, you do Workouts that draw attention to yourself and make you feel more comfortable and confident in front of an "audience."

You join new groups as well as try to change roles and become more active in groups you're already a part of. You increase your attractiveness to the group through congeniality, participation, and contribution. You practice making alliances, influencing group decisions, delegating tasks to others, and working your way into positions of influence. You try to gain personal ends with group help. You start new groups of your own, including both social and special purpose groups.

The object is to learn to move in and about groups and organizations with ease and mobilize groups to your own ends.

The Workouts provide a wealth of off-the-job organizing experience in situations where the game is real but personal risk is low.

The high degree of comfort and confidence you gain serves you well in every area of your life at the same time that it prepares you to go for the big win in the next Round.

I was at the gym and realized that the combination of guys around was bound to lead to an impromptu basketball game. I called them all together and suggested it. Everyone was agreeable, so I went a step farther—I picked four guys and said, "OK, us [sic] five will take you other five guys on." Everyone went along with my decision. Then I announced to my team that I'd play guard and asked the others if they had a preference. Each one looked to me for approval as we quickly decided what positions everyone would play. I'd never done anything like this before, but I was able to maintain my role as coach for the entire game. Everyone seemed to accept my directions without question, and I thought we were better organized and played better as a team than groups like this usually do.

ROUND 8: MANAGING TOUGH TRANSACTIONS AND TERRITORIES

You take on the top contenders in this Round. The object is to win at whatever cost you're willing and able to pay.

At this point you have all the basic skills you need in your repertoire. From now on it's a matter of refining them through practice. By using what you've learned over and over again in many different situations with many different people you learn to spontaneously draw out and apply the skills and strategies you need to accomplish specific results.

Instead of backing off when you meet opposition as you did earlier, now you try to overcome others' resistance to get what *you* want. For that reason, learning to bargain and negotiate is an important part of this Round.

With your own ends in mind, you practice getting, withholding, and prudently dispensing information. You avoid dependence on friends and advisors and practice making independent decisions. You devise and practice ways of getting into inaccessible places to see prestigious or hard-to-reach people. You associate with adversaries and people you don't especially like to make them like *you* and to use their cooperation to gain your ends.

You learn to recognize devious behavior by adversaries and you discover whether or not you're willing to use such means yourself—to fight fire with fire.

As you become more aware of the "big picture" perspective you see the advantage of forgoing immediate satisfactions in favor of long-term gains.

Learning to "cut it" and enjoy your victory over top adversaries in tough territories gives you the CLOUT you need to apply your skills to on-the-job interactions next.

Two friends and I traveled to a nearby city to go to a nightclub. When we arrived we found that we had to be on a guest list to get in. I stood behind some people who were unsuccessfully arguing with the host. I was able to see the guest list and I found one name with the notation "three guests." We stepped back a few paces until the others had left. Then I walked up confidently and said, without hesitation, "McCormick plus two." As we were ushered in I remarked sincerely, "Glad to see you're doing such a good job of keeping the crashers out."

ROUND 9: MANAGING PROFESSIONAL CHALLENGE

You put all your learning together in this Round as you apply your skills on the job. Professional and career development become your primary goals. You use your talents to benefit both yourself and the organization.

You redo exercises from earlier Rounds in the work environment. This way you acclimate yourself to the new practice locale as well as accustom others to your new style.

Gradually you apply your new skills to matters of consequence. You seek a "big picture" perspective. You set career and job objectives and keep on track. You emphasize managing resources effectively as well as managing operations efficiently. You shape your job for effective and efficient use of time, energy, and talent. By extending your influence and control and by demonstrating your upward mobility, you also advance your career.

Learning how to use your skills effectively on the job prepares you to successfully meet all contenders and stay on top in the final Round.

I made the plunge this week. I quit my job and got another. I've thought a lot about my career lately, particularly as my skills and confidence have built through the program. I applied for a job in personnel at the headquarters of a large corporation. I know I should use contacts, but I didn't have any and I applied blind. They tested me and told me in preliminary interviews that I did well. I was set for a key interview later in the day. I decided to take matters into my own hands: I told the girl, "I'd rather not wait. I'm here and ready, and if he's here, I'd like to have the interview now." I got it. We hit it off well. He knew some of the people I worked with in my old job. When he got down to basics, he asked me what my three greatest strengths were. I was ready. I said, "I have four," and proceeded to elaborate, briefly, but with examples. The interview went uphill even from there. I knew I'd made an impression. While I was there he called my boss-to-be to recommend me. I really felt great when he said, "She's the most self-confident person for her age that I've ever seen." That was 5' 1" me he was talking about!

My second day on the job I had to call a woman in Atlanta. The people in the office warned me she was a bitch. I called her, told her my name, and said, "I've only been on the job here ten hours, so you're going to have to put up with me and what I don't know. I need your help. . . ." She was as cordial and helpful as could be. I've gotten off to a great start.

ROUND 10: MANAGING MASTERY

In the final Round you learn to keep your CLOUT. You apply your skills to boost your authority and add to your credibility.

Your strategy is to stay on the offensive—initiating change, adapting to the reality of changing conditions, and taking dramatic action to survive and stay ahead. You keep your strategy and intentions to yourself and manage reciprocation to your advantage. You attract and hold loyal followers. You strive for excellence, make creative contributions, and resolutely pursue your goals. You enjoy your mastery and the rewards it provides. You take satisfaction in seeing your ideas and accomplishments endure in your absence.

From here on you're on your own. You have the experience, competence, and confidence to get whatever you want. You can cut it!

I'm executive director of a small community service agency. I got wind that a new board member who was recently appointed to our Management Audit Committee was raising questions about some of my past practices. I haven't been doing anything out of line, but I felt it would be an annoyance to have to answer any charges. I got together with some of the board members of longer standing whose support I could count on and convinced them that we needed to revamp the committee structure. Then I arranged for the president of the board, who's also in my corner, to sponsor an incorporation of the audit duties into the executive committee. Subsequently he appointed the activist to a newly formed Auxiliary and Fund-Raising Committee where I think his energies will be better spent.

GOING ALL OUT
FOR CLOUT

What style contender will you be if you go the distance in the Bout for CLOUT?

Whatever your particular style, you'll be your own person. You'll know what you believe in and you'll have the strength of your convictions.

You'll know what you want and actively press toward accomplishing self-defined goals. You'll concentrate on what works—what gets the job done. You'll seek ends, not accolades or ego satisfactions.

You'll be confident, imaginative, decisive, commanding, energetic, and responsible. You'll do what you think needs doing, not merely accomplish what others ask. You'll try the unique and uncertain, not just stick with tried and predictable ways. You'll take command to get things your way, not always follow the suggestions of others.

You'll see the big picture, size up the situa-

tion, and shape it to your advantage. You'll see people as resources, not simply as friends or adversaries, and you'll assess their qualities in terms of how they can help or hurt you. You'll prefer to enlist their voluntary help and choose to treat all people with respect, but you'll also recognize the need to win. Thus you'll be quick to grasp opportunities and willing to take calculated risks. You'll adjust means to accomplish ends when you feel that your cause justifies it. The higher the stakes, the more committed you'll be to meeting your goals and the more effective you'll be in selling and defending your position.

You'll appraise people objectively, comparing them to one another instead of to yourself. You'll be more apt to accept people for what they are instead of moralizing, judging, blaming, and punishing. You'll enjoy competence, high self-esteem, and feelings of inner security

SEE THE BIG PICTURE

"I was trying to see the forest . . . I didn't see the tree."

which make it unnecessary to proclaim your superiority or cut others down to feed your own ego.

You'll cooperate, compromise, and give credit where credit is due.

Your power will stem from your personal strength instead of from the prestige of title or position, but it will enhance whatever formal or official authority you hold. You'll be more gentle with the powerless than you are with the powerful.

Your inner strengths and commitment to goals will help you manage your emotions. Fixing your attention firmly on your objectives will keep you from being pulled off target by the emotional static of the ongoing situation.

Your inner strengths will also help you tolerate ambiguity. You'll see the benefits of intentionally fostering doubt, keeping secrets, and clouding intent to gain advantage over others.

You'll be able to take impromptu action in the face of uncertainty as well as to structure unstructured situations so that those who have a need for certainty will accept your way of doing things without question.

Your actions will be self-directed, not externally determined by social pressure, authority, allegiance, rules, traditional standards of rightness, or a mystical belief in luck and fate. You'll care about what "other people think," but when you choose to comply with social and moral conventions it will be because they coincide with your own self-determined, experience-tested values.

You'll believe in the values you display, not merely defend the values you imitate. You'll live with the consequences you bring about, not blame others when things go wrong.

You won't scorn custom, but you'll be able to deviate from accepted behavior when it's the advantageous thing to do. Your competence in dealing with others will help you carry off your deviance so smoothly that it will often go unnoticed or unchallenged.

You'll be seen as attractive, judged as effective, preferred as a partner, chosen as a leader. You'll enjoy the thrill of victory far more often than you'll suffer the agony of defeat.

NOTTIMS:
KEYS TO CLOUT

You acquire a wide variety of action skills on the route to CLOUT. We call these skills *nottims.*

The name is our own. But credit for the idea goes to Frank Gilbreth, a pioneer industrial engineer who introduced scientific techniques into work and management routines in the early 1900s. His purpose was to increase the efficiency of labor by breaking jobs into their basic elements in order to understand the work better and to reconstruct work activity into a more effective sequence of movements. He labeled these basic work elements *Therbligs*—Gilbreth spelled backward.

In developing our training program we took a long and careful look at what managers do—because managers are "take-charge" people, whose job entails the ultimate in action demands. We broke the managerial job down into the basic behavioral skills required to carry off the total function with CLOUT. We labeled these basic managerial elements *nottims*—Mitton spelled backward. What's good enough for Gilbreth is good enough for us!*

These nottims are the keys to CLOUT. They open the doors to both personal and managerial effectiveness and excellence. There are, we discovered, a great many of them. In fact, when we pared our list of nottims to the core, we still came out with an awesome number of action skills and subskills. The reason is, of course, that the job of management is complex. Managers do a lot of things.

The complete list of nottims is presented in Appendix A for easy reference. We suggest that you skim it to get an overall picture of what CLOUT'S about.

*I gratefully acknowledge my wife's generosity in not insisting that they be called "nergillil-nottims"—DGM.

KEYS TO CLOUT

". . . and here's the key to the executive washroom."

You'll see that the nottims are divided into six basic categories. They concern the management of Appearance, Exposure, Attitudes and Perspectives, Circumstance, Action, and Transaction. In other words, people with CLOUT manage how they're seen; what they look at, who they see, and who sees them; how they look at things; how they plan, stage, and direct action; what they do; and the way they do it with and through people.

The Rounds don't necessarily deal with the nottims in this order. Instead, you take them up in a variety of combinations and sequences. This lets you master them in the realistic context of each level of training, starting with the easier skills and building gradually toward the more advanced ones. Not only do the nottims take on more meaning in this learn-as-you-do approach, but you also see them in better perspective.

DOUBTS ABOUT *CLOUT*

As you glance through the list of nottims, some of them may seem to contradict your current notions about the managerial job. Others may seem to contradict each other. This is to be expected, because effective managers use different skills in different situations. They need to own a large inventory of different, even opposite skills, to accomplish their goals. For example, there are times when it's important to *appear prestigious* in order to give an impression of power. There are other times when it's to your advantage to *appear ordinary* to gain the trust of someone whose help you need.

Similarly, managers often have to *seek information only and shun advice* in order to make independent decisions. Other times they *seek consensus* to gain the support of others in accomplishing a goal.

In other words, what skills managers use in any given situation depends on circumstance and the particular results they're after. Your personal experience in the program will show you how the skills are utilized selectively to handle any contingency as well as support the validity of the nottims.

ETHICAL DISSONANCE

Many people say they have mixed feelings after reading our description of the person with CLOUT or nottims like *clouding intent, breaking rules, subordinating friends to ends, ignoring the immediate consequences of actions affecting others to achieve "big picture" goals, and accepting what works as right.* Especially when they're viewed apart from the particular circumstances where managers use them, behaviors like these seem to go against some people's personal code of ethics. A few people even experience doubts about whether or not they really want CLOUT.

In this respect it's important to note that no nottims are included here arbitrarily or because we, personally, believe they're "right." They're included for one reason only:

because this is how effective managers and people with CLOUT operate.

OUR DECISION

We realize that we risk being accused of teaching people how to become scoundrels by listing behaviors that seem to disregard ethical standards which people generally support. We also wholeheartedly agree that the world already has more than enough scoundrels. We recognize, too, that we have no control over how people ultimately use the leadership skills they acquire in our training program. For these reasons we did some serious soul searching before proceeding with this book.

Finally we decided that even though keeping our program under wraps might possibly prevent a few unscrupulous people from gaining influence, *sharing* it would also teach many people of good will how to accomplish their goals. In fact, it seemed to us that scoundrels have a natural talent for getting what they want—they don't have to be taught.

Our decision was to try to even the score in favor of benevolence. We want to teach the "good" guys and gals how to win, too, so they *won't* always finish last.

It should be noted here that we don't advocate riding roughshod over others, nor do we believe that such behavior is necessary to win. On the contrary, the most successful leaders are those who can get others to *willingly* help them accomplish their goals, leaving those involved glad that they shared in the action. This is the kind of leader our program aims to produce. In fact, as you get into the Rounds you'll see that the Workouts promote respect and consideration for other people, not the use of force and disregard for feelings.

YOUR DECISION

Regardless of our intentions, whether you can accept the values and take the actions that bring about CLOUT is for you alone to decide.

THINKING OUT YOUR FEELINGS ABOUT *CLOUT*

Here are some things to consider as you contemplate your own doubts about CLOUT.

Practicing effective management requires continual examination and adjustment of ends, means, values, and circumstance. What you want to accomplish, how you will do it,

YOUR DECISION

KEEP OUT

the principles you believe in, and the conditions and resources available—these are the main variables in any situation you'll encounter.

All of these elements are mutually dependent on one another. Your challenge, as an effective manager or as a serious contender in any venture, is to modify or shape the various elements so that you achieve a harmonious blend of what circumstance permits with what you're both willing and able to do.

In examining circumstance you consider the raw situation as you find it: What are the available resources? Who and what will you include or exclude as you make your moves? Where and when will you arrange for the action and outcomes to take place? You evaluate the data you gather in light of both your ability and your sense of propriety in order to determine how you'll proceed.

Sometimes everything fits and all systems are go. Other times you face dilemmas that can be resolved only by modifying one or more of the variables involved. You can, for example, settle for lesser ends—or change your way of doing things—or alter some aspect of the total circumstance. Or you can stretch the limits of your ethical boundaries.

A "Good" Cause Justifies Deviation

At first glance, stretching ethical limits may seem unacceptable to you. Yet as a manager, you'll encounter situations where you have to choose between doing what's "right" to maintain your principles and proprieties—or what's "right" for accomplishing your goal.

You may believe, for example, that all men—*and* women—are created equal. Yet to manage effectively and get results, you have to act somewhat more than equal to those you deal with: you have to delegate, ask favors, and impose on people.

Or perhaps you believe in "absolute" truth. But you can see that beating a competitor to the punch or negotiating a deal to your advantage calls for bluffing and withholding information.

Actually, most people have the *ability* to tell a white lie or withhold the truth. And most people also are *willing* to do so under certain circumstances. Take these common fibs, for example:

No, I'm not hurt that you want to go without me. (Translation: I really am hurt, but I don't want you to know it.)

Yes, I think that scarf looks nice. (Translation: I don't really think it does, but I want you to like me.)

The self-punishing have no trouble lying in the first instance. The self-serving have no trouble lying in the second. In both cases it's easy to justify the "harmless fibs" because they make the other person feel better. But unconventional action choices that go beyond the white lie stage get much tougher and call for more sophisticated skills and greater justification. In this respect the buccaneerlike manager has a definite advantage over the strict moralist: It's easier for the buccaneer to act saintly than it is for the saint to act unprincipled.

Even so, if you can identify with the cause, you can often endorse behavior that might otherwise be considered unacceptable.

What Christian would argue, for example, that Jesus should not have defied some of the prevailing customs and laws of his times? Would there be a Christian religion if he hadn't?

Would the D-Day landings in Normandy during World War II have succeeded as well as they did if General Dwight D. Eisenhower hadn't authorized sending false signals to the enemy about the location and timing of the invasion? Was he "wrong" to cloud his intent?

Most would agree that the "good" ends in these cases—Christ's brotherhood of man and Eisenhower's victory in Europe—make the means seem almost incidental. Indeed,

[17]

they seem to be literal examples of the "all's fair in love and war" attitude.

Managers, especially, are frequently faced with hard choices between ends and means—between "propriety" and practicality.

Suppose, for instance, you value loyalty to friends. Can you fire a close friend who's doing substandard work? Can you live with the effect it has on your relationship if you fire your friend? Can you live with the consequences to the organization if you don't?

Or suppose you value obeying the law but you also pride yourself on keeping your word. Can you push plant capacity to meet a critical delivery deadline you've promised, knowing you'll exceed air emission standards for several days (and there's no way it will be detected!)? Can you slip the delivery knowing the financial hardship that it would cause your customer? Can you live with the effects of a broken promise?

Royal Little, the driving force behind Textron's expansion in the fifties, had to make hard choices in the process of building an impressive conglomerate. He started with the firm's textile activity as a base, but as his organization grew and prospered, textiles became one of the least attractive of the firm's activities. Yet the textile division was what had spawned the company's growth. Nevertheless, he abandoned it. In essence, he deemphasized old loyalties, allegiances, and conventions. He downplayed the traumatic effect on the people and the communities involved. He made these moves in accordance with what he saw as the best long-run interest of the firm, its survival, prosperity, and growth. In the long run more customers were serviced, more people were employed, more communities were involved, more investment opportunities were uncovered.

Little's "big picture" goals made him willing to take bold actions. His skills allowed him to do it successfully. Textron became a distinctly different firm because of him, and he carved out a unique and commanding style for himself in the process. In 1975, when *Fortune* magazine initiated its Hall of Fame of Business Leadership, Royal Little was one of only four living executives to be honored on the charter list of nineteen Americans.[1]

Success Determines "Rightness"

The *Fortune* list includes many individuals whose methods were controversial during the time in which they lived—John D. Rockefeller, J. P. Morgan, Andrew Carnegie, Henry Ford. In fact, the list suggests that historians are kinder to people who dare to be different than are their contemporaries. It's also a testimonial to the idea that if it works, it's right: Success, itself, *is* a determiner of rightness.

Actions Need Value "Endorsement"

None of the leaders above had doubts about CLOUT. They set a direction for themselves and pushed to get where they were going. They were characterized by strong skills and equally strong convictions.

In any circumstance where values play a significant role in determining action, the *will* to be different is as important as the ability to act. How you *feel* about stretching ethical boundaries is a deciding factor in how well you can carry off deviance. In fact, certain managerial behaviors are virtually impossible unless they're "endorsed" by compatible values.

Thus if you don't really *feel* a little more than equal to others, you'll be embarrassed to give orders. And your image, your relationship with subordinates, and the task at hand will all be jeopardized. Similarly, if you *feel* hesitant or guilty about clouding your intentions to gain the advantage in bargaining, you'll probably botch the deal.

On the other hand, if your particular set of values allows you to accept the necessary deviation and satisfy both conscience and reason—because your goal is so important or the

ACTION TESTS VALUES

"My big sister says kissing's fun . . . maybe we should try it."

deviation is so harmless, for example—then you can act appropriately and also feel good about yourself and what you've done.

When you achieve this kind of freedom and ability to act, you interpret the environment as opportunity-filled rather than restriction-laden. You perceive fewer "don'ts" and more "dos." You see choices instead of constraints. You feel less compelled to obey—to follow the past or other people.

You see policy, procedures, and rules as roadmaps, not as roadblocks. You can put friendships, loyalties, allegiances, and tradition into proper perspective with change, commitment, goals, results, and personal and institutional values.

FINDING OUT
IF YOU CAN HANDLE *CLOUT*

You need to know what you can do and what you really stand for—when it counts. You need to know how your values will affect your actions. You need to know if your values will allow you to act at all. You need to know early in the game whether you want to—or indeed can—keep your ethical "virginity" intact.

Taking action tests value limits. You have to really experience the heat of the kitchen before you know if you can stay in it—or have to get out. Values, in turn, set action limits. Only through doing can you find out how far you can go before your inner voice says, "Stop!"

As the developmental program unfolds you encounter many opportunities to test your values and strengthen your skills in low-risk, real-life circumstances.

If you find that you can live with the philosophy that's implied in the nottims, you have the potential for CLOUT in your personal, social, and professional life. If you discover that you can't accept the philosophy, you'll still profit from finding it out early so that you can adjust your personal and professional objectives accordingly.

HOW TO BEGIN
TO GET CLOUT IN

For the most part, the suggested Workouts in the ten Rounds are self-explanatory. When necessary in each Round, Training Tips are offered to help you get maximum benefit from the exercises at that level. In addition, the following ground rules, which are based on fundamental principles of the program, make sure that you get started right and continue to use the guidelines correctly.

DON'T SHOUT ABOUT *CLOUT*

Keep your participation in the program to yourself. Don't tell anyone what you're going to do, what you're doing, or what you've done.

The principle of Privacy isn't just a gimmick, it's a necessity. It helps you succeed because it keeps others from influencing your behavior and makes it easier for you to get results.

Privacy prevents self-serving others from deliberately thwarting your plans or putting down your accomplishments. It also keeps well-intentioned helpers from creating artificial successes that give you a false picture of your real abilities.

If others don't know what you're up to, they won't be watching you so closely. Without an "audience" you're less concerned about what other people think. You won't be tempted to overextend yourself simply to please the crowd, nor will you shy away from certain Workouts because you fear criticism or embarrassment. In other words, your motivation comes from within yourself. You're in control and you can do your own thing.

This means, of course, that you also accept full responsibility for the outcomes of your actions. If things go wrong, you can't alibi, "My friends did everything they could to stop me," or "I only did it because everybody expected me to." By the same token, when things

YOU KEEP WHAT YOU'RE DOING TO YOURSELF

". . . I just thought it would be fun."

go right you can take full credit for it. One important effect is that you're encouraged to depend on intrinsic satisfactions more than on external rewards, and your independence and self-reliance increase proportionately.

Privacy also gives you an advantage over others in making things go your way. Secrecy is a well-known ploy whenever competition is tough. Just as a good boxer tries not to telegraph his punches, so do managers try to catch others off guard so they'll offer less resistance to an intended action. By effective information management, you get results. The trick is to encourage others to freely reveal facts and feelings to you, but share your own information only on a "need to know" basis.

HOW TO KEEP A SECRET

The design of the Rounds helps you maintain Privacy because you begin with small changes in your everyday life that are easy to adjust to and affect other people very little. In addition, your first dealings with people you're close to are positive ones that are usually welcomed rather than questioned. Even so, it's wise to plan and mentally rehearse a few ways to keep intact both your secret and relationships you care about.

To begin with, simply *don't volunteer information* unless someone asks a direct question. When someone does ask, *give honest, general answers:*

I did it differently because I was getting in a rut.

I tried it because I wanted to see if I could handle it.

I've never done it before, and I thought it would be interesting.

Avoid evasive answers. Don't say things like "It's a secret" or "None of your business," which only heighten curiosity and offend others.

Don't lie. Lying is a way to escape consequences, which is contradictory to an important goal of the program—learning to be accountable for yourself and your actions.

Don't pass the buck. Don't say things like "I'm taking a self-improvement course, and I'm supposed to do new things." Not only would that blow your cover, but it's not entirely true. Because the program and everything in it are strictly voluntary, any Workout you do is by your own free choice and not because any outside force says you're "supposed to."

STICK TO THE GUIDELINES

No matter how capable you think you are, start with the Workouts in Round 1. Don't skip over any Rounds, and do the Workouts in the order given.

In this way you get a realistic picture of your own abilities. Seeing how you do, how others react, and how you react to what you've done shows you where you're already proficient and where you need improvement. This discourages self-analysis, which is often prejudiced or inaccurate, anyway.

Too often, the apparent ability to direct others is due more to the assumptions that go along with a title or position than to managerial skill: the title on the door, the carpet on the floor, the stars on the collar. This kind of symbolism surrounding the managerial job "announces" loudly, "I'm boss, you're subordinate"—"I say, you obey"—"You perform, I judge." Aids like these make it easy for managers to kid themselves about their true ability, as the following example shows:

Preston Boldly had been a manager for many years and currently directed more than thirty technically oriented people. He was anxious to get on with what he perceived as the "pushy" kinds of exercises that meant CLOUT *to him. So he bypassed the first couple of Rounds of training. As his first self-assigned task he almost condescendingly undertook to talk to an elderly couple strolling along a resort path. To his chagrin, he found that he couldn't even* start *a conversation with them, let alone control it. He was utterly crushed by the experience. In retrospect, he realized that he was too blunt and direct in his approach. By taking a typical superior-subordinate tack, he frightened the couple, and they, in turn, ganged up on him and resisted his intrusion. The episode convinced him to start over, lower and slower.*

On the other hand, many people underestimate their skill with people. But once the incremental design of the program gets them started, they literally sail through their exercises and thoroughly enjoy the contact and control.

Stan Aside, who'd always considered himself a wallflower in new social settings, attended a conference at the same time that he began the Workouts in Round 3. As he gradually worked into the "talking-to-strangers" exercises, he was amazed to find himself very socially adept. For the first time in his life he saw himself as a "popular" person whose company others sought. He saw a side of himself that he never knew existed—and he was delighted.

This kind of authentic feedback also shows you how your own actions pay off. You see that *you* can make it happen. This makes you believe in yourself and your ability to keep on making it happen. It's just the opposite from the usual "think-like-a-winner-and-you'll-be-a-winner" approach. Here you win *first*. That makes you think like a winner. And that helps you keep on winning.

The Rounds and Workouts are deliberately arranged in order of increasing difficulty to help you win your Bout for CLOUT.

You always start with the easiest possible tasks and gradually increase the difficulty of your exercises as your skills improve and your confidence rises. Yet you always stay within the limits of your ability to handle the experience successfully. If you make mistakes, they're small and easily correctible. Disappointment and embarrassment are similarly small and easy to handle. The overall result is that you accumulate a progression of successes.

As success raises your self-confidence and self-esteem, you begin to view action and change as exciting and satisfying instead of fearful and unpleasant. This encourages you to keep on taking action—and to enjoy even more success.

"Hadley never leaves anything to chance."

This unique use of the principle of Gradualism also helps other people adjust to changes in you.

Suppose, for example, that you're an easygoing, considerate, complaisant kind of person, always willing to go along with what others want. Suddenly you become more assertive and self-serving. Could your friends and associates who like the "old you" handle the radical change? If it damaged a relationship you care about, could *you* handle it? Making changes gradually gives the important others in your life a chance to get used to the new you and gives you time to find ways to save valued associations.

Gradualism also helps you adjust to changes in yourself. Making too big a change too soon, even if you carry it off, frequently leads to discomfort or regret. When you're not comfortable about a change, it doesn't usually stick. In fact, feeling uncomfortable may actually reinforce your resistance to the change and discourage you from trying again.

Sally Forth discovered this when she decided to kick the blue jeans habit cold turkey. When

GRADUALISM HELPS OTHERS ADJUST

she put on a dress one morning for the first time in over a year, she got a "funny" feeling. She went through with her plan, but all day she felt conspicuous and uncomfortably self-conscious. Even though nobody made any unfavorable remarks, she imagined people were looking at her critically. By the end of the day she felt so anxious that she could hardly wait to get home and change back into her security-blanket jeans. When she did, she breathed a sigh of relief and promised herself, "I certainly won't do that *again." And she didn't—not for a long time.*

Finally she tried a more gradual approach. She wore "dressier" pants occasionally. Next she put on a long dress now and then. Eventually when she tried a short dress again she carried it off with very little "emotional static."

Gradualism helps you enjoy winning, too. Paradoxical as it may seem, many people have mixed feelings about getting their own way. Unassertive people, especially, or those who are in the habit of giving in, have to learn to give priority to their own needs and desires without feeling guilty or regretful.

The experience of Gil T. DeMurrer is a case in point. Gil's job kept him on the road a lot. In between trips he would have preferred quiet evenings at home. After being home alone for weeks at a time, however, his wife preferred going out. So he usually gave in to her wishes. Finally, after a particularly tiring trip, he put his foot down and refused to go to a party with his wife. She said she understood and stayed home, too, but he could see that she was disappointed. Instead of enjoying his evening at home, he felt guilty about imposing his will on his wife, and he wished he'd gone to the party in the first place.

By using Gradualism you get used to getting your own way a little at a time. This makes you—and others, too—feel better about your victories, and it encourages you to continue asserting yourself.

SET YOUR OWN PACE

Take as much time as you need to master the particular nottims you're learning.

Since everyone has different needs and aptitudes at the start, everyone will need different amounts of time to complete the exercises. In general, stay with a particular Round until you feel somewhat comfortable and confident when doing the kinds of Workouts suggested.

Keep the intervals between Rounds brief. Once you start the training, keep going. Each Round conditions you for the next. To keep your momentum and assure success, avoid gaps of inactivity.

PRACTICE OFTEN

"We need to do this over and over and over . . ."

Work out continually. Once is *not* enough. Do each kind of Workout again and again, varying slightly what you do as well as where and with whom you do it. The more you do, the more competent and confident you become.

MAP OUT YOUR OWN MOVES

Design your own Workouts, being careful to follow the guidelines and the intent of each Round.

Plan tasks that fit your own needs—your individual life style, skill level, capacity for assimilating new experience, expectations, and goals. Even relatively simple tasks bring a real sense of satisfaction when you can say to yourself, "I did it all—it was my own idea, and I carried it off."

PSYCH OUT YOUR WORKOUTS

Mentally rehearse what you're going to do.

Make sure the task you plan is within your range of the ability at the time. Anticipate possible consequences: What will you say and do? What might others say and do? What will

you do in return if they do one thing or the other? See it through in your mind, from beginning to end, so you'll meet as few surprises as possible.

BE A FAIR JUDGE

Try to evaluate your performance objectively. Remember that trying is succeeding.

First ask yourself, "Did I do it, or didn't I?" Then ask, "How well did it go?" Positive outcomes are an added bonus, but if things don't go right, you still have the satisfaction of knowing that you tried.

Concentrate on remedies, not reprimands. Ask yourself, "What happened?" (*not* "Whose fault is it?"). Ask, "What went wrong?" (*not* "Why did I fail?"). Ask, "How can I improve my performance?" (*not* "Why can't I ever do anything right?").

Don't dwell on personal weaknesses or unfavorable results. See the experience in perspective: What were you trying to do? What circumstances were present? What did you do? How did it work? What did others do? How did it affect you? What can you do differently to make it happen more to your liking next time?

USE YOUR HEAD

Use good sense in planning and carrying out Workouts. Stay within the law. Don't endanger your health and safety or the health and safety of others. Don't take foolhardy chances.

Design your exercises so that *you* keep the upper hand. If you're not sure that you're willing and able to cope with the consequences, don't do it!

PUT IT IN WRITING

Keep a diary of your experiences.

Record what you've tried and how you feel

MENTALLY REHEARSE
WHAT YOU'RE GOING TO DO

about the results. Write your diary in any form you choose. The writing isn't as important as the thinking that goes into it. This rehash is a way of discussing your progress with yourself. It helps clarify your thoughts, reinforces learning, and puts your experiences into a perspective that helps you set new directions.

Your diary is for your private use only. Don't share it with anyone.

ROUND 1:

MANAGING
SIMPLE CHANGE

Your first bout for CLOUT is a preliminary Round. It gets you into the ring, firmly but gently, and prepares you to expand experience.

THE CHALLENGE

The challenge is threefold: to begin managing a bigger share of your life, to recognize and seek alternative ways of doing things, and to start feeling more comfortable with change.

THE STRATEGY

Your strategy employs Gradualism. You initiate changes that have little effect on your own immediate welfare and no particular significance in your relationships with others. You practice self-direction and choice by breaking the hold of self-imposed routines.

THE MOVES

Your first maneuver is to vary trivial personal routines and break insignificant habits. You change eating and sleeping habits; personal appearance, buying, travel, and leisure patterns; other personal routines.

WINNING THE ROUND

You know you've won big when you begin to make choices and do things differently; when you feel yourself actually enjoying change; when you realize you're making things happen your way; and when you feel eager to go on to bigger challenges. You don't lose the Round unless you fail to try.

WHY FIGHT ROUTINES

You take on trivial routines as your first "opponent" because they provide an easy, risk-free place to begin changing behavior. Furthermore, self-imposed routines often are unsuspected tyrants that hinder personal and professional progress more than you realize.

MAKING CHANGE EASY

Changing trivial personal routines lets you experience change with a minimum of discomfort to yourself and the least possible apprehension for others. The things you change are *personal*, so they concern and affect others very little, if at all. The changes you make are insignificant, so the risk of unpleasant consequences is virtually nonexistent. This makes it easy to try new things, while you still get a genuine feeling of initiating and managing change.

OVERCOMING ROUTINE TYRANNY

When you just let things happen *to* you instead of making things happen *for* you, you hinder your personal growth and progress. If habits control you more than you control them, your routines are tyrants just as certainly as if they were other people forcing you to do their will.

The first step toward effective management of others is self-management. In this Round you try to discover areas in your personal life

FEEL COMFORTABLE WITH CHANGE

"Caspar says you can get used to anything if you do it often enough."

where you have relinquished control, and you take steps to overcome the self-imposed tyranny of habit and routine.

Degrees of Addiction

Different people have different degrees of dependence on habit and routine. Quite often they don't even realize how dependent they are until the routine is interrupted, as in the following examples of slight dependence:

I don't care if all the forks are dirty, I can't eat pie with a spoon.

Something has to be done about that paper carrier. This is the third time this week the paper's been five minutes late.

Who put this roll of toilet paper on the spindle backwards? The paper's supposed to come out over the top, not from behind.

Still more dependent on habit are the kind of people who start to salivate like Pavlov's dog when the clock strikes twelve. Their co-workers say things like, "It must be Tuesday, Phyllis is wearing her red dress." Or they call the TV network and berate them for preempting an "I Love Lucy" rerun to show the astronauts landing on the moon.

Most serious of all are the "routine addicts" who've become overdependent on habit. They're hooked on the feeling of well-being that sameness creates. They gain a false sense of security and expertise from habit that keeps them from building genuine security and competence through accomplishment. They don't welcome new experience or try new things. They become rigid in thought as well as action. They have trouble innovating and improvising. If forced to vary their routines the littlest bit they become upset—even sick.

Joe and Jane Plain are like this. You can find them at six o'clock any Friday evening at the third table on the left in the New Shanghai

Restaurant. They ask for Nancy as their waitress. They don't have to order—she knows they always have the No. 5 special. They tip 15 percent to the penny and leave at exactly seven o'clock in a Plymouth they've driven for twelve years. Their previous car was a Plymouth, too.

They go to a movie once a month, if they can find a Western, which is the only kind of movie they like. They watch the eleven o'clock news on television every night, and on Saturday they make love from eleven-thirty to eleven-thirty-five, whether they need it or not.

Sameness rules every area of their lives. Jane washes clothes on Monday, irons on Tuesday, cleans on Saturday, and cooks a big Sunday dinner just like her mother did. Her neighbors say she's extremely self-righteous and critical. Joe gets to work half an hour early so he'll get the same parking space he's had for ten years. He always takes the stairs to and from the chemistry lab where he works. He resists innovations on the job. One time his supervisor assumed he was bored because he ran the same kind of test on crude oil every day, so he assigned him to test lube oils part of the time. Joe complained to the boss and got the assignment changed back.

A Safe and "Same" Escape from Change

Like other kinds of addicts, people who are hooked on routine don't see their dependence as a problem—they could change if they wanted to. But will they ever want to?

Probably not, because routine serves a definite purpose in their lives. It helps them avoid choices, decisions, and surprises. They escape the anxiety of not knowing exactly what will happen in a new situation, because they never allow themselves to face new situations. They avert self-blame and criticism from others for making "wrong" choices because they never waver from "proven" routine behavior. In short, sameness is the routine addicts' pleasant, comfortable security blanket. They're not likely to change unless they realize they're being smothered—cut off from life by a blanket of self-imposed routine.

WHY MANAGERS CAN'T AFFORD TO BE RUT-BOUND

The mandate of leadership is change. The viability of any enterprise or undertaking depends on its dynamics—its pattern of change and growth. The object of effective management is to create new conditions in order to maintain an advantage.

To have CLOUT managers must be able to initiate change and deal with the consequences of change—their own or that initiated elsewhere: Changes in strategies, policies, structures, procedures, technologies, and environmental factors; changes in personnel, resources, products, services, suppliers, users, and competitors. Clearly, effective managers can't afford to be rut-bound.

NOTTIMS THAT START YOUR BOUT FOR *CLOUT*

CLOUT means consciously guiding your own behavior instead of being driven by other people or restrictive routines. It means *making decisions, initiating action, finding alternatives, implementing change, getting results, accepting responsibility for outcomes,* and *living with consequences.* These are the nottims you start to learn in this Round, simply by kicking the "routine habit."

THE WORKOUTS

The Workouts offered here are suggestions to stimulate your imagination, not hard and fast assignments. Use them as guidelines to design your own "custom-tailored" tasks to fit your individual needs and circumstances.

Although it's useful to try something in every division of activity, it isn't absolutely necessary as long as certain standards of quan-

tity and quality are met in your Workouts: First, do lots of different things—or do lots of things differently. The more you do, the better you learn. Second, be sure your exercises meet the requirements of the Round: trivial, personal behavior that won't affect yourself or others significantly or meet with external resistance. Finally, make your exercises serve the purpose of the Round: to take charge of your behavior, become aware of alternatives, and begin to handle change.

Even if you feel you already manage change and routine satisfactorily, it's important to start the program at this simple level. Don't start analyzing your routines or weeding out certain habits and cultivating others at the start, either. Just start making changes. As you do the exercises you'll learn who has the upper hand, you or your routines. You'll also learn from experience which routines help you and which ones hinder your progress.

Change Eating Habits

▶ Eat out if you usually eat at home.

▶ Eat at home if you usually eat out.

▶ When you eat at home:
Try new foods.
Try different combinations of foods.
Prepare foods new ways.
Eat different amounts.
Eat more slowly.
Improve your table manners.
Eat your meal in a different order.
Try different times for eating.
Change where you sit at the table.
Eat in a different room or outside.
Vary your before- and after-meal rituals.

▶ When you eat out:
Sit in a different seat at your favorite table in your favorite restaurant.

Request a different table than usual.

Order something new.

Try a different restaurant.

Vary your choice of companions.

Dine after the movie instead of before, or vice versa.

Change Sleep and Rest Routines

- Go to bed, get up, and rest at different times.

- Give up something you do in excess (TV watching or partying) in favor of sleep.

- Trade sleep for physical exercise, reading, hobbies.

- Change your sleeping attire.

- Change the color or kind of your bed-clothes.

- Sleep on a different side of the bed.

- Get up on the "wrong" side of the bed.

- Move the bed to a different location.

- Change your pattern of getting ready for bed or getting up—your bedroom and bathroom rituals.

CHANGE SLEEP ROUTINES

- Shower at bedtime instead of first thing in the morning, or vice versa.

- Use a different kind of toothpaste or soap.

Change Travel and Transportation Patterns

- Take different routes when you go places.
  Try a new way home from work.
  Take the "scenic route" to go shopping.
  Take a different route to another city.
  Vary your route to other parts of a building or complex.

- Vary your mode of transportation.
  Take a bus, taxi, train, or airplane, if you never have.
  Use stairs, elevators, or escalators alternately.
  Ride a bicycle or go on foot.

- Change your style of walking.
  Pick up your pace if you usually saunter.
  Slow down if you usually rush.

- Change your driving habits.
  Join a carpool.
  Try riding as a passenger if you usually drive.
  Offer to drive if you usually ride.
  Park in a different place.
  Park different ways—parallel, diagonal, head-in, back-in.
  Go to a different station for gasoline or service.
  Take a different traffic lane than usual.
  Drive at a different speed.
  Turn off your car radio, or listen to a different station.

- Change your arrival and departure times.

Change Personal Appearance

- Try new styles and colors of clothing.

- Try new combinations of clothes and accessories.

- Alternate between casual and more formal attire.

- Change hair length, style, or color.

- Try different frames for your glasses or sunglasses.

- Wear more, less, or different jewelry.

- Wear your watch on the other wrist.

- Practice standing and sitting erect if you usually slouch.

- Try a more relaxed bearing if you're usually stiff and formal.

- Upgrade your grooming.
  Wash more often—hands, face, body, clothing.
  Change your deodorant (or start to use one).
  Manicure your nails.
  Clean, polish, or mend your shoes.
  Eliminate saggy socks and baggy hose.
  Coordinate colors and styles of clothing.

Change Buying Habits

- Vary your usual "route" through your usual store.

- Change the times you shop.

- Buy a new brand or a new product.

- Change where you buy groceries, gasoline, clothing, household furnishings, sporting goods—whatever you spend your money on.

- Go in or out a different door of your usual grocery store.

- Go to an "exclusive" shop.

- Try a discount store.

- Shop by mail.

- Have things delivered.

- Buy something expensive on impulse.

Change Leisure Patterns

- Play more if you usually work.

- Try new ways to enjoy old interests.
  Read different books, magazines, or newspapers.
  Read a section of the newspaper you don't usually read.
  Listen to classical music if you usually hear rock, or vice versa.
  Watch TV from a different chair.
  Watch different programs on TV.
  Watch a different team play your favorite game.
  Mentally coach the team you watch.
  Attend an athletic event you've never seen before.
  Participate in games and sports instead of watching.

- Try new entertainments and activities.
  Try new recreations or hobbies at home.
  Try new kinds of activities and new places of entertainment away from home.

- Go out more often if you usually stay home.

- Stay home more often if you usually go out.

Change Other Personal Habits

- Go without a watch, or start wearing one occasionally.

- Write more boldly or legibly.

[32]

- Rearrange the furniture in your room or change the accessories.

- Vary housekeeping and yard care routines.

- Grow a different kind of flower or vegetable.

- Firm up your handshake.

LEARNING THE ROPES

Here are some training tips to get you off to a successful start.

START SMALL

Don't change too much too fast. Small changes make it easier to get started and easier to succeed. In turn, they condition you for bigger things.

Go from french fries to baked potatoes before jumping from hot dogs to escargot. Try getting up fifteen minutes earlier on a work day before trying to get up three hours earlier on Sunday. Switch channels and give up a TV rerun you didn't like the first time you saw it, before flicking off the set "cold turkey."

In other words, plan your mission so that it's achievable. Be realistic and make changes you know you can manage. Gradually increase the difficulty or kinds of change as you see you can handle it without undue anxiety or discouragement.

TRY TO MAKE CHANGES FOR THE BETTER

In general, make constructive changes. Don't dwell on whether a change will help or hinder you. Use good sense and avoid doing unconstructive—especially destructive—kinds of things.

- Diet, instead of stuffing yourself.

- Eat more slowly, not faster.

- Smoke or drink less, not more.

- Show consideration to others, not rudeness.

- Be neat, not sloppy-looking.

In later Rounds you'll deliberately draw attention to yourself in order to stand being noticed and condition yourself for the unpopu-

START SMALL

lar kinds of actions managers sometimes have to take. For now, try not to shock or antagonize others.

DO THINGS THAT AFFECT OTHERS AS LITTLE AS POSSIBLE

Forcing or even expecting others to change is too advanced an exercise for Round 1. If what you want to do involves other people, think it through carefully. Consider how they might react and how you'll act in return. Anticipate your ability to deal with consequences or explain your behavior. If you aren't sure you can handle it, wait until later to try it.

Suppose someone else prepares your meals at home. Better not bring home the ingredients for a seven-course gourmet dinner when the cook had cold cuts and a tossed salad in mind. Instead, use your imagination to vary routines in ways others will accept. Offer to help in the kitchen or plan and prepare a meal. Clear the table or help wash the dishes.

Even when the changes are pleasant, those around you may question your motives (or sanity) if helping is out of character for you. Be prepared with a simple explanation: "I just want to show my appreciation for all the times you do it alone." Be ready to avoid feeling hurt if your offer is rejected: "I've got my own system and you'd only be a bother." Or be prepared to resist being defensive if the cook replies with sarcasm: "It's about time!"

You might think that making changes away from home is easier. Think them through just as carefully.

Suppose you decide to sit at a different table in a restaurant you go to regularly. What would you do if the host refused to seat you at the table you request? If changing your table means you'll have someone different serving you, can you handle the hurt or displeasure of your regular waiter or waitress? Would you feel you should explain your wanting to change? Could you? If you're not sure of your-self, wait until a later Round when you'll have skills to deal with unsatisfactory reactions from others. Meanwhile, do something easier: order a different food; or try your favorite food in a different restaurant.

DON'T TRY FOR ENDS TOO SOON

It's too soon to concentrate on achieving specific ends in this Round because you haven't yet learned new ways of dealing with that kind of undertaking. At this level of expertise your emphasis should be on the *experience* of change itself, not on the *results* of a particular change.

If you live with someone else and most of your activities involve other people, it's easy to slip into goal-oriented activity. The temptation to change *their* behavior is almost irresistible. *Resist it!* In this Round, concentrate on changing your own behavior only.

Go slow in making changes that involve others and predetermined ends. Trying too much too soon can backfire, causing discouragement and making you reluctant to try more changes.

That's what happened to Peter Eager when he decided to make some changes in his bedtime routines. Instead of flopping into bed after his wife retired and watching TV until he fell asleep as he usually did, he started to bed early one night. He did twenty-five sit-ups, showered, shaved, brushed his teeth, turned off the TV, got into bed nude on his wife's side, and waited—expecting his personal changes to lead to some interesting changes in his wife's behavior.

Meanwhile his wife didn't even notice what he was doing because she was busy cleaning the kitchen floor and baking pies for a dinner party the next day. When she finally went to bed, much later than usual, Peter was so sound asleep that he didn't even wake up when she rolled him over to his own side of the bed.

The next morning, to Peter's dismay, she re-marked, "You must have been pretty tired last night. You forgot to put on your pajamas and you fell asleep on my side of the bed."

Peter wisely decided not to tell her otherwise. In retrospect he decided things could have been worse. She might have come to bed on time and been shocked by all the sudden changes, laughed in his face, or claimed to have a head-ache.

As it turned out, Peter survived the disap-pointment. He might have avoided it entirely if he'd taken things one at a time and concen-trated on the changes themselves instead of on a predetermined goal. Who knows what pleasant "side effects" might have occurred naturally in time as a result of more gradual changes in his personal appearance and bou-doir behavior?

DON'T LET OTHERS
CALL YOUR SHOTS

Make a change because *you* want to. Just as you should avoid deliberately trying to influ-ence others, you should also avoid letting oth-ers' responses (or how you think or hope they'll respond) influence the kinds of changes you make.

Many of the things you do, even if they don't affect others directly, are bound to at least be noticed. Some of the changes you make will please others; some may cause dis-pleasure, arouse suspicions, or threaten the habit-bound security of others. If you go easy, you'll enjoy approval from others more often than you'll suffer criticism.

You must be careful, however, that you don't let your natural preference for approval instead of disapproval dictate your choice of exercises or determine when an experience has been "successful." When that happens, other people control your behavior as surely as if they issued direct orders. Approval makes you

feel you've succeeded. Disapproval makes you feel you've failed. As a result you end up doing what "they" want you to instead of taking charge of your own behavior.

Vera Amiable found this out when she decided to use a forthcoming anniversary date with her boyfriend as an opportunity to buy something "different" to wear. Hoping to please him, she bought a narrow skirt with a side slit like one he'd admired on a friend—instead of the full skirt she preferred herself.

When he arrived for the date he asked, "Is that what you're wearing?"

"Why, what's wrong with it?" she responded, her confidence shaken.

"Isn't the slit kind of high?" he asked.

"Well, you didn't seem to think so when Mary Minx was wearing one like it last week," she said, on the verge of tears.

"That was different," he explained lamely.

Nevertheless, she changed into another dress, whereupon her boyfriend commented, "Now that's better!"

It's no wonder Vera felt that her exercise in change was a complete failure. In a sense she suffered a double disappointment. Not only had she not bought the skirt *she* liked best, but her boyfriend wasn't pleased anyway when she bought the one she thought *he'd* like.

Furthermore, her boyfriend called the shots from the start. She bought the skirt for him. She took it off and put on a different one for him. His responses dictated the action as well as her feelings about the outcome.

How do you avoid Vera's predicament?

You begin with a change *you* like. At least you'll be sure of pleasing yourself. That also lends strength to your conviction so you can pay less attention to comments from others.

You don't invite opinion or judgment. To a question like "Are you going to wear that?"

you give an answer like "Yes, I like it," instead of "Why, what's wrong with it?" In that way you make it harder for someone else to volunteer a contrary point of view—and easier for yourself to carry out the change.

You deliberately substitute intrinsic satisfactions for external rewards in the form of approval from others. As a result your satisfaction comes from choosing a change, carrying it out, and, if necessary, at least "living through" the consequences.

In other words, you call the shots.

DON'T TRAIN ON THE JOB

In this Round and for several more to come you should confine your workouts to off-the-job situations and people.

This minimizes unnecessary risk to your career if you should goof. A blunder off the job isn't nearly as costly. It's only good sense to practice in low-risk circumstances until you learn to use your new tools proficiently.

Training off the job also gives you time to acquire a generous supply of nottims to successfully handle a variety of possible challenges. A little bit of know-how may actually prove to be a disadvantage if you try to use it on the job too soon. As with any real-life situation, your action causes a reaction and one thing leads to another. Until you have a repertoire of skills that enables you to manage the various responses and repercussions you may set in motion, it's best to avoid practicing on the job entirely.

Finally, the particular skills you're practicing in any given Round will not necessarily be the ones a current job situation calls for. Giving yourself time to develop a "big picture" viewpoint allows you to pinpoint needs and problems in the organization. Then you can choose the appropriate skills from your fully developed repertoire and apply them selectively and effectively to get results.

WHEN THINGS GO WRONG

Every now and then your Workouts won't work out the way you want them to. What should you do when that happens?

If you see that an exercise you've planned is going to fizzle, even if you're already into it, back off. If it's something that affects only you and you've kept your plans to yourself, nobody will be the wiser. Then go ahead with another similar activity or an easier one you know you can carry off.

When Sid Sack decided to cut down on his sleeping time, he tried setting the alarm for eight-fifteen instead of eight-thirty. But he turned it off, rolled over, and slept until eight-thirty anyway. The third time that happened he gave up. Instead he tried taking a short nap after dinner and stayed up later at night. He was able to carry that off with no difficulty.

Similarly, Lotta Sweets decided to try eating carrots, something she hadn't tasted since babyhood. After they were cooked, the smell of them turned her stomach and she couldn't bring herself to taste them. Determined to do what she said she would, she bought more carrots. But this time she cut them in strips and ate them raw.

When something doesn't work, don't indulge in self-blame. Just try something else. If the particular change you try doesn't stick—if you switch back to your previous behavior because you didn't like the change—don't worry about it. Trying and living through the change constitute success.

Finally, if you have an unsatisfactory experience that involves other people, don't blame them for your inability to carry it off. Like Peter Eager's wife in our earlier example, the others may not have the slightest idea what you're up to. This is as it should be if you've maintained your privacy. Don't shift the responsibility for your disappointment to others.

Just try something similar another time, using Gradualism more effectively to help others adjust to your change.

LIVE ACTION REPORTS

Got my hair cut shorter than usual. I decided I wanted it that way. Funny—I knew if anyone made a negative comment about it, it wasn't going to bother me.

Spent more money than usual on a present for my wife. It felt good.

Got up and went to an early high Mass for a change. I really enjoyed the choir singing in Latin.

Took a leisurely bubble bath instead of a quick shower before bed. Read a report in bed instead of watching TV.

Sat at my usual table in my favorite restaurant, but across the table from where I usually sit. I was surprised at the crummy view. My wife's been looking at the kitchen while I've been enjoying a view of the garden all these years.

When I woke up this morning it was raining. I turned off my radio and listened to the rain, instead. Listening to the rain intentionally made it sound pleasant—almost inviting.

Postponed dinner for an hour and a half. I found I could accomplish more in that period than I could in the same amount of time after dinner.

Turned off the news station on my car radio and listened to music instead. I found I was mentally practicing dance steps as I listened. A real bonus!

Decided to wear a dress to work. Got it out, but couldn't do it. Put it on after work and went shopping. It felt good to be dressed up. Wore it the next day to work. I'm glad I did. I'm going to wear dresses more often.

I rearranged the food on my plate. Putting the meat on the right side of my plate instead of the left side really bothered me—and I didn't think I was a victim of routine!

Turned off the freeway at the exit before my usual route and noticed the new building activity in the industrial park south of our plant. A lot of expansion that I didn't know about has taken place.

Instead of eating alone in the cafeteria on campus before class, I ate at a small restaurant off campus after class with another class member. Dinner tasted better than usual.

Parked my car in a different parking lot. You guessed it—at the end of the day, I went to the usual lot and wondered where my car was.

INSTANT REPLAY

In Round 1 you practice managing simple change by varying trivial personal routines that don't affect others.

The suggested Workouts are:

- Change eating habits.
- Change sleep and rest routines.
- Change travel and transportation patterns.
- Change personal appearance.
- Change buying habits.
- Change leisure patterns.
- Change other personal habits.

ROUND 2:
MANAGING PERSONAL MOBILITY

In Round 2 you start on a program of "Roadwork," and while you're out and about you "scout the field." Specifically, you actively seek new experience in the community and purposely watch other people and their interactions with each other. It's primarily a "noncontact" Round, however, because you try not to get personally involved with the people you observe.

THE CHALLENGE

The challenge of the Roadwork is to become physically mobile and begin to feel easier about moving around in new surroundings. The challenge of scouting is to look at people and things around you with greater perception and flexibility.

THE STRATEGY

Your strategy involves going new places and doing new things. You actively explore your surroundings. You try to see things differently; express feelings carefully; get an overall picture of what's happening around you; notice what works and what doesn't work for others.

THE MOVES

Your maneuvers include exploring new geographic areas; discovering different cultural, public, civic, educational, recreational, and spiritual activities; looking at commercial establishments; watching people.

WINNING THE ROUND

Your Roadwork is successful when you turn more of the strange and unknown into a familiar part of your life. Your scouting pays off when you can start to recognize resources, opportunities, and challenges in your surroundings instead of feeling vulnerable and insecure in new situations.

WHY DO ROADWORK

Roadwork for athletes is a way to get in shape for competition. Your "Roadwork" exercises in this Round serve a similar purpose. They start you on a path of physical and mental mobility that will make you a winner, both personally and professionally.

EXPANDING EXPERIENCE

To learn from experience you have to have some. To get it, you embark on a continuing, deliberate exploration of your surroundings in this Round. You look for new experience and you experience new ways of looking at familiar things. The immediate result is greater physical mobility—quite literally, an increased ability to move around freely. The ongoing effect is ever-increasing intellectual mobility—the ability to use all the information and resources at hand alertly and flexibly.

GROWING PERSONALLY

You have fun in your Roadwork exercises. You learn about a lot of things. You become more interested *in* others and more interesting *to* others. You see yourself and others in different perspective. Your self-management skills grow stronger. Your self-confidence and self-esteem improve because you're actually doing things instead of only wishing or thinking about it. The very fact that you're moving around makes you more action-minded.

Ann Lightend found that out when she went to two new shopping centers, a high school football game, a college campus, a park in an old section of town, and a "classy" hotel, all in a single weekend. "At first I even surprised myself by actually doing it," she reported. "Then I felt proud that I did. I realized that going somewhere new and really noticing the people made me see myself and others in a different light. And going places I've wanted to—but never got around to—was enjoyable and really didn't seem like extra work at all."

BEGINNING TO FEEL COMFORTABLE IN NEW SITUATIONS

The more you move around, the more comfortable you feel with "newness" wherever you

EXPAND EXPERIENCE

"Don't tell me . . . you've had another interesting new experience."

meet it. Each new experience you carry off well makes it easier to meet and manage the ones that follow. Self-assurance grows as you accumulate successes. Before long you virtually eliminate emotional static and begin to enjoy new experience.

Doug Diddalot was obviously pleased when that happened to him. "New experiences are getting to be old hat to me," he boasted. "I never realized I was missing out on so much, and it's starting to change my life already. I get to feeling at home in strange situations much sooner. I think it's because of my new priority on exploring and satisfying my curiosity. I get so interested in what's going on around me that I forget myself—I find myself following a kind of pattern when I go someplace new. I try to take in the whole scene first, and then I concentrate on particulars. I look at the buildings: architecture, interior design, arrangement of merchandise or displays, art work, colors, mood—heavy and sedate or informal and lighthearted. I look at the people: who works there, who goes there, how they're dressed, what they're talking about, what their mood is— somber, intense, cheerful. I look at how I feel about what's going on: how it's different from other experiences, places, and people; what I like about it; what I'd do differently if I were in charge. It's surprising—but reassuring, I have to admit—to find that so many different kinds of situations—from swap meets to operas—have so much in common. They all have their jargon and their rituals. It's fun finding out what they are. When I do I feel like an "instant insider."

HOW MOBILITY HELPS YOU MANAGE

The fluidity of mind and body that you develop in your Roadwork gives you an edge on the job and a boost in career advancement.

ADVANCING PROFESSIONALLY

"Be mobile" is the first thing we tell budding managers. The second thing is "If you can't be mobile, look like you are." The Workouts help you do both. You not only *see* more people and places as you move around, you're also seen *by* more people *in* more places. The first develops genuine mobility. The last gives you the appearance of mobility.

In either case, the advantage is that you'll be treated better by those in the organization who decide promotions and transfers. The fact that you're not restricted to what's familiar shows the willingness as well as the ability to take on broader as well as broadening managerial assignments.

In addition, if your superiors think you'll move out if you don't move up, they're more apt to move you up. If they don't move you up, you're still better off—because you have the mobility to voluntarily move on to an organization where your future is brighter.

ENCOUNTERING OPPORTUNITIES

Mobility puts you in the "right place at the right time."

Many famous people tell of "chance" encounters that led to important breaks professionally. Actually, successful people don't wait for good fortune to drop into their laps. They manage their mobility so they're likely to be where the action is. They're quick to recognize the breaks, size up the situation, make decisions, and take appropriate action.

Henry J. Kaiser, the industrialist, is a case in point. As a photographic supply salesman, he was walking down a street in Lake Placid, New York, when he happened upon a man named Brownell. After a very short conversation, they made a deal to become partners in Brownell's

*photographic supply store if Kaiser could dou-
ble the sales in a year. He tripled them, bought
Brownell out and expanded to three other stores
on the Atlantic coast. The business flourished,
and Kaiser enjoyed the first taste of the fruits
of entrepreneurship.*

*Fifteen years later he was in the construction
business in the northwestern United States. One
of his employees overheard two competitors discussing a road building job in Redding, California. When Kaiser learned of it, he responded
by going to Redding himself. He actually
jumped off the moving train at a slow-down
spot near Redding when he learned that the
train didn't stop there. He underbid the competition and won the contract for over half a million dollars—the biggest job they'd had up to
that time. Subsequently, his industrial empire
grew to include building dams, bridges, ships,
resorts and housing developments; manufacturing cement, steel, aluminum and even automobiles; pioneering a low cost health delivery system and building hospitals.*[1]

ACCUMULATING INFORMATION

Physical and intellectual mobility work hand
in hand to help you gather information and
ideas, identify resources, and bank data for
future use. What you don't know, you'll know
where to find—or at least know how to go
about looking for it—in your organization,
community, or area of expertise. From the
best lobster in town for a client who's a seafood fanatic to electrostatic precipitators for
separating colloidal chain suspensions to prevent reverse osmosis—you're more apt to have
the answer if you've been around.

BECOMING AWARE OF ALTERNATIVES

As you see new things you also see things
in new ways. You become more flexible, more
imaginative in your thinking. You establish
an ongoing option-seeking habit.

When you combine input from accumulated data with knowledge of alternatives, you
increase the ways you can go to get the results
you want, depending on your priorities at the
time.

Suppose, for example, a manager's production schedule calls for delivery of certain
parts to an out-of-town customer by rail. A
plant shutdown delays completion of the order. Late delivery will invoke a penalty
clause—besides causing costly delays in the
customer's organization and possibly resulting
in the cancellation of future orders from the
customer. In this case the alternatives may
seem obvious: ship the first finished parts by
a faster, though costlier means—truck express, air freight, or even by courier to meet
the deadline and keep the customer's business.

In other situations your alternatives might
concern sources of supply, manufacturing
methods, organization structure, recruiting
and training personnel. Whatever the problem, an overall attitude of mobility will help
you work smart, while the tunnel vision that
comes from immobility will keep you working
unnecessarily hard and long—often with disappointing results besides.

STAYING ON TOP OF YOUR JOB

As a manager, the ability to tour in and about
your jurisdiction is essential. You won't know
what's going on in your managerial territory
if you sit in self-imposed solitary confinement
in your office, never seeing the operations or
the people who perform them.

When you move around in the organization
you see what's going on; spot possible trouble
brewing; notice good performance and bad;
get ideas for improving methods and processes; have opportunities for brief personal

contacts with those you work for, those you work with, and those who work for you. By seeing more of the operation and establishing rapport with personnel, you facilitate the flow of information that allows you to stay on top of things.

Moving around to explore the broader range of your industry or field keeps you abreast of what's happening there, too. You become aware of trends, technologies, needs of customers, strategies of competitors, competence of suppliers, requirements of the community, and the thinking of your professional counterparts.

LEARNING TO THINK LOOSE

Mobility also nurtures discovery. An expanded world, actively observed, frees your thinking from the restrictions of familiarity and current acceptance. This often makes it possible to unite seemingly unrelated bits of information and come up with new conclusions.

Isaac Newton claimed that the concept of a universal force came to him when he saw an apple fall as he was sitting in a garden drinking tea. He was able to relate the characteristics of the very close falling apple to the characteristics of the very far "non-falling" moon. Combining what he knew about attraction of objects, their distance from one another and centrifugal force, he was able to formulate a law of gravity.

In somewhat the same manner, Edwin Land invented the Polaroid instant camera. When his young daughter asked him why she couldn't see the picture he took of her right away, he was challenged to find an answer. All of the information he used was known technology in optics, chemistry, mechanics and electronics. He was able to put it together in a way that paid off.

More recently, a young man named Frank Nasworthy made a revolutionary impact on the sports world by combining two ideas that were already in existence. He literally reinvented the wheel—for skateboards. Actually he took the idea of the polyurethane wheel, already in use on some roller skates, and redesigned it for the skateboard, which until then had used steel or clay wheels. The increased traction of the plastic wheel provided much more control and maneuverability for the skateboard rider. The invention repopularized and expanded the sport and gave rise to the phenomenon of the skateboard park.[2]

Thus creativity and uniqueness are often not so much coming up with something new as they are putting what's known into new combinations and relationships to answer questions and solve problems. Gathering information and identifying resources is the essential first step that makes this kind of intellectual mobility possible.

SEEING THE "BIG PICTURE"

Even when you don't deliberately set out to see the "big picture," you can hardly avoid it if you make curiosity and exploration a usual part of your life. The more you expand your horizons physically and intellectually, the more perspective you gain. You learn to view things in terms of their relative importance. Ultimately, in combination with the skills you'll acquire in successive Rounds, "big picture" perspective helps you do right things instead of merely doing things right; keeps your mind on objectives; lessens emotional distractions; enables you to resist instant gain and tolerate immediate inconvenience in favor of greater long-term satisfactions.

ACCUMULATING NOTTIMS

The specific nottims you begin to learn in this Round include *maintaining geographic mobil-*

ity, making exploring a habit, and *seeking new experiences and new places; maintaining intellectual mobility, making inquiry a habit,* and *seeking new information and perspectives; maintaining high visibility* and *drawing positive attention to self.*

WORKOUTS

Adapt the following suggestions to suit your needs and circumstances. Find more ideas from maps, guide books, TV and radio announcements, the Yellow Pages of the phone book.

Scout the Field

Explore your surroundings. Use all your senses—look, listen, smell, touch, even taste—to extend yourself beyond your present physical and intellectual boundaries.

Geographical Areas

Go to different sections of town—uptown, downtown, east side, west side, the "other side" of the freeway, Mortgage Gulch, Snob Hill.

Visit the inner city, suburbia, outlying towns, and nearby cities; open spaces; quiet places; noisy places; residential developments, model homes, buildings under construction.

Notice and compare roadways, landscapes, structures, and people in different areas.

If you travel out of town—look for landmarks, key streets; learn the history of the area; notice the ethnic makeup of the population, the main industries.

Cultural Centers and Events

Explore museums and galleries. Notice similarities and differences—in architecture, displays, decor, employees, visitors.

Attend theaters, concerts, and shows. Compare different art forms, performers, directors, choreography, stage settings, costumes, sound, lighting, stories, music, lyrics. Explore the physical facility before the performance and during intermission. "Overhear" conversations.

Community Facilities and Public Events

Go to parks, concourses, malls, community centers, information centers.

ACTIVELY EXPLORE
YOUR SURROUNDINGS

Visit botanical gardens, aviaries, aquariums, zoos, fish hatcheries.

Attend a council meeting, public hearing, political rally, election headquarters.

Visit a courthouse, courtroom; observe a trial.

Notice what kinds of services and activities take place in the facilities you visit.

Educational Facilities and Events

Visit different kinds of schools and facilities—preschools to college campuses.

Attend open houses, lectures, forums, exhibits, special entertainment.

Religious Facilities and Events

Visit churches, synagogues, cathedrals.

Attend services—worship, wedding, funeral.

Observe the people, the settings, and the procedures.

Notice sameness and difference.

Commercial Establishments and Industrial Districts

Go to establishments you've never been to in commercial areas you usually patronize.

Visit places you've never been—large shopping centers, small business strips, mom-and-pop operations, center-city stores, suburban vegetable stands, discount outlets, exclusive shops, swap meets or flea markets, ethnic food and merchandise outlets.

Browse in book stores, banks, stock brokerages, hospitals, hotels, convention facilities.

Tour industrial parks and wholesale areas.

Visit airports, bus and train depots, waterfronts. Notice both passenger and shipping activity and services.

Go to food-processing and packaging centers, bottling plants, and other companies that have tours for the public.

Notice what kinds of products and services are available; how courteous and efficient employees are; how you'd change things if you could.

Recreation and Entertainment Facilities and Events

Expand the habit breaking you started in Round 1. Go to new kinds of activities—games, races, tournaments, matches, discos, concerts, carnivals, arcades; shows—flower, fashion, pet, horse, home, hobby.

Visit places you're not familiar with—stadiums, arenas, amusement parks, fairgrounds, theaters, drive-ins, restaurants, convenience food establishments.

See what there is to do—from skydiving to frog jumping, arm wrestling to baton twirling, skeet shooting to shuffleboard. Notice how it's done and who does it.

TRAINING TIPS

Here are some suggestions to help you get the most out of your Roadwork.

Go solo. As much as possible, do your Roadwork alone. This helps you maintain privacy and gradually increases your self-depen-

TRY NEW RECREATION

"Skiing looked like a lot of fun on TV, so . . ."

dence, self-assurance, and self-direction. The ultimate goal is to be able to *choose* to have company instead of *need* to have support and security from the company of others.

Stretch out the things you already do alone. Expand personal routines—going to work or shopping—to include some exploring. Go to work a different way or shop in a different store. Gradually ease yourself into doing more and more things on your own.

Look for new things in old places. If you're apprehensive about going to unfamiliar places alone, start your Roadwork by exploring familiar locations for things you haven't noticed before: homes, businesses, landscaping, open spaces on the route you take to work; architecture, interior decorating, people in the hallways or elevators in the building or complex where you work; flowers, trees, animals, the personal appearance of others in the park where you jog.

Do easy, fun things. Start with interests you already enjoy when you begin to explore new places alone. Go to nearby, accessible places at first. Take part in guided activities like nature walks or bus tours; go back later by yourself and spend more time with things that interest you most.

Keep the upper hand. If you have to take along a friend, try to control the action. Make the plan clear ahead of time. *You* decide where, when, how, and how long.

Vary companions so you don't build a dependency on one person. Gradually try to break away and do some new things alone.

Use different modes of travel. Explore by car, bicycle, or on foot; go by land, water, or air. Things look different when you see them close up or far away, when you pass them quickly or can stop and linger awhile.

Do as much as you can. Don't try to do everything at once—but do *something* at once.

Explore, physically and mentally, in the course of your everyday activities. Use some of your leisure time for exploring. Work, sleep, or fool around less so you'll have more leisure time.

The more you do, the more you'll benefit. Just moving around more is good. Doing many different things is better. Making exploration a way of life is best.

Look Smart

Observe your surroundings carefully, alertly, and purposefully. Notice, perceive, and comprehend what's happening. Gather, process, and store the information and ideas you encounter. Fit the whole into your own frame of reference. (*Note:* While "look smart" doesn't mean "appear intelligent" in this context, it can't hurt.)

Look for Pleasing Things

Deliberately notice things in your surroundings that please you. Look for beauty, uniqueness, simplicity, elegance, newness, oldness, sparkle, humor—whatever you find enjoyable.

Don't pretend to like things you don't, but try to think of how you'd change them if you could instead of only criticizing:

Art Major saw a challenge in doing just that in this Round: "I must have gone past this one house on my way home from work hundreds of times. They have a big picture window in front, and right smack in the center of it is the back side of an upright piano. It pains me every time I see it because it ruins the appearance of the whole house.

"Today, for the first time, instead of being irritated, I tried to think about what I'd do differently if I lived there—besides selling the piano and learning to play a harmonica. My first choice would be to move the piano out about a foot and put a decorative folding screen just

[45]

its height between the piano and the window. You could also attach some kind of attractive cloth or paper to the back of the piano, or hang sheer curtains in the window. It was a lot more fun thinking about the changes I'd make than it was complaining about it like I used to. I felt like I'd been doing something constructive with my thoughts."

Start doing this kind of constructive thinking now, and continue to make it a habit. In any kind of problem, but especially when you're a manager dealing with employees and trying to get results, discovering what's right and what's wrong is only half of the solution. Finding alternative answers and telling employees what you want them to do about it is the other essential part of it.

Talk to Yourself

Say what you think and how you feel about what you observe—silently, to yourself. Try expressing positive feelings first. Start with phrases like "I enjoy . . ." or "I like. . . ." Finish with a factual reason to back up your feelings. Avoid using adjectives that express subjective judgments—words like *nice, beautiful,* and *good.*

I like that tree. It makes me feel good to see its leaves sparkling in the sun. (Not: That's a pretty tree.)

I enjoy that television commercial. It makes me laugh. (Not: That's a good commercial. It's so funny.)

TRAINING TIPS

Expressing your thoughts to yourself isn't just a gimmick. Nor are we advocating a Pollyanna, positive-thinking kind of approach to life. This is the important mental groundwork for a simple, effective way of communicating that you'll soon be learning to add to the ways you already use.

Start with positive feelings because they're the easiest for others to accept (when you *do* begin to say them out loud), even though they're often the hardest kind to express. "I like your tie" is certainly more acceptable to someone you're addressing than "I hate your tie."

Express your *feelings,* rather than an evaluative statement (positive or otherwise) because feelings are harder to contradict. "That's a beautiful painting" can easily be contested with "No it's not—it's ugly." But if you say, "I like that painting," it sounds ridiculous for someone to contradict, "No you don't—you hate it."

By stating your feelings instead of making evaluations you're less apt to trigger argument from others. As a leader anything you can do to get people to agree with you and follow your directions or help you achieve your goals is useful.

Expressing feelings this way also stretches your imagination and gets you in the habit of backing up your statements with observable facts. This is invaluable when you want to express contradictory feelings and opinions later on.

Find new words for feelings. Enlarge your vocabulary of words that express positive feelings. Try not to overdo "I like" or "I dig." Instead try "I enjoy, appreciate, prefer, admire, delight in, get a kick out of, welcome . . . ." Instead of "I feel mellow" try "I feel good, lighthearted, pleased, content, glad, ecstatic, cheerful, comfortable, delighted, relieved." Instead of "I'm happy" try "I'm charmed, in high spirits, satisfied, awed, enthusiastic, excited, fascinated." Listen to others or look in the dictionary for more suggestions.

Start with "I," express a feeling, and avoid evaluating. Fix this formula in your memory. Remember that merely starting with "I think" doesn't make what you say nonevaluative. "I think that's a pretty dress—I think blue looks good on her" means exactly the same thing as "That's a pretty dress—blue looks good on her." Using the feelings formula, you'd say, "I like that dress—the blue matches her eyes," or "I'm glad she wore blue tonight—it's my favorite color."

Watch People

Observe interactions between and among people.

Notice how they deal with each other—what works or doesn't work for them. Imagine what you might do if you were in a similar situation.

Here are some basic things to look for:

◆ Their degree of assurance:

Do they hesitate, hold back, ask permission, apologize, back away when challenged? Or do they press forward, state their needs clearly, ask for facts, and stand up to challenge? How do people act in familiar situations—positive, direct, commanding, self-assured? How do they act in strange circumstances—hesitant, indirect, apologetic, belligerent? Do they demand—or beg—or state what they want politely? In a restaurant, who demands, "Give me a cup of coffee"? Who begs, "Can I have a cup of coffee?" And who states matter of factly, "I'd like a cup of coffee, please"?

◆ Their self-image:

How do people seem to see themselves in relation to others—superior, inferior, equal? How does this vary in different situations or with different people? Is their power an inner strength or a function of their formal position?
Are some "Uncle Tom" to the boss and "Simon Legree" to their subordinates?

◆ Their regard for others:

Do they treat others with respect and consideration? Do they treat others like total human beings, or do they treat them like things? Do they stereotype people by a characteristic like sex, skin color, nationality, religion, physical appearance, social class, or occupation? Do they deal with others only in terms of their usefulness, ignoring personal worth? Notice how treating people like objects with stereotyped characteristics or functions dehumanizes relationships: individuals become "women," "Jews," "hippies," "foreigners," "secretaries," "waitresses," "clerks," "customers," "gas station attendants," "business contacts," "dates."

When a waitress is viewed in terms of her occupational function, for example, she becomes an order pad, a food deliverer, and a hand grabbing for money. In self-defense, the depersonalized waitress fights back in kind. She sees the "customer" as a mouth with a wallet appendage.

Notice what kind of results personal recognition brings as compared to treating people like things—in terms of the general climate of the interaction as well as the quality of the outcome—affecting:

◆ Their different roles:

How do different relationships affect people's behavior? Notice the "roles" people play—man-woman, wife-husband, boss-employee, girl-boy, woman-woman, man-man, parent-child, old-young, clerk-customer, policeman-citizen, and so on.

◆ Their interactions in groups:

Watch the behavior and relationships in informal gatherings like cocktail parties, theater intermissions, meeting breaks.

Notice how some "hold forth" and attract a following while some are ignored. How

some cut in and out of groups easily while others stay glued to one spot. Notice people's body language. Listen to what they say and how they say it.

▶ Their conduct in bargaining encounters:

Observe people bargaining—salesperson and customer in a used car lot; parent and child at a carnival; woman and man in a singles bar; friends in the neighborhood. How much aggression, intimidation, deceit, persistence is there? Who uses it? What's the reaction to it?

Observe people arguing—at home, in meetings, at work, at play. Notice what usually happens—charge and countercharge; everybody anxious to talk and nobody willing to listen; the inevitable switch from original issues to irrelevant matters and personalities. Notice the feelings, motives, efficiency, and effectiveness of those arguing both during and after the confrontation. Notice how seldom people are able to handle confrontation easily or successfully. Try to think what you might do differently.

Observe with a Particular End in Mind

Imagine that you have a particular purpose or end in mind as you do your Roadwork.

Mentally record things as you think a reporter would to cover a story. Get the facts; search for compassion, humor, causes; look for meaning in what's happening.

Seek "clues" the way a private eye on television does. "Search" the scene for details. Notice the clothes and accessories people wear; the bags, packages, or books they carry. Observe their bearing, composure, mood, degree of humility or self-importance, sense of humor or lack of it. Notice people's concern for time, perfection, appearance, their own welfare or that of others. Listen for names and other information that might explain relationships or connections. Mentally try to make something out of your clues. What's taking place?

[48]

Why? How do the various "characters" fit into the scene? Who has the most influence? Who has the least? Who are the "good guys?" Who are the "villains?"

Think of other "roles" you could "play" to gather information purposefully—artist, teacher, playwright, engineer, tour guide.

This Workout stretches your imagination, improves the accuracy of your observations, and increases your intellectual mobility. Also, even though your goals are make-believe, you get a taste of gathering information with a definite goal in mind—a skill that's essential for the manager who wants CLOUT.

Caution: Even though other people are an unavoidable part of most of your Workouts, *don't deliberately seek interactions with them in this Round.* In the Rounds that follow you'll be learning new ways to approach people. To get off on the right foot it's important to stick to our gradual guidelines. By not jumping the gun you're more likely to have satisfactory encounters with people when you do begin to deal with them later.

LIVE ACTION REPORTS

I visited a luxury hotel. I noticed that the "wealthier" guests treated the help like servants, expecting them to wait on them hand and foot. Women who were alone were extremely independent. Those with their husbands let the men take over.

I drove out of the city into the back country. It was warm but not hot. I turned the air conditioner off and opened the car window. The warm air felt good as it brushed past my face and arm. I stopped in a little town and went into the drugstore. They had an old-fashioned soda fountain. The smell of the store reminded me of the drugstore I knew as a child. I had a chocolate soda and got lost in daydreaming about my childhood.

Took my car to an automatic car wash. This doesn't sound like much, but to me it's significant because it's the first time I've ever done it. I always wash my car myself. I felt very apprehensive about it. I guess it was partly the unknown procedure, and partly because I wondered whether it would damage the car. I watched my car all the way through. I found the car got nice and clean. My worries were for nothing. I felt pleased with myself for trying something new. Next time I'll just go out front and sit down and wait instead of walking along and watching it go through.

Drove through the alleys around my neighborhood. Noticed the backyards weren't as neat as the fronts of the houses. Decided you can tell a lot about people by how they keep their front yards—but you can tell a lot more about them by what you see from the alley.

I spent several hours exploring an outlying community. Strangely, the people and their cars attracted my attention. People in dirty T-shirts and Levis riding in hotrods and pickups. Stopped cruising and went into a big discount store—part of the same chain as one where I trade in the city. On closer inspection I discovered the people weren't dirty—just casual. I'd have stereotyped them if I hadn't had a closer look. Their casual manner seemed to create a more congenial atmosphere in the store as compared to the one I normally trade in.

I saw an auction advertised in the Sunday paper. I'd never been to one, so I went. When the bidding started I almost got swept up in the action. I felt excited by the auctioneer's lingo. I got enthusiastic about the good deals he described. I felt the urge to bid on things I didn't need, they sounded like such great bargains. I managed to use restraint and only watch. I couldn't believe the hostility between some of the bidders. They'd angrily bid prices up way out of line, as if they were more inter-

ested in getting their own way than in getting a good deal. It was a perfect example of people satisfying egos instead of ends.

I was waiting while a clerk wrote up my purchase in a department store when a woman and a little girl came up. The woman looked at the clerk and asked in a very soft voice if there was a telephone she could use. The clerk didn't look up from what she was doing and didn't answer. The woman turned away in disgust, mumbling to her daughter, "Well, she's no help. Let's get out of here." I felt embarrassed by the incident, but I don't think the clerk even knew she was talking to her. I decided that if you want something from someone, it's a good idea to be sure you have their attention when you ask.

I went over to the practice field to watch the football team in their afternoon practice drills. I decided to try to "see" with all my senses.

The playing field looked bigger without players benches, people along the sidelines, or stadium seats hemming it in like they do at the games. I liked the open look—green grass, blue sky, lengthening shadows. I enjoyed the feeling of the cool breeze on my face.

I walked along the sidelines until I was even with a group running a scrimmage play. I noticed how dirty and grass-stained their uniforms were, and I could see sweat running down their faces and soaking their shirts. The guys look a lot bigger close up.

But it wasn't their appearance that impressed me most. I was almost shocked to hear the sounds of the players' bodies smacking together. The more expected sounds—the coaches barking instructions, whistles screeching, the players' shouts, grunts, and even their heavy breath—seemed muted in comparison. Suddenly football seemed a lot more violent than it appears on TV.

One play ended in a pileup at my feet. I could actually feel the players' body heat. I could smell dust and crushed grass, but the smell of sweat from the players was much stronger. I realized how much hard work and punishment goes into football. I gained a lot of respect for the coaches and the players.

I sat in the courtyard of the building where I work and watched the people around me as I ate lunch. I tried to guess what they did for a living by their appearance.

Toured an industrial area across town from our plant. From a side street I could see into one sheet-metal forming shop. I stopped to watch. The fellow nearest the door was thin—about fifty-five. He wore a black suit coat, gray slacks, and a white shirt buttoned at the neck. The coat and slacks were worn and dirty. He worked mechanically, but skillfully. When the buzzer sounded for a break he got his lunch pail and sat cross-legged on the pavement outside the building, drinking coffee. The other workers went across the alley to play horseshoes. He sat alone until the buzzer sounded again. Then he went back to work without a word to or from anyone. I wondered about his isolation. I tried to think how I'd deal differently with him than with the others if I managed the shop. I decided to notice what our own employees do on their breaks.

I'm Jewish. I'd never been in a church before. Went to an Easter service. Found it all very beautiful. I liked the singing and the flowers.

I watched the people during intermission at the opera. The "dressier" ones seemed to assume a position of superiority. Sophistication seemed to go with jewelry and fancy clothing.

Watched trash collectors—joking, laughing, and slinging that garbage onto the truck. They *seemed to know how to do the job easily and quickly. I was glad to see they found something to enjoy about their work.*

I was waiting for my order at a fast-food counter when I overheard this exchange between a red-faced waitress and a large, loud woman who came up to the counter to get a free refill of coffee.

"I thought the Super Burgers came with cheese."

"They do."

"I didn't get no cheese on mine."

"You ordered yours with sauce, only."

"I didn't want none of that other stuff besides the sauce, but I wanted cheese."

"When you said you only wanted sauce we thought you didn't want cheese, either."

"That's a stupid way to do it. I've been coming here for three years and I never had this happen before. What kind of a way is that to run a restaurant? I was a waitress for twenty-one years and I know that's not the way you should do it. The hamburger is all dried out, too. I only ate half of it. What am I supposed to do—I'm still hungry."

"All I can say is, next time be sure you tell us that you want only the sauce, but you want cheese, too."

What a great example of the wrong way to handle a situation! I was really uncomfortable listening to the abusive way the woman talked to the waitress. The other people standing around seemed to be embarrassed for the waitress, too. I couldn't help thinking how much abuse service personnel must have to take from customers as a part of their jobs. I made a few jokes and tried to be extra polite, myself.

INSTANT REPLAY

Your Roadwork in this Round takes you out into the community on an exploring expedition where you continue to develop self-mastery and increase control over your environment by going new places and seeing different things. Expanding experience helps you to become aware of alternatives, recognize resources, and practice flexibility in combining information and resources to get results. Observing people and interrelationships conditions you to deal directly with people in succeeding Rounds.

The suggested Workouts are:

◆ Scout the field. Explore:

geographical areas

cultural centers and events

community facilities and public events

educational facilities and events

religious facilities and events

commercial establishments and industrial districts

recreation and entertainment facilities and events.

◆ Look smart.

Look for pleasing things.

Talk to yourself.

◆ Watch people. Notice their:

degree of assurance

self-image

regard for others

different roles

interactions in groups

conduct in bargaining encounters.

◆ Observe with a particular end in mind.

ROUND 3:

MANAGING
SIMPLE SOCIAL RELATIONSHIPS
(TRANSIENT STRANGERS)

You take on your first "sparring partners" in Round 3. For the first time you intentionally initiate contacts with other people. You deal with transient strangers—people you don't know, with whom you have only brief, passing relationships.

THE CHALLENGE

The challenge of this Round is to begin to manage verbal interactions. You learn to approach strangers more easily; to increase spontaneity; to shape conversations and circumstance the way you want them to go; to leave others feeling good about the contact; to further develop your ability to make decisions, carry out plans, and take responsibility for consequences. The emphasis is on the *process* of social exchange rather than on tangible results of any kind. In other words, you're not

after anything from strangers except the experience of the contact.

THE STRATEGY

The strategy employs Gradualism. You purposely start with transient strangers because you'll probably never see them again, so what they might think of you doesn't matter enough to keep you from trying. At the same time, your contacts are brief, inconsequential, and positive, so other people aren't affected adversely.

THE MOVES

Your first moves are simply smiling or greeting people pleasantly as you pass them. Then you talk to waiting people—in lines, lobbies, bus stops; "captive audiences" on elevators, buses, or airplanes; personnel in commercial establishments you usually don't patronize—clerks, bartenders, receptionists, managers; other visitors in new places you explore.

You keep your contacts on a one-to-one basis as much as possible, even if other people are around. You practice ways of starting, maintaining, and ending brief conversations, reducing apprehension, asking questions, making positive comments.

WINNING THE ROUND

You'll know that your sparring exercises are doing some good when you start to be more spontaneous and feel more comfortable talking to people you don't know; when you find yourself getting the upper hand over emotional static that otherwise keeps you from concentrating on goals; when you begin to enjoy the sweet realization that you can influence the behavior of others.

WHY SPAR WITH
TRANSIENT STRANGERS

The sparring Workouts give you experience in greeting and talking to people. Specifically, they offer a few remedies for the familiar complaint, "I wouldn't know what to say."

A typical example of this often incapacitating concern was dramatized on the Mary Tyler Moore television show a few years ago. In one episode the make-believe newsroom staff learned that the real Walter Cronkite was going to visit his old buddy, Lou Grant, producer of the make-believe news program. Everyone was excited and awestruck. Although Ted Baxter, the egocentric, boorish anchorman of the news show wanted to meet Cronkite, he obviously felt apprehensive about the impending encounter. The ensuing dialogue went something like this:

"Gee, what can I say to him?" Ted queried.

"Why don't you just say 'hello'?" someone suggested.

"Yeah," replied Ted anxiously, "I'll say 'hello,' then he'll say 'hello,' and then it'll be my turn again."[1]

Needless to say, none of the newsroom staff said the "right" thing when the time came. Embarrassing silences were punctuated by inane remarks.

It was hilarious to watch them flounder the way so many of us have in similar real-life situations. Who hasn't felt at a loss for words at some time or another, especially when meeting prestigious people for the first time?

STRANGERS ARE EASIER

Although you may think at first glance that learning "what to say" would be easier with people you know, contacts with strangers actually offer several advantages.

First, you start with a clean slate, because strangers take you for what you are at the moment they meet you. They have no preset expectations, so you don't have to worry about living up or down to any previous pattern of behavior. As a result, you feel freer about trying new things.

Second, by practicing at first with strangers, you protect relationships that you care about—personal, social, family, or business—where saying the "wrong" thing could have an adverse effect. Like the producer who tries out a new musical off Broadway to get the kinks out of the performance before the New York critics review it, you build basic skills and self-confidence in low-risk situations where the effects on your reputation and your future are minimal.

Third, since you practice with many different strangers, the lasting impact on any one individual is practically nonexistent. At the same time you accumulate a great many satisfactory experiences that help you shape more important future relationships.

Fourth, the brief, passing contacts you have with strangers are easy to manage: You speak first; you choose the topic of conversation; you end the interchange on your own terms. You never get stuck with an unpleasant situation because the contacts virtually terminate themselves: You say "hi" and walk on by. Or you chat with someone waiting in the same line and one or the other of you gets served and you go on your separate ways, making it easy for you to keep the upper hand.

Finally, you don't have to worry about losing face because you don't know your sparring partners and you'll probably never see them again. Unlike Ted Baxter's situation in the newsroom, none of your friends or coworkers will see or hear you. If you goof, you don't need to worry that the word will get around. Those you see regularly won't know about or remember your embarrassment, so you won't relive it every time you see them. As a result, it's easier to initiate contacts and easier to correct mistakes. You merely assess what went wrong, make a few adjustments, try again with a different stranger in a different situation—and set a successful experience instead of an unsatisfactory one in your memory.

TO BEGIN TO ACQUIRE "PEOPLE SKILLS"

Your Workouts in this Round introduce you to the first of a series of mastery-of-people skills which you'll acquire in the program. The nottims you practice are *increasing visibility and exposure, managing appearance, drawing positive attention to self, seeking new contacts and experience, moving in and about people easily, meeting and talking to new people with ease, building quick rapport and friendships, making and using contacts and connections, setting a positive climate for relationships,* *making others feel good, getting desired responses from others, shaping circumstance to accomplish own ends, terminating conversations easily and gracefully, enjoying the action.*

Here are some ways that the sparring Workouts help you acquire skills like these and how the skills contribute to your personal development and prepare you for bigger challenges.

Getting the Greeting Habit

Your beginning exercises get you in the habit of greeting people. Getting started is often the hardest part of talking to people you don't know. But the more you greet people, the easier it becomes. And once you can handle the "hellos" without the interference of emotional static, you can turn your attention to ways of maintaining and terminating conversations successfully.

Since people like to be recognized, you also make others feel good when you say "hello." As a result of the positive attention you draw to yourself in this way, others form a favorable opinion of you.

Establishing Quick Rapport

You learn how to establish harmonious relationships quickly with people you don't know. This is a useful skill in all your personal dealings. Clerks, receptionists, switchboard

MANAGE VERBAL INTERACTION

"Tell me what else is new . . . and make it snappy!"

operators—anyone you talk to in casual transactions—will give you more attention and better service when you let them know that you recognize them as people of individual worth.

"Mining" Information

You learn effective ways to get others to answer questions and volunteer information. This helps you guide ongoing conversations. It also perfects your "mining" techniques for picking others' brains—to find out things that are both useful and interesting.

Making Friends and Contacts

When you talk to lots of different people in lots of different places you're bound to meet at least a few with mutual interests who give you important information, become friends, or pave the way for useful future contacts.

Ben Traynen ran into such a stranger while he was in Seattle on a business trip. In the hotel elevator he struck up this conversation with an elderly gentleman.

"Good morning. It's a nice day, isn't it?"

"Sure is! I'm glad I'm not at home today. I just heard they're having a blizzard back there."

"Is that right? Where are you from?"

"Des Moines, Iowa."

"No kidding! I know Des Moines. That's where National Packing used to be headquartered. They're in San Diego now."

"That's right. They did move to San Diego. Do you happen to know Bob Keyman there?"

"Sure I do. As a matter of fact I saw him about six weeks ago." (Ben didn't volunteer that it was the first and only time he'd seen him and the meeting didn't go well.)

"Is that right! We used to be golf buddies. When you get home call him up and say 'hi' to him from Mark Ketting."

They continued talking as they got off the elevator and headed for the coffee shop. During *breakfast Ben learned that Ketting was a top executive for Lowco before he retired. He set up their whole discount operation. He told Ben about his career, his strategy and reasoning in going discount, and some interesting stories about his association with Keyman. He invited him to visit him if he was ever in Des Moines, and he insisted that Ben call Keyman to say "hello" for him. Ben did. Keyman's attitude became cordial when he told him he'd seen Ketting. They arranged to have lunch the following week. Ben was looking forward to a much better meeting than their first one.*

Experiencing a Sense of Mastery

Your Workouts show you how to shape situations. You set the limits of the circumstances according to *your* abilities and *your* objectives. You pick the time, the place, and the people. You decide what you'll do and how. You're the initiator, the shaper, and the terminator. The stranger is the responder, the shaped, and the terminated. You discover how it feels to be in control.

Furthermore, the people you talk to in waiting situations are often your temporary captives, because to get away from you they'd have to lose their priority for whatever they've been waiting for. If the situation is one you've designed just for practice, you can end the contact merely by leaving—*you* don't *have* to wait. This greater freedom and mobility gives you the edge.

If you're a temporary captive of the waiting situation, too, you still have an advantage. You know the contact will end when the waiting does. Like seeing the light at the end of the tunnel, anticipating the natural end of the interaction gives you the determination to get through the encounter. It also allows you to structure the exchange to fit the time available and pace yourself to be ready to end the contact with appropriate behavior. You can practice terminating with various comments and gestures to discover what feels and works best.

[55]

The fact that the contact is ending naturally anyway makes the leave-taking smoother.

All this is invaluable preparation for anytime you want to end discussions or interviews, leave small groups or end a conversation with one person and move on to another.

Knowing that you can manage conversations in this way also helps you overcome reluctance to meet people. And you discover that it's fun to be on top!

HOW SKILL WITH STRANGERS HELPS YOU MANAGE

Besides preparing you for interactions with people you know in the next Round, sparring with strangers conditions you for dealing effectively with strangers you'll meet in your job as manager.

GETTING THE RIGHT START

The nature of business is such that you continually come into contact with new people—customers, suppliers, competitors, new employees, potential employees, intraorganizational line and staff personnel, receptionists, clerks, hosts and hostesses, secretaries, telephone operators, regulating agents, government employees, representatives of financial institutions or the community, your counterparts at meetings and conventions, board members, casual social contacts while entertaining.

It's important for you to get started right so that people in situations like these will like you, so they'll remember you, and so you'll reap the full extent of the help and services they can make available to you. You only have one chance to make a first impression. You can't afford a bad one.

MAKING QUICK CONNECTIONS

As a manager you also have to work fast. Not only is your time valuable, but you can't

risk missing the right time to act or take the chance that a competitor or rival will beat you to the punch while you take your sweet time establishing a useful connection. It's important to establish positive relationships quickly.

The fluent connections you make in this manner help you in many ways:

▶ To get information—"What's going on?" "What's the ball park range?" "Who's been around?" "What's the main concern?" "Who needs to be seen?" "How can I get to them?" "What's coming up next?" "Who's holding it up?" "When is it going to break?"

▶ To get people to make allowances—"I shouldn't, but I will for you just this one time."

▶ To get past buffer personnel—"She'll be back at three o'clock. You can catch her then." "He'll be coming out in five minutes. Stick around." "See Ray Jones. He can get you in. I'll call him."

▶ To get favors—"I'll pit you against the high bidders." "I'll waive the qualifying tests for you." "I'll come in on Saturday to finish up." "I'll schedule your work ahead of the others." "I'll specify your brand."

▶ To get people on your side—"To be honest with you, Jones made a very tempting offer—but I like your style." "I'll go along with you—because I think you can handle it."

Smooth and easy associations with people you're meeting for the first time also help to get contracts, make sales, select talent, determine suppliers, form alliances, decide tactics, and generally influence outcome.

SPARRING WORKOUTS

Your Workouts with strangers are carefully arranged in order of difficulty so that the first ones condition you for the ones that come after them. Follow the order in which they're given carefully. Don't do Workouts on the job yet. Practice with people you don't expect to be a regular part of your future.

Greet People

Go for a walk in an area where you'll meet quite a few people coming your way—a shopping mall, a city street, a path in the park, or the corridors of a public building, for example. Notice that most of the people you pass pay little or no attention to you or to anyone else.

Now *keep walking,* and *look directly at people* as you pass. Anytime you catch someone's eye, *nod and smile.* You'll get nods and smiles in return from some of the people. A few will ignore you, seem surprised or even affronted. That's to be expected. Most people aren't used to being greeted by strangers, especially in metropolitan areas.

Continue the exercise, but now *add "hello," "hi," "good morning,"* or whatever greeting feels natural for you and fits the occasion. You'll get more nods, smiles, or greetings in

return now, because they can't pretend they don't know you're greeting them when you reinforce it vocally.

Finally, *call out a cordial salutation* as you approach others, even if they don't look at you.

TRAINING TIPS

Make your intentions clear. Smile an obvious smile, move your head in a definite nod, and speak loudly and clearly enough to be heard and understood. Speak as you approach people rather than as you pass, to give them the chance to respond. Avoid wearing dark glasses so your eye contact is very evident. Make your greeting unmistakably friendly and enthusiastic.

Carefully choose the places you practice. Choose places that have a fairly heavy foot traffic pattern so that you have plenty of opportunity to practice and so that your intent is interpreted as only casual and friendly. Obviously, too, use discretion in the people you greet if you have any doubts about their intentions. In some sections of all cities you may happen on panhandlers, prostitutes, and fanatics who won't be content to pass on by if you encourage them in any way.

Talk to People with Limited Mobility

Talk to people standing in lines—at box offices, checkout counters, in stores or banks, at entertainment events or public receptions.

Talk to people who are waiting very briefly—to cross a street, for a bus, for an elevator, for the doors of a business establishment to open.

Talk to people where the wait is longer—in medical reception rooms, at a car wash, in a public agency like the department of motor vehicles or Social Security office, on elevators, escalators, buses, trains, airplanes, or boats.

GREET PASSING STRANGERS

"Good morning . . . how are you today?"

Talk to people whose mobility is limited by their jobs—clerks who aren't busy, security guards, receptionists, ushers, museum personnel, hosts and hostesses, bartenders.

Talk to people engaged in the same activity as you—watching entertainment, browsing through books in a bookstore, shopping for the same items, eating at lunch counters, viewing exhibits, attending public meetings, conventions, or banquets.

TRAINING TIPS

Carefully choose your sparring partners and the places you meet. Pick places and people that promise the best chances of success. Try your first exercises with people who are most likely to respond favorably—in general, those who are most like yourself: same age, sex, race, style of dress. Be wary of little children. They're apt to be very honest or very shy, leading them to ignore social conventions. In addition, their parents may have wisely cautioned them not to talk to strangers.

Choose both the people and the places where you meet them with an eye to your own safety. To avoid becoming involved in embarrassing or potentially dangerous situations with strangers, pick crowded places in daylight hours, not remote, deserted locations after dark. Remember, your goal is for *you* to manage the interaction, ending it on *your* terms. Getting mugged doesn't fit those requirements.

Say something right away. As soon as you find yourself next to someone you can talk to, say something. It's easiest to break the ice just as one or the other of you arrives:

I'm glad to see so many people waiting here. I was afraid I'd missed the bus.

A delay makes starting more awkward, more suspicious, less spontaneous, and less comfortable for either of you. But if you don't get started right away, start later anyway when you notice something happening to comment about:

I admire people who climb utility poles like that. A stepladder's about as high as I care to go.

Don't come on too strong. Remember, others are as apprehensive of strangers as you are. Be friendly and pleasant, not aggressive. Make small talk instead of personal remarks about the other person. State positive feelings instead of criticism or advice. Comment about things you both are aware of in the situation. Try to be light and humorous:

What a busy place this is today. Looks like everybody got hungry at once.

I get a kick out of that Norman Rockwell picture of the dogs and their owners waiting to see the vet.

Lots of people seem to be taking these elevators up, but I don't see hardly anyone coming down. I wonder what happens to them up there.

Choose sparring partners and conditions that match your level of expertise. Begin with short-lived situations like waiting on the curb for a traffic light to change and work up to longer ones like a block-long box-office line. Talk to the person next to you on a short bus ride before you start a conversation with someone you'll be stuck next to in a reserved seat at a show that lasts two hours.

Start with people you're least apprehensive about—less striking, less prestigious, more friendly-looking. Talk to those who give an easy return to your initial greeting. Talk to the unpretentious, shy guy before you approach the smooth operator. Talk to the friendly, down-to-earth girl before you try the aloof sophisticate.

Establish eye contact. If you usually wear sunglasses, make it a point to take them off when you're talking to people. Not only do your eyes give expression to what you say, but eye contact shows others that they have your undivided attention. It projects confidence, competence, sincerity, and genuine interest in others, which in turn inspires trust and cooperation from others.

Deal one-to-one. Do your first "waiting people" exercises with just one other stranger, unaccompanied by people you know. It's easier to deal with one pair of strange eyes than with several, and you'll have less emotional static than if you feel you have an "audience." When you're dealing one-to-one you're more willing to try new approaches, and you're more apt to succeed, because you'll avoid interference from others. Neither will you push beyond your readiness just to impress your friends.

Show respect to yourself and others. Don't put yourself down by feigning humility. Don't "sir" or "madam" people.

Don't talk down to others or use flattery. Look for something you honestly like or find interesting in a person and express it sincerely. (Your positive observation exercises in Round 2 will help you here.) Talk to people as equals, showing respect and expecting respect.

WHAT TO SAY AFTER YOU SAY HELLO

There's no set formula for talking to people that fits every situation you'll ever face. People and circumstances differ, calling for a variety of approaches and a degree of spontaneity in using them. The more skills you can use effectively and the faster you can size up what's needed in a particular situation, the easier it will be to manage interactions. Before you're

through with the training program you'll have a full supply of conversational skills. The following suggestions are some that will get you started talking with casual strangers and will also become a useful, permanent part of your repertoire.

Use Traditional Openers

Ask, "How are you, today?" "Do you think it's going to rain?" "Is it hot/cold enough for you?"

Questions like these may be lacking in originality, but they're easily said and readily received. The fact that they are common and traditional makes them unthreatening and acceptable: We all know the answer to how we are, and everyone has an opinion about the weather.

Openers like these extend the salutation. They give you time to survey the scene and decide what your best approach is. The answers you get give you clues as to what kind of challenge you face—a grouch, a joker, a straight arrow, a shrinking violet—or, more often than not, a pleasant, agreeable person.

The first responses of others also give you leads for expanding the conversation if you like:

How are you today?

Fine, except for this cast on my foot.

What happened to your foot? . . .

Do you think it's going to rain?

Gee, I hope not. I'm going to a barbecue as soon as I'm off work.

That sounds like fun. Where are you going? . . .

Make Favorable Comments

If you did your observation workouts conscientiously in Round 2, you've acquired the habit of noticing things you like and expressing your feelings to yourself. Now begin to express them aloud to people you encounter.

Comment on things that the person is responsible for or is associated with in some way.

I don't think I've ever seen a '66 Buick that's in as good shape as this. You must spend a lot of time keeping it up.

I like the way you keep your dog under control. He heels like his nose is glued to your knee.

Comment on clothes, accessories, purchases, packages—without getting too personal, of course.

It reminds me of spring to see that flower in your lapel. It cheers me up just to look at you.

I couldn't help noticing your sunglasses. I've been looking for a pair like that myself.

I'm glad you decided on the plaid suit. I like the color on you. (Warning: Don't give advice before they make up their minds or try to talk them into a purchase in this Round.)

Comment on competence or services that please you.

I appreciate your cleaning the windshield.

I'm really enjoying the bird displays. They look so lifelike.

It was a pleasure to be served by someone with such a ready smile and friendly manner.

Notice how the examples above all follow the rule you learned for expressing positive feelings in Round 2: Start with "I," state a feeling, and avoid evaluating. Back up your statement with *factual* reasons if possible.

Favorable comments create favorable feelings. They're especially effective with strang-

MAKE FAVORABLE COMMENTS

"I like your bandana . . . red is my favorite color."

ers because strangers don't expect compliments from people they don't know. When a friend says, "I like your shoes," you're not surprised. You might even think your friend is only saying it to be nice. But when a casual acquaintance says the same thing, you're apt to think, "They must look pretty good, to bring a compliment from someone I don't even know."

Accept compliments graciously. When others compliment you, try to show appreciation:

That's a lovely ring you're wearing.

I'm glad you like it. I got it as a high school graduation gift and I wouldn't part with it for the world. (Not: It used to be, but it's starting to lose its luster now.)

The second response denies the compliment and puts down the complimenter. But the first reply not only makes the complimenter feel that you're pleased with the remark, it also gives information about yourself which makes it possible to extend the conversation if you wish.

Ask Questions

Ask efficient questions that will give you the information you want.

The way you ask questions is important. If you don't believe it, consider this incident:

A man approached a little girl and a dog waiting to cross the street. "Does your dog bite?" he asked. "No," she answered. Reassured, the man reached down to pat the dog. The dog snarled and snapped, narrowly missing the man's hand as he hastily withdrew it. "I thought you said your dog doesn't bite," he complained to the girl. "It doesn't," she answered, "but that's not my dog."

To avoid this kind of communication breakdown in your contacts with strangers, ask the right kind of questions.

TWO KINDS OF QUESTIONS

In this Round you deal with two kinds of questions—*restrictive* and *expansive*.

Restrictive questions are ones that begin with words like "Do you," "Could you," "Can you," "Are you," "Will you," and "Have you." They can be—and often are—answered with single words like "yes," "no," or "maybe." As such they severely limit the amount of information you get in return for your question. And they tend to discourage, or *restrict*, further conversation.

Expansive questions are questions that start with the words "who," "what," "when," "where," "why," and "how." They can't be answered with a final "yes" or "no." They ordinarily elicit more information than restrictive questions. They are sometimes called open-ended questions because they create openings for *expanding* the conversation.

Judge for yourself what works best in the following examples:

Noah Smoothy wanted to ask a girl coworker he knew only casually for a date. He thought he'd engage her in small talk first, then gradually work around to asking her to go out with

him. He tucked his own indestructible Mitex Accurator under his cuff and asked, "Do you know what time it is?"

"No," the girl replied cooly.

Flustered by her brusk answer, Noah pulled up his sleeve, looked at his watch and said, "It's ten minutes to twelve—how about a date?"

Struggling to keep a straight face, the girl said, "No," and walked away.

Barry Suave had a similar plan but he used expansive questions in his approach:

BARRY: *Excuse me. What time is it?*

GIRL: *I don't know for sure, but it was twelve-thirty when I walked past the clock in front of the jewelry store a few minutes ago.*

BARRY: *Oh, you went out for lunch today. Where did you eat?*

GIRL: *At the Oriental Pizza Pagoda.*

BARRY: *I've never been there. How's the food?*

GIRL: *I love their mozzarella cheese, but I'm always hungry again an hour after I eat.*

BARRY: *That Chinese food will do that—I like the cheese soup at Cup and Cracker. I'd like to take you there for lunch sometime. How about tomorrow?*

GIRL: *OK, it's a date.*

Here are some more examples of restrictive and expansive questions that show the different kinds of answers you get:

Restrictive
Do you have a phone?
Yes.

Expansive
What's your phone number?
555–5555.

Restrictive
Can you tell me if there's a restroom in this building.

Yes.

Well . . . where is it?

There isn't any.

Didn't you just say there was?

No, I said I could tell *you if there was. . . .*

Expansive

Where's the nearest restroom?

There isn't any in this building. You have to go down to the main level and through the arcade. . . ."

Advantages of Expansive Questions

Expansive questions are far more efficient than restrictive ones. They help you avoid this kind of frustrating guessing game:

Restrictive

Are you going to the beach today?

No.

Oh, you're going boating?

No.

Roller skating?

No.

Expansive

Where are you going today?

Downtown.

What are you going to do there?

Shop.

When will you be back?

Dinnertime.

Even when expansive questions get single-word answers like these, they're more informative and efficient than asking a series of "yes-or-no" questions to find out "where," another series to find out "what," and so on.

Expansive questions also give you a better return for the number of words you "spend" on your questions.

Restrictive

Did you see many customers today?

Nope.

Expansive

Who did you see today?

I ran into Greezy from Cartown Industries and learned that they're expanding their used parts department.

Restrictive

Am I cutting this carpet right?

No.

Expansive

How do you want this carpet cut?

Make it one-half inch narrower than the stairway on the sides. . . .

The longer answers you get with expansive questions also give you more time to think what to ask next and provide clues that help you shape the conversation. All in all, restrictive questions keep the ball in your court most of the time, while expansive questions put the greater burden on the responder.

Guidelines for Asking Expansive Questions

Use good judgment as to what kind of information you ask for in your sparring Workouts with strangers, especially.

Don't get personal. Use discretion in private matters. Stay away from direct questions about money and personal appearance. Don't persist with questions that meet with initial reluctance.

Ask easy, noncontroversial questions about shared situations. Avoid questions that call for special knowledge, put people on the spot, or start an argument. Such questions are apt to cause embarrassment all around and defeat the cordial purpose of the interaction.

[62]

Ask questions about shared situations that you're sure people can answer:

What did you think of that fumble in the end zone with only ten seconds left on the clock? (*Not:* What do you think of the changes in the professional football rules this season?)

That's a Hawaiian fruit you have in your cart, isn't it? What's it called? (*Not:* . . . How many calories does it have per serving?)

Mentally rehearse. Practice asking expansive questions covertly so you'll have a few stock ones you feel comfortable with. Anticipate situations you might find yourself in and think of appropriate questions to ask.

Share personal information. Give brief, selective information about yourself, so you won't sound like you're conducting a survey. But don't get carried away and volunteer too much. Try to *get* more information from strangers than you *give.*

When to Ask Restrictive Questions

Ask restrictive questions *when all you really want is a "yes" or "no" answer*—as in "Would you like another serving of mashed potatoes?"

Also use restrictive questions *to break the ice when you sense that strangers are apprehensive* about talking to you. Ask something that you already know the answer to—preferably a question they can answer with "yes":

Is this the gate for Flight 84 to Dallas?

Does this elevator go to the Starlight Room?

The object here isn't to get information, but to start a conversation. Asking questions that call for "yes" answers also establishes a more agreeable atmosphere. Salespeople use this knowledge when they ask a series of ques-

tions that establish a "roll" of "yes" answers. After three or four consecutive "yeses" to "obvious" questions, it's harder for the customer to say "no" to the one that clinches the sale.

Find Commonality

Try to find something in common with the strangers you meet—likes, dislikes, pets, cars, ailments, experiences, schools, professions, hobbies, vacation spots, home towns, friends, or even enemies:

Ask questions
You're on vacation? Me, too. Where are you from?

Comment on the obvious
Looks like you're having trouble deciding what cat food to buy. You must have a finicky cat like mine. What kind of cat do you have?

Volunteer information about yourself
You've got back trouble? Me, too. I've been in traction half a dozen times. What do you find gives you the most relief?

FIND COMMONALITY

Start spontaneous conversations in shared situations like community events, disturbances, or accidents.

At the scene of an accident or fire

What happened? How many people were there? How long ago did it happen?

At a parade

You must have had to get here pretty early to get a front-row seat like that!

At a ball game

Where did you buy the popcorn?

Don't use a pat procedure for everyone. Let the circumstances spontaneously determine what approach you use.

With practice you'll find you can quickly discover that you both like black gumdrops and hate broccoli. When you do, suddenly you're no longer strangers—you're "friends." Anxieties disappear and conversation flows easily. There's more to talk about than you have time for.

End Contacts Cordially

Make clean but cordial breaks when you're ready to terminate a conversation.

When termination is automatic—the contact ends when the waiting ends—use the opportunity to practice various ways of ending anyway.

Be direct, but not rude in contacts with long-winded, overaggressive, or unpleasant people. Simply say, "I have to go now." Don't explain why.

Once you give the break signal with anyone, consciously wind down the contact. Don't take off on tangents or introduce new subjects into the conversation. Don't respond to the other person's statements in ways that tempt him or her to answer back or to take off in a new direction. Be neither too abrupt nor too lingering.

Finish up with a comment like, "I've enjoyed talking with you." If there's a reason to want the stranger to know you, state who you are and reinforce it symbolically with a card, a handshake, or a reminder of the commonality you established. These will all help to reestablish your identity in the future.

A cordial ending to a contact is invaluable if you meet again, but even if you don't, the good feeling you both have at the moment of parting is well worth your effort.

Try All the Moves with All Kinds of People

Use the approaches we suggest in this Round as new ways to add to your present skills and substitutions for things that aren't working well for you now.

Try them all to discover firsthand if there's a better way of doing things than you've been using.

People whose style has been too aggressive or those who try to force their will on others sometimes feel that they don't need these early Workouts because they never have any trouble getting what they want. But if you accomplish your ends by bullying people, you're failing to meet an important criterion for effective management—to leave people glad that they complied with your wishes whenever possible. By trying all the suggested approaches you'll discover through personal experience where they best fit into your own behavior repertoire.

Try all the Workouts with all kinds of people, too. Notice which kinds of people and situations are easiest for you and which kinds are most difficult. Start with the easy ones, but make it a point to tackle the ones you tend to avoid as your confidence and competence increase. Go on to the next Round when you feel you can successfully handle all types under all conditions.

LIVE ACTION REPORTS

The thing that impressed me most in starting to talk to strangers today is that it's easier to treat strangers like they are furniture, but it's not as much fun. I find that I feel much less like I'm "alone in a crowd" if I go out of my way to be friendly.

At the county fair I was fascinated by a man selling kitchen gadgets. I commented to an old guy next to me, "He's got some spiel, hasn't he?" I was surprised when the guy grumbled, "Crooks like that oughta be tarred and feathered and run outa town on a rail." I wanted to argue with him but I controlled myself. I asked him if he'd been stung by one of these guys and he went into a long tirade. I didn't have to encourage him to talk, so I tried to think of a way to get away from him. Finally I looked at my watch and said, "Gosh, I didn't realize what time it is. I've gotta go!"—and I walked away real fast.

When I arrived at my friend's place he was busy changing the oil in his car. I struck up a conversation with his neighbor, a fellow in his forties, I'd guess. We really hit it off when I discovered he was an experienced skin diver and I told him that I was about to take lessons. He told me a lot about the sport in return for just a few open-ended questions from me. Then he invited me into his house to show me his gear he was thinking of selling, since his doctor had told him to give up the sport. He let me have everything he had for thirty dollars. It was all top-quality stuff. I figure I saved myself about three or four hundred bucks. The ironic thing is that my friend who lived next door is going to take up skin diving, too. He's lived right next to this guy for a year, but they've never even said "hi."

I went into a little post office in a ski resort to buy stamps for some postcards. The postal clerk was really cheerful, so when I paid for the stamps I said, "I want you to know that I think this is the best bargain I've found all day—getting these cards delivered hundreds of miles away for only a few cents each. And I get your good-natured, courteous service as a bonus, besides."

The clerk literally beamed and said, "It's a real pleasure to hear you say that. Everybody remembers to complain to us, but very few people express their appreciation." I felt especially glad that I'd commented.

When I go into a store just to look around I usually try to ignore the clerks so they won't hover around and try to high-pressure me. Today I tried a different approach. When I entered a shop I deliberately caught the clerk's eye and said, "Hello, how are you today?" Everyone seemed more cordial than usual. They even seemed to hover less—as if they were willing to leave me alone once I'd recognized their presence. I made it a point to say, "Thank you. I've really enjoyed looking around," when I left. I felt a little uneasy in the first store I went into. But each time I tried the approach, the easier it got. I felt really good about the whole thing. I think I left the clerks feeling better, too.

People waiting in lines are the easiest strangers to talk to. You can always comment on how long the line is.

I was really apprehensive about talking to strangers—particularly getting them to talk. That hasn't been my problem. Getting them to stop is a bigger problem. Thank goodness most situations do terminate by themselves. I need more practice in ending conversations smoothly.

A young woman sat down next to me in a theater Saturday night just as the performance started. I'm shy around strangers, so I told myself it wasn't a good time to talk to her. Later it seemed awkward to say "hello," after we'd been sitting silently next to each other for a while. Finally I decided I'd say something at intermission—but she got up and left as soon as the lights went on. I almost decided to take the easy way out and forget the whole thing— but I knew I'd be mad at myself later if I didn't try. When she came back I smiled and nodded and asked her, "How do you like the play?" She said she loved it—and she was sorry her friend didn't make it (there was an empty seat next to her). That gave me a chance to ask more questions. She was very friendly and we talked until the second act started. I'm glad I carried through, and the next time I'll say "hello" right away.

Went to my wife's class reunion with her. I didn't know a soul there. Found immediate commonality with all the other mates who weren't a part of the class. Knowing they were in the same situation as I, and seeing this as a real opportunity to talk with strangers, made it an interesting evening as my wife continually roamed about seeing friends she knew.

I talked to a man on an elevator. I've always been uncomfortable when alone with a man before. Speaking to him actually made the ride more comfortable.

I was amazed at how much information people "volunteered" without my revealing anything about myself. With the "right" questions and a "sympathetic ear" I could lead them just where I wanted them to go.

At an arts and crafts sale I saw an unusual plant container. I asked the woman in charge the price of it and told her much I liked her wares. I asked her some questions about how they were made and how she got into the business. I wasn't doing it just for practice—I was

really interested—but I never would have done it before I started the program.

She seemed happy to answer all my questions. Finally I bought a twenty-five-dollar container. Then I told her I liked the plant she had displayed in it and asked her what kind it was. She told me the name and then she said, "I'll tell you what. I'm going to give you the plant, too. It needs a home, and I don't have time to care for it properly."

Later I noticed the plant still had a $5.99 price sticker on it. I doubt if she would have given it to me if I'd just walked up and handed her my purchase. I think the friendly conversation made the difference.

INSTANT REPLAY

In this Round you begin to impose your will on others at the simplest possible level. You "force" people to respond to your greetings. You take advantage of "captive audiences" to practice initiating and maintaining conversations. You terminate contacts at your pleasure. The emphasis is still on the social interaction process here instead of on getting tangible results. Unobtrusive as it is, this is your first taste of managing circumstances and the behavior of others.

The suggested Workouts are:

▶ Greet people.

▶ Talk to people with limited mobility.

▶ Use traditional openers.

▶ Make favorable comments.

▶ Ask questions.

▶ Find commonality.

▶ End contacts cordially.

▶ Try all the moves with all kinds of people.

ROUND 4:

MANAGING SIMPLE SOCIAL RELATIONSHIPS (PEOPLE YOU KNOW)

Your fourth Bout for CLOUT sends you back into your "own corner" to talk with people you know—friends, relatives, and acquaintances. However, you still avoid doing Workouts with people on the job.

THE CHALLENGE

The challenge is to improve existing relationships—to make them stronger, more meaningful, and more enjoyable. You try to improve the quality of your communication with people you see frequently, and you try to increase your contact with those you see less often.

THE STRATEGY

The strategy involves expressing more understanding, warmth, and cordiality to others; encouraging conversation; listening so that you hear the total message others send; mak-

ing responses that show understanding as well as stating your own feelings constructively so that the lines of communication are kept open.

THE MOVES

Your maneuvers include personalizing and symbolically reinforcing "hellos" and "goodbyes," listening for feelings as well as for substance; making reflective responses; stating facts and feelings in ways that neither tune others out nor turn them off.

WINNING THE ROUND

Success in this Round is managing contacts so that there's greater mutual enjoyment with the people in your own corner. It's discovering that you can be understanding, considerate, and supportive of others. It's seeing that you can present your own views and feelings so they'll be understood by others. It's recognizing that you can cool down emotions and encourage a return to reason by the way you talk and listen. In other words, it's gaining ground in all of your personal relationships.

WHY WORK OUT
IN YOUR OWN CORNER

Your Workouts with people in your own corner give you experience in managing simple social interactions where you have slightly more emotional involvement than you have with strangers. Yet there's neither as much emotional involvement nor as much risk as there will be later on when you'll seek specific ends.

Working out with people you know provides a double opportunity—to improve relationships with those you care about at the same time that you're learning important new skills.

Some of the nottims you begin to acquire here include *appearing friendly, understanding, pleasant, flexible, open, and trustworthy; keeping objectives constantly in mind and avoiding being distracted by emotions; managing information* (especially gathering facts); *making friends;* and *nurturing relationships.* The last includes *improving existing relationships, setting a positive climate for interactions, making others feel good, listening reflectively,* *avoiding moralizing, eliciting desired responses from others,* and *terminating contacts easily and cordially.*

These communication skills are basic to successful relationships. Through them you control the climate of interactions. This, in turn, helps you to get and maintain the upper hand in personal as well as professional transactions.

HOW IMPROVING RELATIONSHIPS
HELPS YOU MANAGE

There are always a few who approach these Workouts with skepticism. They're usually people who currently hold management positions and feel that their hierarchical position in the organization is enough to assure compliance with their wishes. Their argument goes something like this:

"What does nurturing relationships have to do with management? I'm not interested in making the people who work for me feel good. I want results. I'm the boss. I tell them what to do. They do it! If they don't, they find another job."

Managers like this see their jobs in terms of superior-to-subordinate instead of in terms of person-to-person relationships. Besides seeing people more as objects than as individual human beings, they overlook the fact that managers engage in other kinds of interactions

IMPROVE EXISTING RELATIONSHIPS

"You blockhead! Can't you see I'm trying to be friendly?"

[68]

than purely vertical ones. In practice, more managerial exchange takes place laterally, peer-to-peer, than with subordinates—both inside and outside the organization walls. Equally important are relationships where managers themselves are subordinate to those of higher rank.

BUILDING A SPIRIT OF COOPERATION

In all your managerial transactions you'll find that cordial relationships help you get results. When you get off on the wrong foot, you waste valuable time trying to rebuild *esprit de corps*. The story of "Honeymoon" Harry illustrates this:

Harry Hipshot was hired by the Laggard Company to take over their manufacturing operation. The previous manager had allowed things to slide so that production schedules were behind, quality was poor, and the once-capable work crew was disintegrating.

When Hipshot came in and surveyed the situation he quickly sensed the casual pattern of the employees. He called the entire crew together, foremen, leadmen, and workers. "Gentlemen," he said arrogantly, "the honeymoon is over." He went on to tell them things would be different now. He would determine what was done, who would do it, and how it would be done.

Minutes after the meeting the locker room talk established both his nickname, "Honeymoon" Harry, and the conspiracy against him that would take place immediately—"Sit on your hands until he tells you what to do."

Harry learned quickly that you have to have a two-way relationship to run a plant. After a slowdown that took on ridiculous proportions (straightfaced workers asked questions like, "How exactly do you want these boxes stacked, Mr. Hipshot?"), Harry set about mending the shattered relationship. Fortunately he was tech-nically and operationally competent—and flexible enough to recognize his error and take steps to overcome it. Finally, six months later, schedule, quality, and morale had been restored—and the workers were good-naturedly calling him "Honeymoon" to his face.

Hipshot realized, in time to recoup, that management is a two-way street: Managers have unique contributions to make and so do the people they work with. It isn't necessary to pull rank. Nor is it necessary to be overfamiliar or even informal. As a manager you can popularize and legitimize your actions and get commitment and support for your ends by establishing a spirit of cooperation based on respectful, authentic relationships.

GETTING NEEDED INFORMATION

Since people are usually your best source of information, cordial relationships with subordinates, peers, and superiors alike will help you develop a healthy climate of information exchange.

You're best off when you know *everything* that they know and *everything* that they feel about *everything* that's relevant to your own performance and objectives. When you're viewed as a deserving person, information comes to you voluntarily or with minimum encouragement, in a form and spirit that's easily translatable and useful to your ends.

GETTING OVER ROUGH SPOTS

Solidly built relationships also stand up better under the strain of occasional affront, misunderstanding, or mistakes which are bound to occur in the give and take of the managerial arena.

MAKING YOURSELF LOOK BETTER

Finally, good relationships amplify competence. In the eyes of people who feel cordial

GETTING OVER ROUGH SPOTS

*"OK, so I made a mistake that cost the firm $50 million . . .
I hope you're not going to let that affect our relationship."*

toward you, you look better than you may actually be.

To sum up, effective communication helps you to get and disseminate needed information, to give and receive directions, to delegate and receive assignments, to represent and be represented. It also helps you prevent and resolve conflict and effect favorable negotiations.

In a nutshell, that's the answer to the question, "What does nurturing relationships have to do with management?"

WORKOUTS WITH PEOPLE YOU KNOW

Many of the skills you learn in this Round can be used with strangers, just as the ones you learned with strangers can be used with people you know. But don't practice in the workplace yet.

Start your Workouts with "easy marks"— your most approachable parent or offspring; the sister or brother with whom you have most in common. Talk to your friends, aunts, uncles, cousins, or grandparents who like to lis-

ten, and listen to those who love to talk. Try the easiest things first. But make it a point to try the harder Workouts with people you feel are more difficult to deal with before going on to the next Round.

Personalize Your Greeting

*Greet the person by name,
or use a suitable term of endearment.*

Good morning, Victor.

Hello, dear.

Hi there, good friend.

Choose a way of personalizing your "hello" that suits the particular relationship. Don't be too familiar or endearing with acquaintances you don't know well. Some people are offended rather than flattered when addressed as "honey" or "dear" by casual acquaintances.

To address a person by name—first or last, depending on your relationship—is always appropriate. Just be sure you get it right and pronounce it correctly. Otherwise your effort to show personal recognition will backfire.

[70]

Inquire about an interest

Good morning, Margo. How's the new puppy getting along?

Refer to a shared interest or experience

Hi, Jim. That was some game last night, wasn't it? How about that basket in the last three seconds of the second overtime?

Recognize an achievement

Shirley! Hi—I hear you nearly broke the bank at Las Vegas on your vacation!

Take notice of an absence

Hello, Peggy. I'm glad you're back. I missed you.

Avoid clichés that depersonalize your greeting. Don't say, "Hello, there. Long time no see. Where have you been hiding?" Instead, say something like, "Hello, George! I'm really glad to see you. It's been a while. What's new with you and the family/tire business/golf game?"

Personalized greetings like the examples above show that you're interested in people as individuals, because you've taken the trouble to remember their names and some personal information about them. Even if it's only a passing contact, it makes a favorable impression. If it's the beginning of a longer conversation, it gets you off to a good start and sets a cordial tone for the interaction that follows.

Use Reinforcing Gestures

Strengthen your verbal message with a physical gesture: Smile, nod, shake hands, hug, kiss, squeeze an arm, or give a friendly pat on the back.

Use the reinforcer that best fits your relationship with the other person. The closer you are, the more personal your show of affection can be. A good rule is to do what you believe the recipient would enjoy.

Generally speaking, reserve the hugs, pats, and kisses that emphasize your "hellos," "thank yous," and "goodbyes" for close friends and family members. Use a firm handshake or a friendly slap on the back with more casual acquaintances. Offer elderly distant relatives a kiss on the cheek or a supportive arm.

Remember, some people don't enjoy any touching at all, so don't defeat your purpose by trying to force physical contacts on them.

Give Positive Verbal Strokes

Say things which show that you recognize a person's worth and that you value your relationship with one another.

Purposely express your esteem, respect, admiration, or affection for others directly to them. In other words, compliment people.

Use these guidelines for compliments:

Start with "I," tell how you feel, tell why you feel that way whenever you can, and avoid evaluating. For example

I got a kick out of that joke you told yesterday. I keep thinking about it and laughing all over again.

I'm glad you're here. I feel relaxed and comfortable around you.

I love everything about you.

I like to hear you laugh. It makes me smile.

I really enjoyed that apple pie—and I appreciate your making my favorite.

Avoid ritualized compliments or flattery that smack of insincerity, because these are people you know and you may see them again and again. Anticipate with whom you'll be talking when possible and covertly rehearse

[71]

GIVE POSITIVE VERBAL STROKES

"Ms. Jones, your vision and decisive action earned my company $15 million last year . . . thanks a lot!"

a few personalized comments when you're first learning this skill. Look for additional clues in a person's appearance or conversation to develop a knack for making spontaneous comments.

Ask questions

Ask the same kinds of questions you asked of strangers in your Workouts with people you know. Build rapport gradually in the same way you did with strangers.

Use what you know about the people you talk with to guide your questioning. For example, use information they contribute or subjects they've discussed previously to construct appropriate questions:

To a man who's told you earlier that his wife is out of town: "With your wife away in Vermont, what do you do about meals?"

To someone who's informed you about a change in an athletic team lineup: "If Johnson is out for the season, who on earth will they get to replace him?"

Give a little information about yourself to set the stage for questions and keep a conversation in balance:

"Say, you've got a dog, haven't you? Our dogs are having a terrible time with fleas this year. What do you use on your dog for fleas?"

After asking for advice, don't take over with lengthy opinions, anecdotes, or advice of your own. Try to keep the other person talking. Ask how the insecticide is applied, for example; how long it lasts, what it smells like, or how the dogs like it.

Listen Smart

Listen for the total message a person gives, whether it's verbal, vocal, or visual. Use all the senses at your disposal to discover what's going on with the person you're listening to, just like you do when you *look* smart. Use the input to respond appropriately in conversation and to manage the direction of the interaction.

For the purposes of the training program

there are two main kinds of smart listening: *substantive listening* and *reflective listening*. In the first you listen primarily for content; you try to follow the story line, gather information, and comprehend verbal messages. In the second you listen for and respond to feelings which may be expressed verbally but which may also be expressed nonverbally, or "hidden between the lines" of the spoken words.

In both kinds of listening you're an active participant. In both kinds your responses to what is said can manage the conversation to a great extent. In both kinds, the object in this Round is to encourage the other person to talk, to keep the conversation going on a level of cordiality, and to improve your overall relationship with your conversation partner. Thus you seek out and create opportunities to listen to others.

Although you sometimes listen for meaning or feelings only, more often than not you'll find yourself listening for both substantive and emotional messages in the same conversation. Sometimes the feelings messages are intended, but not stated in words. Other times the person unintentionally reveals them by actions or appearance.

For the most part the particular circumstances and specific topic of conversation determine whether you listen for content or feelings in a given interaction. With a little experience you'll become quite proficient in discerning what each interaction calls for—which, of course, determines what kinds of answers you give. In turn, what kind of answers you give influences the nature of the contact and directs the progress of the interaction.

SUBSTANTIVE LISTENING

If you're like most people, substantive listening—listening for content or factual information—is easiest and most familiar. Although emotional overtones sometimes punctuate this kind of message, for the most part it's the words themselves and the story they tell or the information they give that you listen for in substantive listening.

Do's and Don't's for Substantive Listening
Easy as it may seem, some people are better substantive listeners than others. Here are a few "do's" and "don'ts" to help you keep conversation flowing and increase the satisfaction of the encounter for yourself and others.

Show interest in what others are saying by paying attention to them. Look directly at them when they talk. Look up from your newspaper, look away from the TV set, or take off the stereo headphone.

Encourage a storyteller with comments like "What happened next?" "Good Lord! What did you do then?" "That blows my mind! What else did you hear?"

Reinforce your verbal remarks with facial expressions and body language. Smile, frown, or raise your eyebrows to show interest, enthusiasm, concern, or surprise. Nod or shake your head to show you agree or understand what's being said.

Don't punctuate every statement another person makes with a mechanical "uh-huh." It gives an air of insincerity and makes people feel you're urging them to hurry up and finish the story.

Don't do distracting things, like tapping your fingers on the table, swinging your crossed leg, or jiggling a seat you're sharing.

Don't turn your back or walk away while someone's talking—but if you must for some reason (the telephone rings, the dog just ran off with the steak for the barbecue, or the storeroom's on fire), explain and excuse yourself.

Don't interject disruptive comments like "That reminds me, I heard it's supposed to rain tomorrow" or "Incidentally, is that drive-through massage parlor still in that shopping center?"

Don't take the floor away from a speaker by remarks like "I know what you're going to say—the same thing happened to me. I. . . ." They show that you consider your own story more important than the other person's, which naturally hampers good relationships.

Don't jump in and finish a story someone else has started, no matter how obvious the conclusion is. "Stealing" the story steals the glory, especially with jokes, where the punch-line is the best part.

Don't shut people up in mid-story by bluntly reminding them, "You already told me that." If they've started a story, let them finish. Then if there's some good reason to tell them you already know (simply letting them know they've made a mistake to tell you again isn't a good reason), do so with a remark like "I know—I couldn't believe my ears when you told me about it last week." If someone askes you, "Did I tell you about . . . ?" use the same approach in your answer: "Yes, you did, and I was shocked to hear it." Most of the time when people tell a story over again, it's because it's very important to them for some reason. By listening, you show them that you care about what's important to them.

Don't correct or make fun of people's grammar, pronunciation, or slips of the tongue. If you get their meaning, let it go. It's possible that *you* are wrong—or that you're both right, as often happens when there are two acceptable pronunciations for a word, for example. In any case, rebuking and ridiculing are put-downs which defeat the purpose of the Work-outs.

Don't correct people's stories, especially if their error doesn't really matter. If someone says, "There were at least two hundred flies on the potato salad," don't challenge their harmless exaggeration with a question like, "How do you know? Did you count them?" Hear their statement as, "There were lots of flies at the picnic," and let it go at that.

Don't interrupt an ongoing narrative with corrections or questions that are irrelevant to the point of a story. Such interruptions send a clear, if unintentional, message that you're not really interested in the other person's story.

Don't monopolize conversations. Don't be the kind of person who never seems to hear what anyone says, listening only for key words and chances to break into a conversation and take over with their own stories.

Ima Tawker was like that. Her daughter Lil phoned her long-distance to tell her she was in the hospital recovering from an emergency appendectomy. "Hi, mom," she said. "I'm in the hospital. I had my appendix removed, but I'm getting along just fine."

Like someone had pushed the buttons marked "appendectomy" and "hospital" on a tape re-corder, Ima began reciting stories about friends, relatives, acquaintances, and distant relatives of casual acquaintances who had had appendicitis or were in the hospital at some time or other for everything from brain surgery to hangnails. Lil, who didn't feel too chipper anyway, listened politely for about fifteen min-utes, contributing only an occasional "uh-huh" or "izzat so?" Then she ended the conversation and hung up. Minutes later the phone rang. It was her brother, Les, calling from another distant city. "Mom called and told me you were in the hospital," he said, "but she didn't seem to know much about what happened to you so she asked me to call you and find out why you're in the hospital and call her back."

An inability to listen like this not only leaves you without important information, but it also makes others feel that you don't really care much about their concerns.

Don't try to take part in two separate conversations at the same time. When someone's talking to you, don't break in to comment on something going on in another conversation across the room. Give your conversation partner your undivided attention, at least until you find a cordial way of breaking away.

Don't make jokes when the other person's trying to be serious.

Mayda Laffingstock's boyfriend makes puns out of everything she says. He's so busy trying to get a laugh that he never listens to what she's trying to tell him. If she complains, he accuses her of not having a sense of humor. She thinks he's insensitive and uncaring. He does the same thing to everybody. Lots of people think he's funny—until they're the target of his wit. Then they think he's a self-centered drip.

Refusing to take a person seriously is a kind of putdown. In effect, the joker is saying, "I don't care about what you're trying to tell me—listen to how funny *I* am."

Don't practice one-upmanship. When others tell you about their experiences—good or bad—resist the temptation to go them one better.

Sue Purlative never has anything ordinary happen to her. She lives a life of extremes—the best or the worst; the biggest or the smallest; the easiest or the most difficult; the best bargain or the most expensive purchase. It's no fun to tell her anything because you know your experience will appear trivial when she's done telling about hers.

We've all played the one-upmanship game. It's the kind of competitive boasting that pops up when one person in a group tells about an experience and others come back with stories that start with "That's nothing, I. . . . ." or "Oh yeah? Well, wait'll you hear what happened to *me.*"

Intentional or not, it's a form of putdown, because it says, "My experience was more important than yours—and that makes me more important than you." (*Note:* Be especially wary of the one-upmanship urge when you're trying to establish commonality. Any points you gain for having a shared experience will be wiped out if others feel you're trying to belittle their own adventure.)

Mind your manners. Much of our advice for successful substantive listening is simply showing consideration for others and practicing good manners. Showing respect for what people say also shows that you recognize their worth.

Old habits die hard, so practice often with a variety of partners. When you catch yourself slipping into behavior that you're trying to change, just stop where you are and redo the Workout. Make a comment or ask a question that will put the interaction back on the track and reestablish rapport.

REFLECTIVE LISTENING

Reflective listening—listening for feelings and reflecting back understanding—is more difficult than substantive listening, mainly because we're not used to doing it.

One reason is that we're in the habit of "hearing" only with our ears, just as we often "see" only with our eyes. Yet when a message has emotional overtones, other kinds of input are necessary to understand the real and total meaning.

Facial expressions, tone of voice, and body language, for example, often betray or confirm feelings that words alone leave in doubt. The staccato click of heels, "letting" a door slam, and putting things down roughly suggest annoyance. Getting up, moving away unexpectedly, and shuffling papers aimlessly may indicate hurt feelings or anger. Drooping shoulders and dragging feet express dejection or sorrow. Hanging one's head may show shame or embarrassment.

Here are some suggestions and illustrations to help you "reflective listen" skillfully.

Recognize and identify emotions. Before you try to reflect back understanding of others' feelings, bone up on recognizing and identifying emotions. Here are some ways to do this:

1. Get in touch with your own feelings.

Express feelings covertly, as you did in Round 2, but now include all kinds of feelings, not just the positive ones. Review an emotional experience at a later time. Try to remember how you behaved, what you said, and how you felt. Try to identify your feelings by name and determine if you expressed them accurately.

2. Expand your vocabulary of negative feeling words.

Think of a variety of new words that express the way you feel. Look in the dictionary or a book of synonyms, if necessary, so that you don't overdo ones like *angry, sad, afraid, mad, turned off,* and *bummed out.*

3. Practice hearing people's wordless feelings.

Observe others' interactions and try to recognize and verbalize to yourself what feelings others are showing. Try some simple experiments to practice "hearing" feelings when you can't hear words. Turn off the sound on your TV set during a dramatic presentation. Try to guess what's going on by the facial expressions, body language, and story-line action.

Do the same thing in crowded public places or at spectator events, where you can see action and facial expressions but you're too far away to hear. Notice what other input in a situation helps you identify feelings. For example, it's obvious what a football player is feeling when he throws the ball down in the end zone after scoring a touchdown—and it's equally obvious that he's feeling something different when he throws it down on the two-yard line when the referee calls a penalty on his team. Similarly, the tears streaming down the face of someone who's just won a marathon race mean something different from those of the person who came in second by less than a minute.

Make noncommittal responses. Acquire a supply of responses that show interest and understanding and invite others to express themselves without sidetracking or stopping the flow of conversation. Interjections like "Mmm-hmm," "I see," or "I understand" take the pressure off the speaker momentarily and reassure him or her that you're listening, besides giving you a few seconds to digest and interpret the feelings you hear.

Avoid getting into a rut by using the same comment over and over again. Vary your responses to break the monotony and show that you are sincere.

Make educated guesses. Make a tentative statement about how you think the other person feels, based on what you know about the person and what you perceive about the particular situation. For example:

It looks like . . . (you're really enjoying that steak).

I'll bet . . . (you're looking forward to your vacation next week).

You must feel . . . (very grateful that no one was seriously hurt in the accident).

I can see that . . . (you're very proud of your daughter).

MAKE EDUCATED GUESSES

"Don't care for my tie, eh?"

You're really . . . (pleased with your new car) *. . . aren't you?*

Sounds like . . . (you were pleasantly surprised to find dinner ready when you got home).

If your guess is correct—or close—the talker is encouraged to agree and contribute additional information and feelings.

I'll bet you can hardly wait to get settled in your new house.

That's for sure. We've been waiting for the escrow to close now for over six weeks.

That must be really frustrating. What's taking so long?

If you guess wrong, you haven't been so dogmatic that the talker doesn't feel free to correct your misunderstanding.

I guess you're pretty happy with the way the election turned out.

Not entirely. I was glad to see Goodfellow win for mayor, but sorry to see Best lose her council seat.

Respond to positive feelings first. Since positive feelings like love, joy, pride, and enthusi-asm are easier to respond to than negative feelings, practice reflecting back that kind of feeling first in your Workouts. Take into account everything you know and can observe about the person and the situation. Then sound out the person's feelings with trial-and-error statements that say what you believe or guess to be the case.

Here's an example that gives two different ways to respond to a positive feeling. As you read it decide which response shows reflective listening.

A young boy runs to his father and blurts out excitedly, "Dad, Dad—I made the team!"

1. That's great, son. I knew you could do it. What position do you play?

2. That really pleases you, doesn't it, son? Me, too! Tell me all about it.

The first response certainly sounds like something a caring parent would say, and in many cases it would make a son happy. But it isn't reflective listening. In addition, there are several possible pitfalls in it.

To begin with, it's a judgment, even though "great" is a positive evaluation. If you allow yourself to get into the habit of judging at all when you're learning to reflective listen, negative judgments are also apt to slip out.

Also, the substantive question assumes that the boy has won an assignment to a particular position on the team. If it turns out that he's a fifth-string substitute, it will be embarrassing to admit it after his dad has evaluated the news as "great." He may even feel inferior and guilty for disappointing his father.

Now notice how the second response clearly reflects back the son's own feeling of pleasure. It shows that the father understands and shares the boy's pleasure and invites the boy to share the whole experience. If it turns out that the son is a fifth-string substitute, but *he* is happy about it, then everything is great.

[77]

Here's another example. Which is the reflective response here?

A little girl runs to her mother, beaming, and says, "Look, Mom, Grandma gave me a whole quarter to spend on candy."

1. She spoils you rotten. You know you aren't allowed to buy candy. Here, give it to me before you lose it. I'll put it in your piggy bank.

2. You really like it when Grandma gives you money, don't you? Where shall we put it so it won't get lost until we have a chance to talk about what to do with it?

Notice how the mother totally squelches the girl's enthusiasm in the first response—moralizing about Grandma's behavior and shaming the child for forgetting a rule. She also implies several putdowns that the child is bound to hear: "You *are* spoiled rotten, you *will* lose it, and you *can't even be trusted* to put it in your piggy bank without my help."

The second, reflective listening response shows that the mother recognizes and understands the girl's delight and creates a pleasant, shared interaction. That sets a receptive climate for the second question, which expresses the mother's concern about the money being lost but gives the girl a say about where it will be put for safekeeping. It also reminds the girl that they must talk about how it can be spent, but implies that they will share that decision, too.

Finally, which one of the responses in the following interaction is most likely to improve the relationship?

The sales rep bursts into the boss's office exclaiming, "Hey boss! Guess what? I just got a hundred-thousand-dollar order for rivets from Jim Philbert. He's always been a hard nut to crack."

1. How stupid can you get? We're already three weeks behind our production schedule in the rivet section. How many times have I told you it's screw orders we need?

2. So you finally got through old Philbert's shell? You must feel really good about that. . . . I hope he'll go for a delay in delivery. . . . We're three weeks behind on our production schedule in the rivet section. . . . And listen, there's going to be a layoff in the screw section in two weeks if we don't get some orders in there. See if you can use that technique of yours to get an order for screws from Bill Thread over at Driver and Sons.

In the first response the boss resorts to name calling and putdown, with no recognition of the sales rep's enthusiasm or pride for having accomplished a difficult feat.

In the reflective listening response the boss first shows that he understands and shares the sales rep's pleasure and then follows up with some factual statements and a respectful suggestion. Both the employee and the employer benefit.

Reflect negative feelings. Once you feel comfortable reflecting back positive feelings, use the same kind of approach to show understanding of negative feelings like anger, fear, jealousy, resentment, shame, or grief.

Reflective listening is especially effective for dealing with outbursts of negative feeling. It helps cool emotions, encourages people to open up, and allows them to find solutions for their problems. Also, the calmer the situation, the easier it is for you to keep your attention on your own objectives or the goals of the interaction.

Avoid turnoffs. Make a conscious effort to recognize and break old habits which either turn people off or only make things worse—fruitless responses that judge, advise, explain, moralize, command, threaten, or ridicule. Such nonreflective responses only hinder conversation and understanding.

By way of illustration, suppose someone

complains bitterly and emphatically, "I hate my job!" Here are some typical nonreflective responses and the comebacks they're likely to evoke:

Advising

If I were you, I'd talk to the personnel manager about getting a transfer to a different division.

Well, you're not me, so you don't really understand the problem.

Threatening

I swear, if you're going to start harping on that again, I'm leaving.

Go ahead and leave! You never care about how I feel, anyway.

Moralizing

Listen, you should be glad you've got a job at all. There are plenty of unemployed people out there who'd love to have your job.

Name two—I'll call 'em and tell 'em where to apply.

Ordering

Quit complaining and do something about it. Like go out and find yourself a job you don't hate.

Listen to the great know-it-all telling me what to do. You're as bad as my supervisor, always bossing me around.

Cross-examining

Who upset you this time?

My boss.

What did he do?

Yelled at me for being late.

Why did he do that?

How should I know. . . . Because he's a jerk, I guess.

Note that it is advisable to avoid expansive

questions—who, what, when, where, and why—in situations like this where you're listening more for feelings than for facts. Asking such questions in an emotionally charged climate turns some people off entirely and limits others to answering only the specific question asked.

Judging, Name-Calling

You're crazy to hate a job that pays so well.

And you're stupid if you think a paycheck can make you like a job.

Explaining

That's really quite normal. Studies show that less than 20 percent of the people engaged in your kind of work really like their jobs.

Yeah? Well just because a lot of people who are dumb enough to have jobs like mine don't like them doesn't mean that it's normal.

Analyzing

You don't really mean that. You're just tired tonight.

How do you know what I mean?

Reassuring

It can't be all that bad. You'll feel better after a good night's sleep.

No I won't! I'll still hate my job tomorrow and next week and next year. It'll never be any different.

Humoring

Well, of course you do. You're much too good for it. You should be giving the orders instead of taking them.

Who are you trying to kid? I couldn't get a starving dog to come to me when I call even if I had my pockets filled with T-bone steaks.

These examples show how nonreflective responses can trigger disagreement, resentment, resistance, counteraccusations, guilt, self-put-downs, and misplaced aggression. They often make it look like you're talking down, causing both resentment and lowered self-esteem. Rather than helping to solve others' problems with such comments, you may unintentionally create more problems for them. If they redirect their feelings or misplace their aggression toward you, you also create a problem that didn't exist before for yourself and the relationship. If feelings heat up on both sides, irrelevant issues pop up and you get sidetracked from your original purpose.

Here's how a conversation might go when you respond reflectively to the same complaint, "I hate my job!"

Sounds like you've had it today.

You said it. Everything that could possibly go wrong went wrong.

Just one thing after another, huh?

Yeah. But I was coping until Mr. Foreman came in and gave me a lecture about getting back from lunch ten minutes late.

I can see how that might be the final straw.

For sure! He really makes me mad. You can bet he never complains about all the times I work overtime for ten minutes or more without pay.

Doesn't seem quite fair to you, does it?

You bet it doesn't. I'm the most conscientious, responsible, most punctual employee in the whole damn place—so he sees me come in late one time and he's all over my case.

That must really be discouraging. It seems like he never notices any of the good things you do, he only criticizes the times he notices you making a mistake. . . .

Yeah—but that's nothing new. I know that's just his way. I think he likes my work all right. Most of the time it doesn't bother me that much. But today was such a lousy day! . . . Well, maybe tomorrow will be better.

Notice how reflective responses get the whole story out, without asking direct questions or interjecting disruptive personal opinions or advice. When you reflective listen you don't either agree or disagree that the talker *should* feel that way. You merely show understanding of why the talker *does* feel that way. This usually helps people to solve their own problems.

If nothing else, the fact that you as a listener can understand and accept their feelings helps others understand and accept their own negative feelings. It helps them avoid guilt, fear of reprisal, and lowered self-esteem and gives them a noncommittal sounding board for their feelings. Getting it out in the open defuses "dangerous" feelings and helps to put the whole matter in proper perspective.

Listen for feedback. Since your remarks are more exploratory than absolute, reflective listening makes it easy for others to correct you when you read their feelings wrong. This immediate feedback prevents the kind of misunderstanding that occurred in the following situation:

Little Wanda Nannser came home from school and asked her mother, Hedda, "Mother, where did I come from?"

Hedda Nansser launched into a serious, carefully worded explanation about how babies grow in their mothers' bodies for nine months and then the doctor helps to deliver them at the hospital.

Wanda listened politely until her mother finished the long story. Then she said, "Yeah— I know all that—but, like Tommy came from Ohio—where did I come from?"

Be matter-of-fact about misses. If you miss the intended meaning of a question or feeling, simply reflect back the corrected message:

Oh, I understand. You want to know where you were born. OK—You came from Oregon.

Don't apologize or put yourself down: "I'm terribly sorry—how dumb can a person be?" Don't accuse: "Why don't you make yourself clear?" And don't argue: "What do you mean 'maybe' you're worried—of course you're worried."

Look for disguised feelings. If you can't tell for sure what feeling someone is expressing, send out a test "guess" to verify it. People sometimes disguise their real concerns in generalized statements or questions with double meanings to hide guilt, embarrassment, or fear. If you suspect that's the case, look for clues in the circumstance or their current concerns and add them to what you know about people and what they've said to determine your response. For example,

Eighteen-year-old Jess Fretten sat down next to his father and asked, "Dad, what was it like your first day at college?"

Mr. Fretten hesitated a second and then answered, "Sounds like you're a little worried about starting classes tomorrow."

JESS: *Maybe. The campus is so big.*

MR. F.: *I suppose you're afraid you won't be able to find your classes.*

JESS: *Or get there on time—I have to go clear across the campus in ten minutes. And I haven't talked to a single friend who's got the same schedule as mine.*

MR. F.: *It's going to be different, not having your buddies in class with you. Maybe even makes you feel a little insecure, huh? . . .*

Mr. Fretten reflective listened until Jess finally concluded, with growing confidence, "Well, there's one consolation, all the freshmen are in the same boat. Thanks for the help, Dad. I feel a lot better now."

Jess's father read between the lines and guessed what his son's real concerns were because he knew that the next day was Jess's first day of college. He exercised self-control and resisted the temptation to reminisce about his own college days, which he might easily have done if he had taken the question literally. He stayed away from turnoffs like "Don't be silly, you're not a little boy anymore" or "Everything will be just fine—in a week you'll know your way around blindfolded" or "It's just as well—when you and your buddies get in a class together, all you do is goof off."

By showing understanding and acceptance that enabled Jess to get his feelings into words and out into the open, they both felt better when they parted—Jess because someone understood his problem and his father because he'd been able to help.

Retreat, review, and repeat. When your reflective listening Workouts miss their mark you'll know it immediately from the reactions of others: You may get blank stares, quizzical looks, and awkward silences. Or raised voices, tears, and slammed doors. When negative feelings accelerate like this, back off as gracefully as possible and review what happened. Did you misunderstand the feeling or did you misapply the skill? Reconstruct the circumstances and try to discover what went wrong. Then correct your approach when you repeat the Workout another time.

Avoid wild punches. The following suggestions will help you avoid the most common pitfalls faced by beginning reflective listeners:

Don't merely echo the verbal message. If your efforts at reflective listening get responses like "What's the matter, didn't you hear me?" or "Stop talking funny," you're probably merely echoing words instead of reflecting feelings.

Here are two examples that show the subtle difference between echoing and reflecting:

I've had about all the barking I can stand from that neighbor's dog. I haven't had a wink of sleep all night.

Echoing

You're fed up with that dog barking and you didn't get any sleep last night.

Reflective listening

You must be pretty tired and annoyed if that dog's barking kept you awake all night.

The dumbest thing we ever did was to buy that camper. It cost a bundle and we never use it.

Echoing

You think it was really dumb to buy a camper because it cost a lot of money and you never use it, huh?

Reflective listening

Sounds like you regret buying it because you feel you're not getting your money's worth out of it.

If you catch yourself falling into the echo trap, try simply pausing a few extra seconds before you respond. Pinpoint the feeling expressed and choose the appropriate words to reflect your interpretation. Sometimes the other person feels impelled to fill the silence you create, giving you more clues to identify feelings accurately and more time to phrase your response.

Don't pull punches. Don't underplay the feelings of others. Show people that you share their joy, sorrow, anger, fear, or whatever feeling they're experiencing by responding with an intensity of feeling that comes close to their own. Remaining too calm and reasonable in the face of another person's joy or distress may give the impression that you don't understand, or worse, that you don't care.

Nort Withitt's secretary, Iva Greevanss, rushed into his office and blurted out excitedly, "Look at this memo that I just found in the interoffice mail. It says that since I obviously don't have enough to do I'll also be on call for two other departments from now on. This is the work of the boss's haggy secretary, I know it. I hate her."

Hoping to calm her down, Nort responded flatly, "Sounds like you're not pleased with the change."

Iva practically screamed back, "Not pleased! I'm furious! If she was here right now I'd punch her! How can you be so calm? Don't you see that this is an intentional putdown? I don't know about you, but I'm giving notice! Right now!"

Nort recognized his error and tried to recoup: "Boy, you're madder than I realized. And I can understand why. I can hardly believe the boss would do a thing like this to us. What do you think triggered him off?"

Iva began to calm down as she related details of a run-in she'd had earlier with the boss's secretary-mistress. When she had finished she was able to decide on a course of action that would serve her own interests better. She still intended to quit her job, but she would wait until she had another one before giving notice.

Showing genuine understanding lowers the intensity of feelings, while a spiritless, disinterested-sounding response often upsets people more—or compels them to impress you with just how strongly they feel.

The trick to responding appropriately is to try to put yourself in the other person's position. If you really care about the person, and if you keep in mind that your object is to improve the relationship, the right responses come easy. More often than not, what people's emotional outbursts are saying is, "Understand how I feel and tell me that you care." When your reflective response does that, not only is the relationship improved, but many times their own self-understanding is increased and they can solve their own problems.

Don't hit them when their guard is down.

Try to maintain an understanding attitude even when you hear something you don't like. Here's how one well-intentioned friend blew it by letting his own values take over his responses:

Izzy Jellus came home early from a date. His roommate, Maury Lizer, could see he was downhearted and tried to help.

MAURY: *You look like something's got you down. (Reflective listening)*

IZZY: *Peggy and I had a fight.*

MAURY: *You must be pretty upset. (Reflective listening)*

IZZY: *Yeah—but she started it. She was flirting with the waiter at the coffee shop as if I wasn't even there.*

MAURY: *I guess you felt really put down to be ignored like that. (Reflective listening)*

IZZY: *I was really mad. I felt like punching the waiter.*

MAURY: *You were mad at the waiter because you figured it was all his fault? (Reflective listening)*

IZZY: *Not all of it. She encouraged him. I told her to cut it out and she got mad and told me to get lost. So I just got up and left.*

MAURY: *You didn't even take her home? (Translates to: You should have taken her home—Criticizing, Moralizing)*

IZZY (*Sarcastically*): *No I didn't even take her home!*

MAURY: *That's terrible! (Judging) It's not safe for her to be out alone in that neighborhood at night. (Instructing) Wouldn't you feel terrible if something happened to her? (Warning) Maybe she'll still be there. Why don't you go back right away? (Advising)*

IZZY: *Why don't you mind your own business?*

In this case Maury led Izzy to believe he would understand his problem by reflective listening at the beginning of the interaction. Izzy let his guard down and opened up to Maury. When Maury learned that Izzy didn't escort his date home, however, he couldn't hide his disapproval. He let his own feelings take priority over Izzy's problem and socked him with moralistic, judgmental, instructive, threatening, and advisory responses. Izzy hit back with sarcasm, resentment, and defiance.

When you lead others to open up by reflective listening and then you hit them when their guard is down, they often feel betrayed. The resentment and misunderstanding that results is greater than if you'd never tried to listen at all. This doesn't mean that you can never express *your* feelings if you're upset by the other person's behavior. How to do that constructively will be the subject of the next section on using "I-talk." But that's not reflective listening. Remember, reflective listening means expressing your *understanding of the other person's feelings,* not telling your own feelings. There's a right place to use each kind of skill, as you'll see in the section on I-talk.

Don't identify or attribute. Don't try to identify with others' feelings by remarks like "I know just how you feel—I've gone through exactly the same thing myself" or "You're just like me. . . ." To see why statements like these often miss their mark, listen to what they really say.

To begin with, when you say, "I know just how you feel, I've gone through the same thing myself," you make a statement about yourself, not an interpretation of the other person's feeling. Since most people feel that their own suffering is unique, it often triggers at least unspoken disagreement and defensiveness: "You don't either know how I feel. How could anyone possibly know how I feel? I'm the only one who knows how much this means to me."

You also draw attention away from the other person and toward yourself. The troubled person is apt to think, "You want to

[83]

tell how you feel and what you've been through instead of listening to what I've been through."

Finally, by bringing your own experience into it, the other person hears you say, "You're not the only one who's had that happen— it's no big deal."

The second remark, "You're just like me," attributes your feelings to others instead of reflecting back their feelings. It may set off disagreement and resentment in thought, at least, if not out loud: "How do *you* know I'm like you. You haven't let me tell you what my feelings are," or "If you think I'm like you, then you don't understand what I'm trying to say." If you feel you must identify with others in this way, say, "I feel the same way" or "I'm like you" instead of "You're like me."

Don't engage in overkill. Don't try to apply reflective listening to every situation you encounter. It's only one of many useful communication skills. You'll learn from experience when to use reflective listening and when to give other kinds of responses. Meanwhile, here are some common circumstances where reflective listening should never be used:

When a straight, informational response is desired

GUEST: *Where is the bathroom?*

Overkill

You have to use the bathroom, huh?

EMPLOYEE: *When do you think we'll be putting out the Christmas merchandise?*

Overkill

Getting anxious about the Christmas rush already, huh?

EMPLOYEE: *No. I have a customer on the phone who wants to know when strings of Christmas tree lights will be available.*

In the absence of emotional overtones or other knowledge that would lead you to believe that people have a problem they want to talk about, assume that questions like this are requests for straight, informational answers.

When responding reflectively disrupts the spontaneous flow of words

Chris Candor is the kind of person who's able to open up and talk about his feelings very easily. Nevertheless, his girlfriend insisted on trying to reflective listen to him. Even though it was obvious that he just wanted to talk without interruption, she kept reflecting back almost everything he said. Finally he said, impatiently, "I wish you'd stop butting in—or don't you want to hear what I'm trying to say?"

With free talkers, simply keep quiet and listen. Nod agreement or interject an appropriately placed "uh-huh." If it's clear to both parties that you're on the same wavelength, don't ruin the rapport with unnecessary reflective responses.

When other people don't want their feelings exposed

Rob was always reticent about his personal affairs. For that very reason, Bill thought he'd be a challenging person to try reflective listening with. When he saw him come back from making a phone call, visibly disturbed, he made his move.

BILL: *Bad news, huh?*

ROB: *What makes you think so?*

BILL: *You seem upset.*

ROB: *I'm OK.*

BILL: *You're upset but you think you can handle it.*

ROB: *Look. It's my business. Bug off, will you?*

Don't use reflective listening to pry or to pressure people into talking. For whatever reason, there are times when people don't want to reveal their feelings. Good manners and good sense require that you respect their wishes. If the person's first response to your tentative statement of understanding shows unwillingness to talk (as Rob's "What makes you think so?" did), retreat as gracefully as possible with a comment like "I thought you looked upset, but I guess I was mistaken." This leaves it up to the other person to decide whether to reveal the feelings or drop the subject.

Remember, the object of reflective listening in this Round is to give other people the *opportunity* to talk out feelings *if they want to—* not to force them to do what you want.

When the time is wrong

A mother was on her way out the door to go to the dentist's office when this exchange took place with her daughter, home from college for the weekend:

DAUGHTER: *I want to move out of the dorm. I hate my roommates. They never clean up after themselves. It's like living in a pigpen.*

MOTHER: *Sounds like you feel that they're taking advantage of you. I'd like to hear more about it when I get back from the dentist. I've just got time to make my appointment. Can we talk about it after dinner?*

After dinner the mother made it a point to remember her promise, and opened up the conversation again: "This situation with your roommates must be really upsetting you if you want to move out of the dorm."

If you don't have time enough at a particular moment to listen to all the feelings that your reflective responses may unleash, it may be better not to encourage any at all. But don't ignore the person or the feelings. Recognize them, explain why you can't listen, and make a point of reopening the discussion later. If the person solves the problem in the interim, let it go.

When there's an "audience"

Joe was standing on the front lawn talking with a neighbor when his best friend approached, dragging his feet and looking downcast.

JOE: *Hey—looks like you're carrying all the cares of the world on your shoulders.*

FRIEND (Mumbling): *Mr. Griper fired me.*

JOE: *I can see why you're upset. I'm coming in in just a minute. We can talk about it if you want to.*

Don't encourage a person to reveal intense, private feelings when others are around. Not only is your own behavior likely to be influenced by the "audience," you also often have little control over what the onlookers will say or do. Unless it looks like a simple matter that can be resolved quickly (like showing concern for a bumped head or stubbed toe), delay listening until you're alone.

If someone's feelings seem so urgent (hysterics or violence) that a delay seems inadvisable, interrupt what you're doing and find a place where you can listen in privacy. If the feelings are directly expressed to you and you care about your relationship with the person, never simply ignore them.

When the other person is ready to quit

I feel a lot better after talking about it.

I can see now what I want to do.

It helps just to know someone understands.

Be sensitive to signs that the other person is ready to end the interaction and resist the temptation to keep talking to serve your own needs or wishes. The signs are obvious and the interaction is also very satisfying to the listener when the other person says that the problem is resolved.

Less satisfying to the listener, but still a clear indication of the other person's desire to stop talking, are comments like "Well, I haven't quite got it all together yet, but I can see it a little more clearly," or "No sense talking any more now—I have to think about this."

Other moves that show a person's ready to quit are getting up, walking away, changing the subject, and saying things like, "I didn't realize how long we've been talking," "It's been fun," or "I have to go now."

Graciously accept the other person's decision at times like this. If appropriate, offer, "I'll be around if you want to talk some more."

Once you learn to use reflective listening correctly you'll be pleasantly surprised with the results. You'll notice dramatic improvement in your ability to communicate as well as increased compatibility with friends and relatives. Showing that you care enough to listen and try to understand how others feel generates a warmth that comes back to you. In turn, the satisfaction and appreciation that others feel lead them to express caring, interest, and concern for you. People also become more receptive to what you have to say if you make it a point to first listen and try to understand what they say.

Use I-Talk

Tell others how *you* feel. Use the formula you learned in Round 2: Start with "I," express your feeling, and give a factual reason for why you feel that way.

To illustrate, here are two different ways to handle the same situation—a date who arrives late:

SHE: *You're late again. You really make me mad. You never get here on time. You're just plain inconsiderate. Now we're going to miss the best part of the play.*

HE: *What do you mean I'm late again? When was I late before? You're the one who's always still fussing around with your clothes and makeup when I get here. You're so self-centered that it doesn't even occur to you that I might*

have a good reason for being a few minutes late tonight.

SHE: *I'm upset that you're late. I'm afraid we're going to miss the start of the play. I've heard that the opening scene is the funniest one of all, and I really wanted to see it.*

HE: *I really apologize. I was delayed by a long-distance call just as I started out the door. Come on, we'll park in the higher-cost lot right next to the theater to save time.*

SHE: *What was the call about? Is anything wrong?*

Accusations, generalizations, assumptions, exaggerations, and name-calling fly freely from one side to the other in the first dialog. Most of their sentences start with "you" as they chew each other out. This is the exact opposite of I-talk. We call this kind of chewing out "you-ing out."

In the second dialog, the woman deals only with facts and her feelings about what happened. Instead of feeling threatened and responding defensively, her date is able to deal with the problem at hand and suggest a solution. There's a preponderance of "I's" in their interchange, and the only "you" is in a statement of fact ("you're late"). They're using "I-talk."

When to Use I-Talk

Use I-talk whenever you want to let someone know how you feel about something—especially when your feelings are contrary to the wishes or viewpoint of the other person or are apt to put them on the defensive. Use it when you have a problem or a grievance that you want someone else to know about. It's a way of getting others to listen to you the same way you do to them when you reflective listen.

As both reflective listening and I-talk become a comfortable part of your repertoire, you'll find yourself using the two skills alter-

"I don't care what everybody else says, I like you."

nately in the same conversation. When the *other person* has a problem, you reflect back their feelings to show understanding. When *you* have the problem, you help them to understand it by using I-talk.

Why Use I-Talk

I-talk lets you meet your own needs and gives a better balance of give-and-take in a relationship. It usually lessens resistance and facilitates getting people to do what you want.

At first glance it may seem that you're doing all the work in the relationship, since you have to listen just right and express your own feelings just right. In fact, what you're doing is initiating interchanges in a way that causes others to respond as *you* want them to, giving *you* maximum control of the situation.

The Case against You-ing People out

Before they try it, many program participants are skeptical about I-talk. A few argue, "I don't see anything wrong with you-ing people out. It *works!* There's no doubt in anybody's mind about how *I* feel when *I* tell somebody off."

It's true that you-ing out gets the message across, even if people don't understand what your exact feelings are and why you feel that way. Especially those who see you as having more authority or strength than they may buckle under—at least until they're in a position themselves to get even. But those who see themselves as equal are apt to put up a fight. And those who have more strength or authority than *you* may well clobber you.

Even when it works, you-ing out is a putdown, and like any putdown, it lowers the self-esteem of the objects of your displeasure. It's disrespectful and provokes disrespect in return. It provokes resentment toward you personally and resistance toward complying with your wishes. If you do win by intimidating others in this way, it's at the expense of relationships, future as well as immediate.

Finally, you-ing people out is a communication turnoff. Accusing, judging, criticizing, moralizing, ridiculing, name calling, shaming, threatening, bossing, and making sarcastic comments hamper communication when you're trying to get *your* feelings across, just as they interfere when you're trying to show that you understand the feelings of others.

[87]

Change the "You" to "I"

Here are some examples of typical you-ing out turnoffs and how to change them to I-talk. Notice you simply change the "you" at the beginning of your statement to "I," add your feelings, and back them up with observable (hopefully uncontestable) facts.

You-ing out

You're making me mad. Why don't you look where you're going? (translation: *You don't look where you're going.*) *That's the third time you've bumped my arm and spilled my drink.* (**Accusing**)

I-talk

I'm starting to get mad. When you bump my arm like that my drink spills all over my clothes and on the carpet.

In a case like this, don't say, "*You* make me mad," or "*You* make me spill my drink." Keep the message on a factual and feeling level to lessen argument and resentment. Bumping your arm is a fact that can't be disputed. The drink spilling is a consequence that can't be disputed. Your annoyance is a feeling that can't be disputed.

You-ing out

You're always quick to find fault, but you never think to tell me about it when I do something right. (**Criticizing**)

I-talk

My feelings are really hurt (feeling) *when I do something right and you don't comment on it* (fact).

Even though this I-talk doesn't begin with the word "I," it's still authentic, because a feeling is expressed and no one is you'd out.

Try to avoid using words like "always" and "never," which invariably trigger counteraccusations and arguments.

You-ing out

You should know better than to leave your shoes lying around where the dog can chew them up. Do you think I can afford to buy you new shoes every day of the week? (**Moralizing**)

I-talk

Damn! The dog has chewed up one of your new shoes that cost twenty-five dollars (fact). *I get really angry* (feeling) *when you leave your shoes lying around* (fact).

Don't feel that you have to pull punches here any more than you do when you're reflective listening. A "damn" aimed at no one in particular isn't considered you-talk. But a "damn *you*" is the worst kind of you-ing out.

You-ing out

I wish you'd stop telling funny stories at my expense. (**Bossing**—translates to: *Stop telling . . .*) *I think you were terribly inconsiderate last night at dinner.* (**Judging, name calling.**—translates to: *You were* inconsiderate . . .)

I-talk

I hated it (feeling) *last night when you told that story* (fact) *about me soaking the french toast in the batter for an hour. I don't like* (feeling) *to be laughed at.*

Simply starting a sentence with "I" doesn't necessarily make it I-talk. Avoid camouflaging you-talk by starting a sentence with "I think." "*I think* you're inconsiderate" is still judgmental. "*I think* you should know better" is still moralistic. "*I think* you're going to be sorry" is still a threat. To avoid slip-ups, follow the rule, "Change the 'you' to 'I' and add your feeling and a factual reason."

Watch Your "I's" and "You's"

Just as starting a sentence with "I" doesn't necessarily make it I-talk, neither does merely using "you" in a sentence always mean that you're you-ing someone out.

It's all right to use "you" in an educated guess—for example:

Sounds like you *are worried about what* you *should say in the job interview.*

Or when you're stating an observable fact:

I'm really discouraged because you *walked on the kitchen floor before the wax was dry.*

Avoid using "you" when it will serve as a communication turnoff, either in reflective listening to the feelings of others or in expressing your own feelings. For example:

Don't complain to me about flunking your test ("You" is understood in commands).

If you *had studied last night . . .* (translates to: You should have studied . . .).

That was plain careless of you *. . .* (translates to: You were plain careless . . .)

Analyze Your Anger

If you find yourself expressing anger more often than any other feeling in I-talk, examine your feelings carefully. Sometimes instead of being the first feeling you experience, anger is a reaction to another emotion such as fear or humiliation.

Anne Noyd was standing on the curb waiting for a traffic light to change when a boy on a bicycle came racing down the street toward her. As he hit the mud puddle directly in front of her she was showered with dirt and water. He looked around and laughed—and sped away. She was furious. When she analyzed the incident later, however, she realized that she had two other feelings in a split-second interval before she became enraged. First, she was frightened, because it looked as though the bike would run right into her—and she felt like screaming. Second, she was humiliated, because the boy turned around and laughed—and she felt like crying. The fear and humiliation were so fleeting and so overshadowed by the anger that she only remembered them when she conscientiously recounted the experience to herself later.

Psychologists say that the anger generated in cases like this is partially physiological. It's a kind of primitive reaction to being threatened. In other words, fear starts the adrenaline flowing to prepare you to defend yourself from the danger. When the danger subsides, as it did in Anne's case, the adrenaline keeps on flowing for a while. Anger, and perhaps a desire for revenge, are the result. The same kind of thing can happen when people are worried or grieved, too.

If you find yourself saying "I'm mad/annoyed/irritated/upset" too often, stop and analyze what happened. If you discover that you felt another emotion first, say so.

I'm really discouraged to come home and find the lights have been burning all night, when I'm trying so hard to conserve energy—and then I get mad.

I'm scared when you drive these mountain roads so fast. I feel hurt and angry because you don't slow down when I ask you to.

In general, people react better to expressions like these than they do to anger, because they feel less threatened.

Don't Dig up Old Bones

Don't use I-talk as an excuse to air old gripes. Deal with current concerns to help people understand and accept your feelings and improve relationships you care about.

Catch Yourself if You Slip

Correct yourself on the spot if you inadvertently slip back into the you-talk habit:

Don't you ever think of anyone else's feel-ings?—Wait, I take that back. What I mean to say is, my feelings are hurt when you don't call or write for such a long time.

GENERAL STRATEGY

Here are some suggestions for getting the most out of your Workouts with people you know.

Mix and Match Your Skills

Use the skills you've learned earlier as well as the new ones you're learning in your Work-outs in this Round: Personalize greetings, give positive strokes, ask questions, encourage peo-ple to tell information and feelings by smart listening, tell your own feelings with I-talk. Try to develop the ability to spontaneously choose the skills that are appropriate for the situation and the people you're dealing with.

Here's how mixing and matching skills might work to deal with a disgruntled em-ployee:

EMPLOYEE: *I quit. You can take this job and shove it!*

MANAGER: *Sounds like you're pretty ticked off! (Reflective listening)*

EMPLOYEE: *You said it! This is the third time this month I've been screwed on assignments.*

MANAGER: *You haven't liked your work as-signments lately. (Reflective listening)*

EMPLOYEE: *That's right! It sure looks to me like Lowe Level walks off with all the cherries.*

MANAGER: *The cherries? You think he gets better assignments than you do? (Reflective lis-tening)*

EMPLOYEE: *Yeah. He gets the stuff you can do with your eyes closed. I get the planning jobs that take everything I've got to figure them out and set them up right.*

MANAGER: *You'd like some of the easy stuff so you can coast a little. (Reflective listening)*

EMPLOYEE: *I wouldn't say that. I like some challenge and I don't like to be idle. But the work load that Level gets is a joke! (Emotional temperature is going down some as employee is able to state feelings more clearly.)*

MANAGER: *So you don't really mind your work load as much as you resent Lowe's. You just wish he'd pull his weight. Is that it? (Reflec-tive listening)*

EMPLOYEE: *Yeah. That's what it boils down to.*

MANAGER: *Well, I have a problem here that I've been trying to solve the best way I know how. (I-talk) Tell me this. What do you think would happen if I assigned Lowe the same kind of jobs that you do? (Expansive question)*

EMPLOYEE: *He couldn't do the work in a mil-lion years! He'd goof 'em up for sure!*

MANAGER: *I'm inclined to agree, so I try to load him up with the things I think he can do. He's just not ready to do the kind of things you do—but I think he can learn with you teaching him. (I-talk, factual reasons, and pos-itive strokes)*

EMPLOYEE: *Well—I have to admit he's better than he was a month ago. I guess he's gradually catching on.*

MANAGER: *I've noticed some improvement, myself. But until he develops some of the skill you have, I need you to do the tough stuff so I can be sure it's done right and done on time. I need men like you that I can count on when work gets critical. (I-talk and positive verbal strokes)*

EMPLOYEE: *I always do my best. (Emotional temperature practically back to normal)*

MANAGER: *I know you do and I appreciate it. That's why I assign the ones that really count to you. I especially liked the way you thought of reversing the machining cycle on the Climax job. It prevented a costly pile-up of work on the turrets. (I-talk and positive verbal strokes) I'd like you to explain your thinking on that one to Lowe.* (A managerial request, not I-talk, even though it starts with "I") *It's the kind of thing he needs to learn in order to take on bigger jobs.*

EMPLOYEE: *"I was kind of pleased with that one, myself. Maybe I* can *teach Lowe something. That's one way to get him to take on a heavier load of work, isn't it? I'll give it a try."*

MANAGER: *"I appreciate it. I'm glad you came in and told me how you felt."* (*I-talk*)

Change Your Conversation Habits

If you're naturally talkative and gregarious, listen more—or talk and listen differently.

If you're usually the silent type, or if you keep to yourself a lot, change your routines that encourage silence. Put down your book or newspaper when others are in the room and start a conversation—or at least show that you're available to listen.

Talk more at mealtimes and linger at the table after meals to join and shape conversation.

Actively Seek Sparring Sessions

Talk to others who are doing household chores—cooking, washing dishes, gardening, washing or repairing the car. Instead of relaxing in front of the TV set when others are occupied elsewhere, seek them out and talk, offering an occasional helping hand. Besides creating opportunities to practice your skills, this does wonders for a relationship.

Expand conversations with people you meet in personal business contacts—at the service station, in shops and stores, in government offices.

Make it a point to talk to neighbors when you see them outside their homes.

Plan some of your leisure activities so that there are opportunities for conversation. Go for walks or rides. Go on a picnic. Spend an afternoon or evening talking instead of attending spectator events where your attention is drawn toward the performance and away from each other.

Look for New Sparring Partners

Talk to more people more often—at family gatherings and social events. Seek out friends and relatives who are outside your routine pattern of contacts—former coworkers or neighbors who have moved across town; classmates you haven't seen since graduation; aunts, uncles, cousins, or old friends you've been out of touch with.

Work Out Often

Practice every chance you get, as long as it's off the job. The more you practice, the faster and better you'll learn the skills.

Start Easy

Begin your Workouts with whatever skill is easiest for you. Try listening first. Or share factual information of your own—tell what you did or saw or heard before you try to share your feelings.

Start with casual strangers or with acquaintances you see only occasionally if you're less uncomfortable with them. As your competence and confidence increase, gradually include more and more people you're close to.

LIVE ACTION REPORTS

There are four checkout lines in the cafeteria. I always choose the line with the white-haired woman. She's always pleasant and efficient. Today I decided to tell her so. I said, "I always choose your line because it's the fastest and you're always smiling." She really beamed and as she gave me my change she squeezed my hand very gently. I was really touched. I felt good all day from her simple gesture. Being on the receiving end made me realize how effective reinforcing gestures can be.

A friend of mine made a special trip over to show me her new leather boots and matching purse. My first thought was, "Wow, they must have cost a fortune." Then I guessed that she might be regretting the extravagance and was really looking for some reinforcement. Instead of my first reaction, I told her that I really liked the boots and that I especially liked them with the outfit she had chosen. She smiled and said she was glad I liked them because she worried about spending so much, but now she felt that they were worth it.

Made a point of greeting my roommates. I've tried to be sensitive to their feelings and more reflective in my responses. The change in our relationship has really impressed me—and I've learned more about each one of them in one week than I did the whole previous year.

I decided to talk to my neighbor, Audrey, late this afternoon. I've known her for a long time but I didn't feel as much at ease with her as I do with other friends. I think it's because she's so tall and beautiful. . . . I asked her about her sports car. I said I liked its color and low profile. We went for a ride, and as we got into the car she made a sarcastic comment about her long legs. Instead of saying, "You should be glad you're tall instead of a shrimp like me," I said, "You don't like being tall, huh?" She talked about her trouble getting clothes to fit, about having to sew her own, about being gawky all through her growing up. Understanding her feelings about herself made me fell less threatened by her beauty and stature. Besides, I learned she could sew. She's coming over tomorrow to help me with a dress I'm making.

Today I had what I consider to be my most significant experience to date in connection with the program. This morning I greeted a fellow student on the way to class. As we walked along together I didn't have the usual trouble talking to him . . . then I realized that it was because I was asking questions and listening instead of talking so much.

Just as we got to the classroom, Tom mentioned that his mother is going to have open-heart surgery tomorrow. At that moment a friend of mine met us, told us that class was cancelled, and asked me to join him for coffee. Because personal illnesses, deaths, and other grave problems usually leave me with an embarrassing lack of words, I thought, "Aha! Now I don't have to be uncomfortable listening to Tom's story about his mother." Oddly enough, I asked myself if I was making the right decision to abandon Tom at this point. After all, he probably wouldn't have broached the subject of his mother's surgery if he hadn't felt a need to talk about it.

I decided to risk some discomfort and followed Tom to the accounting lab instead of going for coffee. I asked if he felt like talking about his mom. At first he said, 'No,' but then he launched into a long explanation of his concern for her and the difficulties that a long convalescence would bring. I said very little while he talked and yet I think it was one of the most successful conversations I've ever had with someone—particularly considering the emotional subject matter.

When Tom had to go to his class, he thanked me for asking about his mom. I honestly think he felt better after our talk; I know I felt good about taking the time to listen.

Boy, is my vocabulary limited! I must say, "That's weird," a hundred times a day. I tried to say feelings instead and ended up saying, "I think that's weird." I'm getting better, though. One time today I said, "I get a weird feeling."

I nearly tripped over two little children who were playing hide and seek in the supermarket. I said, "Looks like you're having a lot of fun." They looked surprised and agreed. Then I said, "I nearly tripped over you. I'm afraid someone will get hurt when you run around corners like that so fast." I think it worked better than scolding them. But then their mother walked up and you-ed them out by hollering, "If you kids don't cut it out, you're really gonna get it!"

Set myself a quota of talking to one person a day that I hadn't talked to for a while. Stopped at a service station I hadn't been to since I moved. Went to a coffee shop for lunch—a place I used to go to a lot. Called my sister long-distance. Stopped in at a bar where an old school chum is bartender. Invited a couple we hadn't seen for a while over for dinner. Went to a family reunion out of town on the weekend—something I usually would have avoided. I hit the jackpot there!

A coworker has a habit of putting himself down and wishing he were like somebody else. Today he wished that he had a good sense of humor like the boss. My first thought was to list his good points, but then I reminded myself how that never worked in the past. If I told him he was a good cost analyst, he only answered, "I'm thorough, but I'm way too slow." So I just said, "Fred, I like you the way you are." That put an end to his self-criticism. How could he argue with that?

I continually find myself saying, "That's great," or "That's too bad." I really felt like a winner today when I blurted out, "I'll bet that made you feel good!"

I notice an added benefit of this Workout: people I've made an effort to greet and talk to are showing more friendliness toward me when we meet again.

I saw a friend of mine who is going through a marital crisis. I made a real effort to hear her feelings instead of giving advice. For some reason the conversation seemed more productive than usual. I felt less like an authority figure and more like a friend. And I didn't feel the burden that usually comes with giving advice. When I felt the conversation had run its course, I ended it with "I'm really glad you felt you could confide in me and I hope things work out."

Made it a point to notice the next time I saw my neighbor outside working in his garden. Went over and told him how much I enjoy looking across at his well-kept yard. Asked him some questions about what kind of fertilizer he uses, how often he waters it. It was a really pleasant conversation.

My sister dropped by to tell me her husband was leaving on a business trip to West Germany. He's a nuclear physicist. As she told me about the trip I sensed she was both boasting about his going and sad at being alone for several weeks. Rather than asking about the trip or sympathizing about her loneliness (which is what I'd usually do), I picked up on the boasting. I said, "It must make you really proud that Pete is your husband." She looked at me sort of surprised, but then she smiled and said she really was proud—he'd worked hard to make his success and she was glad he was getting some good opportunities and recognition. I tried to reflect her feeling of pride as she spoke of his accomplishments. When she left she was feeling cheerful instead of complaining about having to be alone.

Three of us share a house and one guy is a real pig. His room is a disaster area, but I don't mind that as much as the messes he leaves in the kitchen. I've tried about everything I can think of—sarcasm, good-natured reminders, threatening to kick him out if he doesn't get his act together. Nothing seems to get *through his thick skull—we just fight a lot. Last night I tried I-talk. I told him I feel imposed on when he leaves his dirty dishes in the sink. I said it was really frustrating for Tim and me because when he leaves a mess in the kitchen and is gone for several days we either have to look at his mess or clean it up. And we don't like either choice. I told him I get mad as hell when I trip over his dirty clothes on the bathroom floor, too.*

I don't know if it will change his sloppy ways, but at least I had the satisfaction of telling him just how I felt. I wouldn't say he was happy about the conversation, but he wasn't defensive or hostile like he usually is when we criticize his "housekeeping" habits. I felt proud of myself for keeping my cool.

Now that I know about these new skills, I often recognize them when I hear other people talk. I even notice them on TV. The best talk show hosts use substantive questions and are careful not to interrupt or monopolize conversations.

When I watch a situation comedy or a drama I catch myself thinking, "That was reflective listening," or "She sure you-ed him out." Lots of people use turnoffs—and that's just what they do, turn people off. It's kind of fun. It's a temptation to tell the other people watching TV about it, but then I remember about practicing privacy and catch myself just in time.

INSTANT REPLAY

In this Round you try to improve relationships with people in your own corner—friends, relatives, and acquaintances—people with whom you have some degree of emotional involvement.

The suggested Workouts are:

◗ Personalize your greeting.
   Use names or endearing terms.
   Inquire about an interest.

Refer to a shared interest or experience.
Recognize an achievement.
Take notice of an absence.

◗ Use reinforcing gestures.

◗ Give positive verbal strokes.

◗ Ask questions.

◗ Listen smart.
   Listen for content and information.
   Listen for feelings and show understanding.
   —Recognize and identify emotions.
   —Make noncommittal responses.
   —Make educated guesses.
   —Respond to positive feelings first.
   —Reflect negative feelings.
   —Avoid turnoffs (advising, threatening, moralizing, ordering, etc.).
   —Listen for feedback.
   —Be matter-of-fact about misinterpretations.
   —Look for disguised feelings.
   —Retreat, review, and repeat.
   —Avoid common pitfalls (echoing, underplaying feelings, overkill, etc.).

◗ Use I-talk.
   Change the "you" to "I" and add feelings and facts.
   Analyze your anger.
   Don't dig up old bones.
   Catch yourself if you slip.

◗ Follow the general strategy.
   Mix and match your skills.
   Change your conversation habits.
   Actively seek sparring sessions.
   Look for new sparring partners.
   Work out often.
   Start easy.

[94]

10

ROUND 5:

MANAGING THE BALANCE OF SOCIAL EXCHANGE (GETTING YOUR FAIR SHARE)

You get a chance to even the score in this Round. Specifically, you work toward an equitable balance of give and take in your personal and social relationships.

You try to balance social exchange so that you get your fair share of both the action and the returns of a contact. This is a small but significant shift in emphasis from previous Rounds where the process or *means* of social interaction was your primary concern. Now, for the first time, the *ends* of the interaction— and your own needs and wishes—are *equally* important.

THE CHALLENGE

In fight jargon, the challenge of the Round is to block more punches from others and land more punches of your own. Your objectives are to begin to shape transactions more to your own advantage; to get what's rightfully

yours; to appear effective and attractive to others; to further develop your ability to make decisions, influence others, and affect outcomes.

THE STRATEGY

In your strategy you employ all the skills you learned previously to improve relationships. But now you also use them to get people to do your wishes or follow your lead. While you continue to enhance relationships, you also try to change unbalanced relationships so that you get a more even share of both leadership and benefits.

You start with pleasant, easily accepted kinds of "impositions." Then you gradually increase your assertiveness: You make your wants known; you make decisions for yourself and for others; you resist being imposed on by others; you widen your pattern of association and increase your independence; you lessen the dependence of others on you.

Although your goal is to get your fair share in personal contacts, you still try to create an atmosphere of goodwill; you try to establish a reputation as an attractive, competent, decisive doer; you show a liking and respect for others that makes you liked in return.

You continue to practice with strangers, family, friends, and acquaintances—everyone in your environment except people on the job. As always, you choose your Workout partners carefully, starting with those you see as most amenable. If a particular relationship already enjoys an equitable balance, you leave it alone. You don't deliberately try to get more than your share in this Round.

THE MOVES

Your moves in this Round include asking pleasant favors; imposing favors; borrowing things; making assertive requests; making more decisions; modifying, resisting, and refusing requests from others; contributing more to conversations; making suggestions; making your wants known; asking for full service; increasing independence; using the telephone to advantage.

WINNING THE ROUND

You know you're gaining ground when more transactions are going your way and you're getting what you want more easily; when you have close yet free associations with a broader variety of people; when others seek you out for support or companionship rather than merely to impose on you; when you don't feel guilty about your new sense of independence; when your influence is not only accepted, but appreciated and valued; when people welcome and enjoy your presence.

WHY BALANCE THE SOCIAL EXCHANGE PATTERN

You have a valid right to a fair share of personal dignity, freedom, material needs, and self-fulfillment in your dealings with others. This alone is reason enough to balance the give-and-take exchange if it's weighted against you now.

GETTING EVEN TO MOVE AHEAD

Getting on an even plane with others also prepares you for your role as a leader. You get even with others first, then you move ahead of them.

CHANGE UNBALANCED RELATIONSHIPS

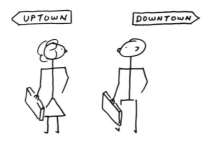

". . . and remember, it's your turn to cook dinner tonight."

As a manager you need to get results. You need to get others to respond to you so that you get what you want. You're the leader. They're the followers. Evening the balance of social exchange in this Round conditions you for influencing others and shaping circumstances to gain your own ends in later Rounds.

GETTING THE SKILLS TO GET EVEN

Some of the nottims you acquire in this Round are *managing appearance*, particularly *appearing attractive, credible, and resourceful; enjoying action, seeking challenge, making decisions, accepting responsibility, managing reciprocation, making quick friendships, influencing others, directing others, taking charge, maintaining independence, resisting external pressures, managing social distance, making assertive requests, and negotiating.* Skills you continue to practice and upgrade are *managing information, making appropriate responses to others' appeals, eliciting the desired response from others,* and *thinking more highly of yourself.* You still work on *initiating and sustaining action* as you begin to place more emphasis on *getting results.*

These nottims give you an edge in action management. They help you get answers and results, and they make you look good in the process. Looking attractive, competent, and action-oriented to a broad constituency maximizes your opportunities for further gain, because when you look good to others, whatever you do looks good to them, too.

Charles Schwab, the steel executive, exhibited these skills early in his career. As a young man he was a clerk in a store where William R. Jones, superintendent of one of Andrew Carnegie's steel plants, bought cigars. Schwab's self-confidence and wit won the attention of Jones, who soon gave him a job in the steel mill. Schwab continually showed his initiative by expanding his jobs. He won the favor of his mentor not only with his work, but by giving piano lessons to Jones' children.

Finally Schwab was given the key role of taking Jones' messages to Carnegie. He took full advantage of the opportunity to attract Carnegie's favorable attention. He learned the music and lyrics of Carnegie's favorite Scottish tunes and ballads and played the piano and sang them in Carnegie's parlor while waiting to see him. The rest is history. He became president of Carnegie Steel, then U.S. Steel and eventually founded the modern Bethlehem Steel Corporation.[1]

Recognizing the right to your fair share often makes the difference in getting your career rolling. The importance of this fact is even more pronounced in the case of women, who are currently finding increasing success in management careers. A few years ago *Business Week* featured several women executives who were making it up the corporate ladder.[2] They all attributed their success to a lot of time and hard work. They all also agreed that they often had to fight for their views and that they allowed no one to push them around.

One of the managers, Kay K. Mazuy, a senior officer of Shawmut Association, Inc. of Boston, had built her career through market research studies at Arthur D. Little, Inc., market research management at Polaroid, and market strategies in her own firm, Mazuy Associations, successively. She was characterized by her former boss at Polaroid as one who "would stick to her guns if she saw the figures differently than others. She had the courage to say, 'No, you're wrong.'"

Maintaining a strong conviction about her right to equality also gained a piece of the executive action for Diane Levine of Continental Airlines, who was interviewed in the same article. She says, "I care about how men feel about woman managers, but I'm not there to resocialize any-one. I'm paid to do a job that will affect sales and profit. If someone won't work with me for whatever reason, I will work around him, under him, over him, whatever is possible to move a project."

You accomplish more if you're convinced that you have a right to a fair share of the action—whether you're women looking for equality with men, men trying to catch up with your peers, or people in general seeking your just deserts in any kind of social exchange. Your Workouts in this Round help you to recognize your rights. When you know what you want and are convinced of your right to it, you've got a fighting chance to even the score.

THE WORKOUTS

As you increase your degree of influence over people and circumstance, selectively pick from your tool kit whatever skills meet your needs. Don't force your will on others. Try to present yourself and your wishes in ways that make others comply willingly. Although you want people to like you, *don't do what others want* to make them like you. *Make them like you* so they'll do what *you* want. This subtle distinction makes the difference in who controls the exchange, you or the other person.

"Impose" Favors

Do things for others that you're sure they'll appreciate.

Make Offers Others Can't Refuse

Hold a door, carry packages, help with household chores, assist someone into or out of a car. Pick up the tab for a companion's meal. Give your place in line to the person behind you. Give up your window seat to the person next to you.

Plan your approach carefully to ensure acceptance of your favor. Communicate your wish clearly and make it plain that you'll be disappointed if the person doesn't accept. Give believable reasons in I-talk:

I want this to be my treat today, because I've enjoyed your company so much.

I'd like you to go ahead of me (in line). *You seem to be in a hurry, and I have plenty of time.*

I'd like you to sit here next to the window so you can enjoy the scenery. I see it often, but I overheard you say that this is your first trip.

Offers like these, made to sound like they're doing you a favor by accepting, are an easy and painless way to impose your will on others. It goes without saying that you must initiate the offer, of course. If you comply with *their* request, you are obviously doing *their* will. This is not to say that you shouldn't comply with the wishes of others if you want to, but don't count that kind of favor as practice in imposing your will on others.

Do Something Unique and Unexpected

Surprise someone with a thoughtful gift or gesture:

I was down at the wharf today, so I picked up a loaf of your favorite sourdough bread.

I came across these wooden toast tongs at an arts and crafts sale and it reminded me of the trouble you had getting that burned English muffin out of your toaster last week.

I saw an ad for a new imported foods store so I called them and found out that they carry the Swedish peas you like.

Favors like these are neither expensive nor difficult to carry out. This makes it easier for

DO SOMETHING UNIQUE AND UNEXPECTED

"It's a towel rack for your bathroom."

others to accept them. They'll appreciate your thoughtfulness, but they won't feel embarrassed or obligated, as might be the case if you went to great expense or inconvenience.

Make your gesture an accomplished fact, not a promise. Don't say, for example, "When I'm down at the wharf I'll pick up some bread for you." To begin with, such a promise obligates you to carry through, subtly implying a servant role instead of the benefactor you want to be.

Promising also gives people a chance to argue or resist your favor if that's their nature. Surprises catch them off guard and give you the advantage.

Also, if you're unable to carry out your offer for some reason, people may see it as a broken promise. This lowers you in their opinion, which is the exact opposite of what you want. Surprising someone with the completed deed, on the other hand, establishes your reputation as a doer, not a promiser.

Finally, you score extra points with surprises because it lets people know that you were thinking of them while you were apart.

Observe others, listen smart, and use your imagination to think of thoughtful, unique favors. When you decide on something, do it promptly, both to emphasize your efficiency and to prevent someone else from beating you to the punch.

When another person expresses appreciation for your thoughtfulness, accept the thanks graciously. Don't say, "It was nothing," or "Anybody could have done it." Such comments only belittle yourself and your favor. Instead say something like, "I'm glad you like it," or "I was happy to do it."

The kind of strokes you give in this Workout create long-lasting respect and good will. More important for your managerial development, you've had your way—you've made others do what you want them to.

Ask Pleasant Favors

Ask people to do things for you that you know they'll enjoy doing. Get them to show off or demonstrate their special skills, knowledge, or interests.

I've always admired your roses. I noticed you took a lot of time and care when you cut them back earlier this month. I'd like you to show me how to prune mine.

I like your taste in wines. They always seem to fit the occasion perfectly. I'd like you to tell me how to choose a good wine for the dinner party I'm having next week.

I admire your skill with photography. I'd be pleased if you'd take a picture of me.

Ask favors of strangers as well as of people you know:

To a piano bar pianist: I like your interpretations of the old favorites. I'd like to hear you play Stardust.

[99]

To the host in a restaurant: I'm fascinated by the way you fold those napkins so they look like flowers. I'd like you to show me how to do it.

Any kind of ability or expertise is a possibility, from juggling oranges to juggling figures. Make sure they're things you know the person enjoys doing and will do for you willingly, so it won't seem like you're imposing. Choose things where you have a real need or can show genuine admiration.

You'll discover that most people like to show off their talents and be helpful to others. In fact, studies show that instead of causing resentment, letting people do you favors actually makes them like you better.[3] They're pleased that you admire their skill or consider them good enough friends to ask. And they like you more in return.

If people offer to do more than you ask—like prune all your rose bushes for you, or buy the wine and loan you the "right" bottle opener and glasses—accept the extra favors graciously, *if* you *want* them. But don't let others force unwanted services or attention on you—like "Let's make a standing date for Saturday mornings and I'll teach you how to care for your other plants, too" or "I'll join you for dinner on Friday and serve the wine for you." The challenge is to manage people and situations. The object is to get others to do *you* a favor, not let them *impose* a favor on you.

In your Workouts with favors, never let it appear that you're giving or asking with reciprocation in mind. Try to look like you're offering a favor as a genuine act of consideration because you think highly of others, not because you expect something in return. Also try not to look like you're asking a favor because the other person "owes" you. For most people, favors create unconscious feelings of obligation anyway—a fact you may find useful later. But if the connection is obvious, it de-

stroys the other person's pleasure in either doing for you or accepting from you.

Maura Fishant was pleased when Will Scheinon, the idol of all the typists in the secretarial pool, asked her out to lunch. Just as they got back to the office Will said, "Incidentally, I need some bids typed up before tomorrow. I like your work better than any of the other girls'. I'd really appreciate it if you'd do them for me this afternoon." Maura said "OK" and stayed after quitting time to finish, but her resentment built as she worked. Later she confided to a friend, "I've always liked Will, and I was pleased that he liked my work. I'd have typed the bids for him without the phony lunch bit. The way it is now, I feel like I made a fool of myself, thinking he took me to lunch because he liked me, when he was really just scheming to get what he wanted."

Will's timing made Maura feel that she'd been used. If the lunch invitation had come after the bids were typed, Maura could have accepted it as a thoughtful gesture of appreciation on Will's part. Even though she might still prefer to be asked out on her personal merits, at least she could sincerely appreciate his effort to say "thank you." As it was, she felt only embarrassment and resentment. And Will blew his chances for any special favors from Maura in the future.

To be on the safe side, practice imposing and requesting favors with different people. Or watch your timing if you use both skills with the same person: *Ask* a favor first and *impose* a favor later. That leaves the other person feeling better about the interaction and keeps the relationship amiable for future contacts.

Get Your Share of the Conversation

Speak up in your conversations with others. Consciously try to balance the give and take in verbal exchanges so that you do your fair share of the talking.

Talk about Your Experiences

Continue to listen, but gradually begin to talk more in your one-to-one contacts. Talk about what you discover as you continue to explore and observe your surroundings and increase your contacts with people in general. Make mental notes of things you think various people would like to hear about. Anticipate who you'll be seeing and plan some general topics of discussion.

If a conversation is running smoothly and you can contribute without using your pre-planned material, don't feel compelled to change the subject. Don't force issues or change a subject abruptly. But if the conversation runs down or there's a lull, move in and fill the gap. When you do, don't say, "Not to change the subject, but . . ." if you are, in fact, changing the subject. Say something like, "I just remembered something I've been wanting to tell you . . ." or "I had an interesting experience I want to share with you. . . ."

Mentally rehearse what you want to say and how you want to say it to make it as interesting as possible. Avoid moralizing, judging, or instructing. Keep your contributions on the light side, to make your presence enjoyed at the time and create an image of adventure, imagination, energy, and curiosity for others to remember.

Practice Giving Opinions

Express your feelings and thoughts on subjects that others bring up in conversation, but also bring up topics of your own.

In one-to-one contacts, ask other people's opinions on subjects about which you have developed a point of view. Listen to their views and reflect understanding of their position. Then tell what you think and why you think it.

Try to avoid controversy. Don't try to get others to agree with you, but don't let them win you over, either. Be content to state your opinion and accept the similarities and differences as they are. The object is to make your views known and to be able to state an opinion whether others agree with it or not.

Express opinions often so you have lots of opportunities to practice keeping your emotions in check. Ask questions and reflectively listen from time to time to "catch your emotional breath" and keep others calm. Show that you understand others' viewpoints without either agreeing or disagreeing with them. Never "you" them out.

If others push too hard for agreement or berate or ridicule you for your viewpoint, try approaches like these:

I understand what you're saying, but I'm going to have to give it some more thought.

No, I don't agree with you, but I respect your right to your opinion.

I can tell that you feel very strongly about this, but so do I. . . .

Make More Decisions

Take over more decisions in matters that concern you and start to make decisions that influence others. Look for decision-making opportunities in your everyday environment. Begin your Workouts with less consequential decisions, amenable people, and easily manageable situations.

State Your Preference When Asked

When someone asks your preference, give it. When a decision is necessary, be the one to make it —without hesitation.

When would you like to go?
I'd like to leave at seven-thirty so we'll be seated by eight o'clock. (Not: Oh, I don't know— what time is convenient for you?)

MAKE MORE DECISIONS

"Well, I think . . . let's see . . . no, that won't work . . . better ask Joe."

What would you like for dinner?

I'm hungry for spaghetti, or *How about soup?* or *Let's go to the drive-through.* (Not: Anything is fine with me. You decide.)

What do you want to watch on TV?

I'd like to see "Sully's Seraphim" or *I'd rather listen to records than watch TV* or *Let's go for a walk instead.* (Not: Whatever you want.)

If, as sometimes happens, the request for a preference was perfunctory and causes resistance, attempt to overcome it without becoming argumentative or defensive.

We don't have any spaghetti.

I'll go out and buy some, or *Let's have soup tonight, and we can have spaghetti tomorrow, after you've been to the market.* (Not: How was I supposed to know you didn't have any spaghetti *or* If you didn't intend to cook what I want, why did you ask me?)

Try to anticipate what kinds of preferences you'll be asked to express, and plan a few possible answers in advance. A ready answer makes you *look* spontaneous, confident, and decisive and, with practice, leads quickly to genuine confidence, spontaneity, and decisiveness.

Stop Letting Others
Make Decisions for You

Start to exercise more independence in decisions you have a right to make for yourself. Just as you freed yourself from the tyranny and seductive security of routine, begin now to assert yourself against the unwanted domination of others.

Make it a point not to ask approval from others for what you eat, how you dress, how you style your hair, where and what you buy, and how you spend some of your free time. Start with things that are most personal and affect others least.

Thanks for offering to pick me up, but I'm going to drive myself tomorrow.

Since you're going to be playing poker Thursday night, I'm going to a movie with some friends.

I'm going to buy the blue shirt this time because I really like it.

Make decisions on your own in the absence of the person or persons who usually influence you.

While you were gone the Volunteer Thrift Shop called and asked me to help out on Saturday mornings for six weeks. I said I would.

The jewelers called to say that it would cost fifteen dollars to service my watch. I couldn't reach you to ask your opinion, so I told them to go ahead.

Help Others Make up Their Minds

When people are in doubt, help them to make up their minds. There are many situations that virtually beg for someone to step in and make a decision.

I can't decide whether to put this picture over the TV set or above the buffet.
I like it over the buffet. I like it better with the white wall in there.

I wish I knew of a good French restaurant to go to on our wedding anniversary.
Go to La Cuilleré Graisseux at Garnet Point. Their specialty is nourriture de hier.

Situations like these are commonplace—where to go, when to go, what to do, how to do it, who to see, what to wear. Look for decision vacuums and don't hesitate to fill them.

Take Responsibility for Outcomes

Don't "delegate" blame for your decisions to other people or to circumstances. Don't argue. Don't apologize.

If you goof, or somebody doesn't like the outcome of your decision, accept full responsibility for the decision anyway.

Suppose you were the one who chose a movie and your companion complains, "That was one lousy movie. I hated it."

Don't say, "Well, I'm certainly sorry that I spoiled your evening" or "That's the last time I'll recommend a movie to you."
Say something like, "I agree with you (if you do). I don't know how it's managed to get so much good publicity," Or state matter of factly, "I enjoyed it. I guess our taste in movies differs. We'll go to one you choose next time."

Practice accepting the outcomes of your decisions honestly and gracefully, whichever way they go. Don't be a chronic apologizer or alibier.

Say No

Learn to refuse requests from others without guilt or fear of being disliked. Don't give in to the urge to say yes just to please others or get them off your back. You may regret it later, as these examples illustrate:

For several years I've been doing my employer's personal gift shopping on my own time as a favor. I feel it's an imposition and I'd like to put a stop to it, but I'm afraid it will cause hard feelings.

I knew I didn't have time to head up the fund drive for SPITE (Society to Prevent Infestive Termites' Extinction), but the person who called made me feel so guilty that I said, "yes"—now I wish I hadn't.

To get what *you* want, practice resisting the pressure others exert to get what *they* want. If you're a soft touch now, don't change too abruptly.

Delay Action on a Request

Say "yes" but make it clear that you'll comply at your convenience.

I'll be glad to help as soon as I finish what I'm doing.

Sure, I can do that—tomorrow.

No problem. I'll pick it up for you next week when I'm out that way.

Delaying action isn't a flat no, but it clearly indicates that your own priority is higher than the other person's. It usually cuts down on the urgency and frequency of future requests and discourages last-minute appeals. This raises your self-esteem because you feel less like you're being imposed upon. You're more in control, and in a small but important way, you have successfully shaped the environment.

Make Compliance Conditional

When others make requests, say yes on the condition that they do something for you in return. By trading off your servant role for theirs, both sides end up even.

Be specific, positive, and matter-of-fact when you state your bargain so that you appear strong, but cordial: Don't threaten or grumble, "No, I won't do it unless you help me first." Say something like, "Yes, I'll be glad to help you wax your car, but I'd like you to help me mow the lawn in return."

If you agree to help others first, don't let them off the hook for their part of the bargain later. If you're not sure they'll carry through, get your service from them first.

Anticipate situations where others habitually impose on you and have a number of things in mind that others can do for you, so that your "yes, but . . ." response will be spontaneous, not contrived and phony-sounding.

Show Others How to Help Themselves

If others claim they "can't" or "don't know how" to do something, offer to show them. Disarmed of their excuse for imposing on you, they're less likely to make the same request again.

I'll go with you to the permit office and we'll go through the procedure for getting the plans approved together so you won't have to depend on me next time.

MAKE COMPLIANCE CONDITIONAL

". . . it works like this. If you take a kitten, I buy a box of cookies. If you take another . . ."

I'll show you where the outdated records are kept in the storeroom. Then next time you can get what you need without my help.

Use this approach whenever people ask you to do something you *don't want* to do which they *can* do for themselves—from checking under the hood of a car to sewing on a button. Don't use it with technical or hard-to-learn skills or proprietary skills. Don't use it in circumstances where it's to your advantage to be "indispensable" to someone.

Since learning to do for themselves frees others from their dependency on you as much as it frees you of their imposition, use this approach only when you're sure it's to your advantage.

Refuse Outright

Simply say no *unhesitatingly, succinctly,* and *firmly.*

Requests in the form of restrictive questions ("would you," "will you," or "can you") reflect a weak posture and make it easy to say no. Direct refusals to such questions are often accepted without a fight.

If a reason for refusing is called for ("I don't want to" is often reason enough), make sure it doesn't suggest that your answer can be disputed or changed to a yes. Be polite but matter-of-fact and firm. Give sound reasons, stating facts and feelings.

No, I can't give you a ride on Tuesday. I'd be late to work because it's out of my way to pick you up and drop you off.

No, I won't wash your breakfast dishes. I don't like to wash dishes. We agreed that all of us would clean up after ourselves in the kitchen.

Don't use the "broken record" technique in relationships you value. That's the approach where you say no, state your reason, and impassively repeat it verbatim, again and again, no matter how much the other party pleads or disagrees. For example:

Can I borrow one of your new suitcases for my trip to Europe?

No. I never lend my luggage.

I only need a small one.

No. I never lend my luggage.

I'll take really good care of it.

No. I never lend my luggage. . . .

This kind of refusal is both aggravating and insulting because you seem to neither hear nor care what the other person is saying.

You can say no firmly without being disrespectful. The trick is to keep the current request the *only* subject of the discussion and remain politely resolute:

Can I borrow one of your new suitcases for my trip to Europe?

No. I don't want to lend them to anyone because they're still so new. I'd feel terrible if they got damaged.

I only need a little one.

I wouldn't want that one damaged, either.

I'd take really good care of it.

I know you would. But baggage handlers are often careless, and I'd feel resentful if it came back with dents and scratches in it, even if it weren't your fault. . . .

If someone tries to make you feel guilty or distract you with tangential arguments, refuse the bait and stay on target:

I think you're being unreasonable to refuse to let me use one measly suitcase! What kind of friend are you, anyway?

I can understand your being disappointed that I'm saying no. And I value your friendship a lot. But I can't help you out this time. (Not:

Look who's talking about friendship! How about the time you refused to let me borrow your tennis racket?)

In other words, reflectively listen to hostility, resentment, disappointment—whatever the feelings are—but then take the conversation back to the point at issue. In this way you prevent negative feelings and antagonistic behavior from escalating. And even though you don't grant the request, you preserve a relationship you value.

Avoid "broken record" refusals even in situations where you feel that the relationship is secondary—door-to-door salespeople, telephone solicitors, or strangers, for example. Simply refuse firmly and follow up with appropriate reinforcing gestures. Say, "No, thank you. I'm not interested." Don't allow yourself to be drawn off target by side issues. As soon as possible, signal termination by closing the door, hanging up the phone, or quickly walking away.

Refuse and Counter with a Request of Your Own

When someone imposes on you with a request that they're perfectly capable of handling themselves, say no and follow up with a request of your own.

Will you carry these card table chairs out to the garage for me?

Gee, I can't. I'm not going to be through installing this window glass for another hour or so. Incidentally, when you go out to the garage, I'd appreciate your bringing back that small stepladder. I'll need it before I'm done here.

On your lunch break today will you take this Mother's Day card to the post office and send it special delivery?

I'd like to help you out, but I have a luncheon engagement that's going to take my whole lunch hour. While you're there, pick up a roll of stamps for me. Here's the money.

Once you put a plan like this into action, see it through:

My grass got so high while I was gone that I can't cut it with my hand mower. Will you do it for me?

Gee, I can't. I'll be busy with my remodeling all week. I can see your lawn needs mowing all right. So does mine. While you're mowing yours, I'd like you to mow mine, too.

But I don't have a mower.

You can use mine.

But I don't know how to run it.

I'll show you right now.

Notice how several skills are combined in the example above—smart listening, I-talk, asking a favor that's hard to refuse, disarming helplessness, refusing a request, and countering with one of your own. And it all seems to happen spontaneously.

Use the refuse-and-counter tactic mainly with habitual imposers in relationships where you feel you're being taken advantage of, and where you feel the imposers are more than able to fend for themselves. Anticipate opportunities with this kind of person and plan and covertly rehearse your refusal.

Besides the fun of evening the score for past impositions, this approach doubly dampens others' urge to impose on you. When they make a request they're not only turned down, they're also faced with a request they must deal with in return. As a result the relationship takes on changed meaning. You serve notice that you can't be counted on to play a passive servant role in the future. And you also make it clear that the price of asking runs high.

Practice your right-to-refuse Workouts selectively. If a relationship enjoys an equal balance of give and take now, leave it alone. If you already dominate a relationship, don't push for even greater influence. Seek more challenging circumstances and people with whom to assert yourself—situations where you feel you presently give too many yes's and receive too many no's.

Using an incremental approach, start with people whom you believe will accept no for an answer most graciously and avoid those who are especially important to you until your skill and confidence increase.

Start with the kinds of refusals that require the least assertiveness or confrontation and gradually move on to those you think take a lot of nerve.

Practice saying no on the telephone before you do so in person, or make your first refusals to especially difficult people over the phone.

Remember that saying no to people you usually say yes to is a two-sided blade. While it cuts you free of a compulsion to comply and increases your independence, it also frees others from dependence on you. By refusing to do for others, you either force them to do for themselves or to find someone else to do for them in your place. Most people find that this creates happier, stronger individuals and improves relationships. To avoid any unwanted backlash and maintain the balance of social exchange you want, however, move carefully until you see how you like the changes your own different behavior causes in those you care about.

Suggest Highly Probable Activities

When you sense that others are leaning strongly toward a particular decision, be the one to finalize it by putting it into words.

What time does the big game start on TV?
Any minute now. Let's go into the family room and watch the pregame show.

Boy that popcorn smells good.
Let's buy some at intermission.

Make a quick survey of the situation, combine it with what you already know about the other person, and make spontaneous suggestions that fit the time and occasion.

I'm burning up in this sun. You must feel hot, too. Let's go over and get a cold drink.

The storm's so bad I could hardly hold the car on the road on the way over.
Then why don't we forget bowling and stay here. I'll light a fire in the fireplace and put on some records.

Make things happen *for* you instead of letting them happen *to* you whenever you can. But if you see that something's probably going to happen anyway—and you're agreeable to it—make it seem like it was your idea.

When you suggest the inevitable, others make a subtle connection between your suggestion and what actually takes place. Since you get credit for making it happen, you also get a reputation for making agreeable decisions and shaping events. With your reputation preceding you, it's easier to exert genuine influence and shape circumstance the next time.

Speak up for What You Want

Go straight to the point and tell others what you want:

I only want to play two sets today. The Athletic Sport Store is having a sale on golf bags. I'd like to stop there on the way home. It's in the new Galactic Center. It's a far-out concept in marketing. I think you'd enjoy seeing their layout. . . .

I'd like to eat out tonight. I'm too tired to cook after the exhausting day I've had.

Don't expect people to guess your preferences or go out of their way to ask you what you want. Speak up and make sure they know.

To carry the greatest weight, express your wishes early. Timing is very important in influencing others. An idea presented first, by itself, stands out. An idea that's been heard before or one that's presented in a field of others easily becomes lost in the crowd.

If you think someone has the same idea, make your wants known first.

The Applied Statistics Society is having its annual meeting in Las Vegas next month. I notice they have a series of seminars on performance tables, card sorting, and rotary scanning and indexing. I'd like to represent our organization. I believe I can personally gain from the trip and also bring back some useful insight into risk-reward ratios.

If it turns out that there's room for others to share in the request, you still get credit for thinking of it first. There's no strength of leadership in "me too." Nor does it make a favorable impression to explain, "I thought of that a long time ago, I just never mentioned it."

Clarify your wants in your own mind and think of incontestable reasons to back them up. State your wants in I-talk, expressing feelings and facts. Make them sound convincing.

Don't worry if you don't "win them all." Some people are incurably stubborn about having their own way. When you have a conflict of desires with this particular breed of mule, it may be impossible to even the score

no matter what you try. Keep testing your skills on them anyway as you improve your persuasive powers, but if you never get your way, realize that it's not your fault. With such people you can either put up with playing second fiddle (if the redeeming features are great enough) or dump the relationship—both of which have disadvantages. As your personal confidence, self-esteem, and managerial competence increase, so does your ability to make such a choice and deal satisfactorily with the consequences.

When you meet situations where the wants of others are equally as strong or important to them as yours are to you, shoot for a compromise or a tradeoff:

Okay, I know I promised I'd go to the church pot luck dinner with you. But I didn't realize this was the Monday they were televising the Recoilers game. I'd be willing to go to the dinner if we can leave by eight-thirty. That way I can see at least part of the game.

I'll make a deal. Both of us can't be gone on Friday. I'll fill in for you next Friday if you'll fill in for me the following week.

Anticipate problems and meet them head on instead of avoiding situations or suffering in silence. Make your wants and needs known in a positive way early in order to shape situations that otherwise might become awkward or work to your disadvantage.

Since either Tuesday or Thursday seems to be all right with you, I suggest that we meet on Thursday. I have a prior commitment on Tuesdays.

I'm looking forward to coming to dinner. But I'd like you to know I'm on a salt-free diet, so there are certain foods I have to avoid. I'll check with you before sitting down to dinner so that I'll know what I can eat.

If someone offers to make special arrangements to accommodate you, accept graciously. Don't make them coax you. Show genuine appreciation that will make them glad they went out of their way for you.

Learning to speak up for what you want in this Workout is good managerial training because it's an exercise in initiatory decision making. This requires more skill and assertiveness than merely reactively choosing what you want from alternatives offered by others.

State Your Problem

Tell people your problem and let them help you solve it. To save time and increase your efficiency, state your problem briefly instead of asking piecemeal questions.

Here are two possible approaches to the same banking problem. Which approach would impress you more favorably if you were the bank employee?

STATE YOUR PROBLEM

"I have a problem . . ."

Is it possible to transfer funds from one city to another?

Yes.

Can you transfer funds from here to Chicago?

Yes.

Can you do it for me?

Do you have an account with us?

Yes.

Then we can handle it for you.

Does it take very long?

Not usually, but it depends on the time of day the transaction is made and the time zone the bank is in.

Do you think it would be deposited before tomorrow night?

It certainly should be if we start the transaction now.

Well, OK. Then I guess I'll go that route. What do I have to do?

I have a problem. I need to send some money from an account I have with you to a bank in Chicago. It has to be deposited before tomorrow night. How do I do it?

I'd be glad to handle that for you. How much money do you want to send and what bank is it going to? . . .

The second statement says it all, clearly and concisely. It requires only a moment's covert rehearsal, but helps the bank personnel deal with the situation efficiently, and it makes the questioner appear far more intelligent and with-it.

Use I-talk to state your problem, not restrictive questions that sound like begging and can easily be answered with a no.

I need your help—I can't find any Finicky Feline cat treats on the shelf. (Not: Will you please help me find . . . ?)

I've got a problem. I promised to call H. S. Cumshaw before closing time about that rebate deal, but his line has been busy and I'm going to be in a meeting for the rest of the day. I need you to get hold of him and tell him I'll get back with him tomorrow. (Not: If it's not too much trouble, could you please call H. S. Cumshaw . . . ?)

Stating your problem usually works like a charm. When you explain that you're in a predicament, most people can't resist the challenge to help you solve your problem, no matter how small it is. It's as if you become partners in a venture. They often identify with your need and go beyond the call of duty to be of assistance:

Melody Wordless called a music store and explained, "I've got a problem I'm hoping you can help me with. I want to start an essay I'm writing with the words of an old song—but I can't for the life of me remember the second line of the lyrics."
The clerk asked her to hold while she looked through all the songbooks in stock, without success. Then she offered, "I've heard my mother sing that song. I'll call her and ask her what the words are and call you back in a few minutes."

The approach makes you feel good because you get what you want without humbling yourself, and it makes others feel good because they were able to help you out.

Try stating your problem instead of ordering or asking people who resent direct requests because they think you're trying to boss them around. Telling what you need instead of ordering or asking for help makes them feel that they have a choice in the matter. Knowing that it's voluntary encourages them to volunteer:

"Will you help me move these desks around?" gives an opportunity to say no even if it's only mumbled inaudibly or expressed in thought. "I need some help moving these desks around" gives others a chance to *offer*, making them feel initiatory and independent instead of responsive and subservient.

Notice how stating a problem instead of asking a question affects the responses in these examples:

Asking

Where's the key to the restroom?

Don't ask me, I haven't used it today.

Who had it last?

How should I know? Am I the key keeper or something?

You don't need to be nasty about it. It was just an innocent question.

Well, I get sick of everybody around here blaming me when something gets lost.

Poor mistreated you, everybody always picking on you. . . . (Notice all the you-ing out in the interchange?)

Stating

I need the key to the restroom. It isn't on the hook beside the counter.

I haven't seen it, but I'll help you look.

Asking

How much longer is it going to take you to finish that job?

Quit bugging me. I'm working as fast as I can.

Stating

I need to know when you'll be finished with the jig so I can plan my work accordingly.

I think it's going to be another two hours. I'll let you know as soon as I'm done.

Request Full Service

Request all the service and attention you feel you're entitled to. In other words, insist on your reasonable rights.

Although what's reasonable is sometimes difficult to resolve to everyone's satisfaction in personal relationships, it's usually fairly clear-cut where paid services are involved. You may not get full service automatically, but certain services are available if you opt for them. At a full-service gasoline station, for example, it's reasonable to have the attendant check the battery, tires, water, or transmission fluid; clean the windows, give travel directions. When making requests, don't order or demand. Use all the skills at your disposal: smile, use traditional openers, make favorable comments, ask questions, establish commonality, reflectively listen, use I-talk, speak up for what you want, state needs and problems:

Hi! How are you this evening?

Wishing it was quitting time.

Fill it with ethyl, please—Had a tiring day, huh?

Must have had a hundred people who discovered they needed new windshield wipers in the rain this afternoon.

And you had to stand in the downpour to install every one of them!

Oh, sure—but some people think I'm all wet even in a drought.

Sounds like your usual good humor survived it all.

Yep, I'm part duck anyway, coming from Seattle.

Oh, you're from Seattle! We were there on vacation last summer. We loved it. I think all the rain must be worth it—the countryside is beautiful.

Yeah, we go back every year.

Say, after you check under the hood I'd like the tires checked. The car steers like they're low. I'll open the trunk so you can get the spare. It was losing air very slowly the last time it was checked. I'd hate to have a flat tire on the freeway and discover the spare was flat too. . . . Thanks a lot. I always feel I can rely on my car when you service it.

Practice telling service personnel how to perform services to your satisfaction.

At the barber's or hairdresser's: Just a little shorter in the back.

In a restaurant. I don't like my steak quite this red. I'd appreciate your putting it back on the broiler until it's just slightly pink.

As a manager you have to be able to direct others without embarrassment. You also have to ask others to extend themselves to accomplish your ends. Take advantage of all the opportunities you meet in service-related situations to practice getting others to comply with your wishes—dealings with clerks, receptionists, attendants, librarians, government agencies, people who perform services or do repairs in your home.

Try to give an impression of mastery to assure compliance, but don't order or command in a rude or disrespectful way. Establish a rapport that makes willing helpers of the people you deal with.

Insist on Getting What's Coming to You

Take a firm stand to get what you've contracted for. Insist on returning merchandise that's not right. Or make sure that you get services you were promised.

INSIST ON GETTING WHAT'S COMING TO YOU

COMPLAINT DEPT.

"So you think you've got something coming, eh?"

Don't deliberately irritate people in hopes that they'll give you what you want just to get rid of you. That approach can easily backfire if they hold the trump card—they already have your money or they won't release your property until you pay, for example.

Avoid temper outbursts, the broken record approach, or you-ing people out. Such tactics trigger defensiveness and resentment and start your own adrenaline flowing unnecessarily.

Be politely firm and reasonable. Know your rights and state your problems or expectations in I-talk. Don't get sidetracked. Carry your request to a higher authority if necessary.

Make your appearance work in your favor by being well-groomed, pleasant, and cooperative.

Return Unwanted Merchandise

Set up a Workout where you return merchandise to a store. If you have any doubts, ask about store policy on guarantees and merchandise returns when you make your purchase:

Eustace Cower went into a men's store to purchase a tie for his new blue suit. He narrowed it down to four that he liked, but he wasn't sure how they'd go with the shade and texture of the suit, which was at home. "I told the clerk that I'd like to buy all four, with the understanding that I could bring any or all back if they weren't right with the suit. He agreed. As it turned out, none of the ties matched, and I returned them all without a hassle. I felt good that I was able to manage the transaction so smoothly, without feeling nervous or guilty."

Get the Services You Were Promised

When you're not satisfied with services you've ordered, say so. Give yourself leverage by getting an "up front" agreement before you give the go-ahead. Settle details about cost, time, and quality of work—in writing, if necessary. Here are two examples that show the advantages of a preservice understanding:

Merilee Rollong took her car in for repair. She asked them to fix whatever was wrong and left. At five o'clock she returned and the car wasn't ready. She complained loudly, "You should have had my car ready. How am I supposed to get home now? My friend who drove me here has already left. And I've got an important meeting tonight that I'll miss because of your incompetence. What kind of an outfit is this anyway? I should have known from the last time I brought my car here that you're irresponsible. You can bet this is the last time I'll ever bring my car to you—and I'll see to it that all my friends know about the lousy kind of service you give, too." Her outburst didn't change the fact that the car wasn't in drivable condition. And the you-ing out made the service manager unwilling to suggest possible solutions to her problem. In fact, when Merilee asked when she could expect the car to be ready, the manager said she'd have to call him around noon the next day. He clearly had the upper hand, and all she could do was storm out and take a bus home.

Willa Ware, who also had car trouble, handled it differently when she took her car in for repair. She and the repair shop foreman, Ole Aginous, agreed on what needed fixing. She watched while he wrote it on the work order. She emphasized that she needed the car by five o'clock because she had to be at an important meeting in neighboring Boone Docks at six o'clock that evening. Ole assured her that it would be ready. She gave him her office phone number and asked him to call before two o'clock if it appeared that the car wouldn't be ready at five, so she could make plans to get a ride to the meeting with someone else.

At five-fifteen Willa arrived to pick up her car and was told by Ole that it wasn't ready. She said firmly but calmly, "I'm really in a spot. As I told you this morning, I have a meeting in forty-five minutes in Boone Docks. When you didn't call before two o'clock as I asked you to, I assumed the car would be ready, so I didn't arrange a ride with someone else. Everyone else has already left now, and there's no way I could possibly make it to the meeting on time by bus."

Ole explained that they didn't discover until after four o'clock that a part they needed was out of stock. He was busy with other customers, and by the time he tried to reach her, she had already left her office.

Willa said, "I understand it's not intentional, but I absolutely must have a car to get to my meeting. I'd be willing to take a loaner."

Ole said, "I'm sorry, we don't have a loaner available."

Willa replied, "Just my luck. Well, let's see— I simply have to get to that meeting. I'd like to talk to your supervisor. Maybe we can work something out."

Willa explained the situation to the supervisor. He decided he'd rather lend her his own car than pay her cab fare to and from Boone Docks. He explained that he could borrow a used car off the lot overnight for himself. The problem was solved and everyone parted feeling satisfied about the transaction.

When dealing with broken promises, serve your ends, not your ego: Remember that the object is to have the "contract" met as promised, not to get revenge if it isn't.

Manage Your Personal Appointments

Handle personal appointments like contracts that you have a right to have fulfilled on time.

Anticipate appointments far enough in advance to request a time when there'll be the least possible waiting. When you arrive for an appointment, make your time needs known to the receptionist. If your appointment time passes without your being seen, re-remind the receptionist. (Even when delays are unavoidable and nothing can be done to change it, you enjoy more self-respect if you make your problem known to those in charge.)

Be polite but assertive. Don't scold the office staff, but don't humble yourself, either. If someone explains or apologizes for your inconvenience, don't say, "Oh, that's all right." Say, "I understand, but. . . . " Consider both your immediate and long-term goals in planning what action to take.

Here are two different ways to deal with a doctor's appointment. The first is more common—the second is more satisfying.

Stew Alott entered the doctor's office five minutes before his three o'clock appointment time. As he brushed past the receptionist's window, he said, "Alott," and sat down in the crowded waiting room. By three-fifteen he was fidgeting; by three-thirty he was agitated; by three-forty-five he was resentful; by four he was really mad and had decided to give the doctor a piece of his mind for making him wait so long. At four-oh-five the doctor saw him and asked "How are you this afternoon, Mr. Alott?"

"Just fine," Stew answered.

"Your blood pressure's up quite a bit, today," the doctor commented. "I hope you're following my advice and not letting little things upset you."

Stew assured him that he always took unimportant matters in stride. After a brief examination and almost no communication between him and the doctor, Stew left. On his way out he made an appointment to return in exactly four weeks—at three o'clock.

Val Yooztime walked into the waiting room, refreshed his memory with a quick glance at the name plate on the receptionist's desk, and said, "Hi, Florence! How are you this morning? I'm Val Yooztime, remember? I'm here for my appointment promptly at ten, just as you suggested."

Florence cheerfully returned his greeting and said, "Dr. Lordlee will see you in just a few minutes."

Before he left her desk Val remarked, "Good! As I told you when I called for the appointment, I have another commitment at eleven, so I'm counting on getting in to see the doctor right away."

Val was still choosing a magazine to look at when the nurse summoned him out of the waiting room. As they walked down the hall the nurse said, "I'm glad you told Florence you were in a hurry. We always try to accommodate people if they've got a tight schedule and we're not swamped."

In the doctor's office Val asked questions about his health that concerned him. He interrupted the doctor when necessary to ask things like, "What does that mean?" "What should I do about that?" and "What kind of side effects does this medication cause?" When the doctor started to move toward the door, Val said, "I have a few more questions to ask." When he had all the information he wanted, he thanked the doctor, "I like the way you do things here. I appreciate your cordiality and thorough answers."

As he left he thanked Florence for getting him in so quickly and added, "I appreciate your recommending an appointment time that fit into my heavy schedule so well."

Don't Slam the Door Behind You

Whether or not you get what you think you have coming in your dealings, try to keep the lines of communication open in case future contacts are necessary.

You won't succeed with everybody, and it won't always be your fault. Among all the generally accommodating and competent organizations and people who provide services there are bound to be a few asses. Try to see them as a challenge rather than a threat. Many hard cases soften when you relate to them as individuals. Sometimes a compromise is the best you can do. Other times you may have to admit defeat—at least until another day. But unless you're sure you won't have to get back in, don't slam the door when you leave.

Do More Things Alone

Decrease others' dependence on you by doing more things alone.

Just as being too dependent on others gives them the upper hand in a relationship, so can being "needed" too much by others become a burden which allows others to virtually run your life by their dependency. Continue to increase your personal freedom and self-direction by breaking the bonds of others' dependency.

Decline invitations occasionally from people who seem not to be able to do anything

BREAK THE BONDS OF DEPENDENCY

"Sorry, Bill . . . I've decided to do more things alone."

without you. Discourage others who regularly impose on you for transportation and suggest alternatives. Do the things you usually do with different people or do different things with your usual companions.

Remember that others might easily interpret such departures from your usual behavior as rejection. They're apt to think, "He's always gone with me before—he must not like me any more," or wonder, "Why did she ask *her* to go this time instead of me—maybe I did something to make her mad."

Whether you're dependent on them or they're dependent on you, if they stand to profit by the relationship, they're bound to resist, resent, or fear a change. Even if others aren't trying to control you, they may feel

hurt if you suddenly stop doing things with them that you usually do. Just as kindness from a stranger brings extra pleasure, a rebuff from a friend gives extra pain. To avoid damaging important relationships and accomplish your own goal of greater independence, make gradual changes and give rational explanations for why you're doing different things.

Here's how two different people managed to ease out of relationships with people who leaned on them too heavily:

Tag Long went everywhere with Brick Wall. Brick figured he could break Tag's dependency to some extent by expanding and changing his recreation patterns. Among other things he became interested in sabot sailing, a one-man boat hobby. He didn't discourage Tag from also getting interested, but Tag had to sail his own boat if he wanted to participate. At least on sailing days, Brick had a degree of freedom.

Evvie Leaner and Eylla Cariyou had lunch together every weekday without fail. To practice breaking a dependency bond (and ask a favor at the same time), Eylla asked her father to take her to lunch at his executive club. Then she told Evvie, "Evvie, I want you to know that I won't be able to have lunch with you this Thursday. I'm having lunch with my dad at the Exec Club. My dad and I don't have many chances to get together for lunch, and I'm really looking forward to it."

Make the Telephone Serve You

Use the telephone instead of writing or going in person whenever it's more efficient or convenient, saves you time or money, or helps to make things go your way.

Call for Information

Call and ask for information from libraries, bureaus, banks, stores, theaters, bus companies. Mentally rehearse what you want to say and practice stating your needs clearly and completely.

I want to take the Easy Street bus from Nth and Poverty Drive to Prosperity Square. What are the nearest stops at either end and which bus do I have to catch to get to my destination by two-thirty? (Not: Can you tell me the schedule of the Easy Street bus?)

Transact Personal Business

Shop or request services by phone. Use toll-free numbers to call long-distance. Try calling collect.

Remember to ask expansive questions and state needs or problems when trying to get past switchboard operators or secretaries:

I need to talk to Dr. Payme. I'm having nausea and dizzy spells and I'd like to know if it could be caused from the medication he prescribed. (Not: If it's not too much trouble, do you think I could speak to Dr. Payme?)

When will the manager be back? I need to settle this today. (Not: Will the manager be back soon?)

USE THE TELEPHONE
TO PERSONAL ADVANTAGE

"I'm afraid you have the wrong number . . . but don't hang up . . . do you have enough life insurance?"

Say No over the Phone

Use the phone to say no when you want to resist a particularly moving request from others. Saying no on the phone is easier than refusing in person because you can't see pleading eyes or be influenced by anguished facial expressions. When you're ready to terminate the conversation, you can make a clean break and forestall a second appeal simply by hanging up. Remember this when you want a yes answer to a request of your own, and try to see the other person face to face where it will be harder for *them* to refuse *you*.

Practice saying no to telephone solicitors. Use the skills you've learned to recognize and counteract the sales pitches of telephone solicitors. Notice how the following example uses traditional greetings, frequent repetition of the customer's name, questions that start a "roll" of yes's, reflective listening, commonality, and expansive questioning to keep the salesperson in charge of the interaction at all times:

Is this Mr. Fallgye?

Yes, it is.

How are you this evening, Mr. Fallgye?

Fine, thank you.

I understand that you own your own home out there, Mr. Fallgye.

Yes, we do.

I guess you're pretty glad you do, with the price of housing as high as it is these days.

That's true.

Mr. Fallgye, our company is installing insulation in the home of one of your neighbors, the Easymarks, and since we're in the neighborhood, our representative can stop by this evening and give you a free inspection of your house to show you how you can save energy and money on fuel bills. What time will be convenient for you?

Fight back against this kind of sales approach, without being impolite, by using your own skills. For instance:

Is this Mr. Turntables?

Who's calling please?

This is Fasstokker at Warmer Houses, Inc. I understand that you own your home out there, Mr. Turntables.

Why do you want to know, Mr. Fasstokker?

Our firm is making a fantastic free offer to homeowners in your neighborhood this month only.

What business are you in, Mr. Fasstokker?

We're home insulation specialists.

I'm not interested in insulating my home right now, thank you. Goodbye.

Notice how Mr. Turntables is able to take charge of the interaction by "answering" a question with a question, instead of playing Fasstokker's game? Turntables never gets rude and never asks a question to which he isn't entitled to know the answer. He firmly terminates the conversation on his own terms, showing that when you're being imposed upon you don't have to adhere to that old rule of etiquette that says the person who starts a phone call has the privilege of ending it.

Another way to discourage an imposer is to explain that the call is inconveniencing you.

Mrs. Plainspeaker? How are you this evening?

Wet and cold and disagreeable. I was in the shower when the phone rang.

Don't lie or make up reasons. Since telephone soliciting is usually a genuine inconvenience, real reasons are easy to come by—watching television, working outside, eating dinner, reading—anything you happen to be doing at the time. Even when you think they "deserve" it, try to avoid you-ing solicitors out—if for no other reason than to practice stating feelings and facts and keeping on target. Using I-talk, say something like, "I resent having my privacy invaded by telephone solicitation," or "I'm not interested and I don't want to talk to you now."

Don't Be a Slave to a Ringing Phone

Let the phone ring a few extra times at home before you answer it. Or don't answer at all if you're busy somewhere else. Prove to yourself that you can live with your curiosity or your fear that it was your best friend using "the last dime I had" to call you from jail. Take the phone off the hook for a short time, just to show it who's boss.

If someone answers the phone for you, ask that calls be held and messages taken. Don't make up excuses. Simply have the person who answers tell the truth:

Mrs. Engroesst has asked me to take her calls for her. What's your name and number so she can return your call? Or I'll take a message if you prefer.

Controlling the telephone's intrusion manages your accessibility to others and gives you blocks of uninterrupted time to devote to your own priorities.

TELEPHONE TRAINING TIPS

Here are a few suggestions to incorporate in your telephone Workouts.

Speak Up

Say, "hello" (or whatever greeting you prefer) briskly and clearly. Don't mumble or whisper. Since people can't see you, they'll judge you by how you sound—so try to sound alive and intelligent.

Identify Yourself

Unless it gives you an edge to remain anonymous—you don't want to tip your hand or receive return calls, for example—tell your name to people you call on the phone.

Introduce yourself at the start of the call. On the job, follow your name with the name of your organization or department or the person you represent if that's the policy:

This is Alpha Bett calling for Mr. Tome at the ABC Bookstore. (Not: This is the ABC Bookstore calling. *or even* This is Mr. Tome's secretary at the ABC Bookstore.)

Repeat your name as you wind up the contact, spelling it for emphasis as well as for clarity:

I'd appreciate hearing from you as soon as possible. My name is spelled B-e-t-t. Alpha is my first name.

Hearing your name out loud, even when you say it yourself, overcomes shyness and gives you a sense of importance.

It helps establish a personal relationship if you call the same place repeatedly—and "friends" are more apt to give you special attention than strangers. It often gives others the impression that you've dealt with them before even when you haven't.

On the job, identify yourself by name when others call you. If they're pleased by their dealings with you they'll ask for you again by name, commend you to your superiors, or recommend you to others.

End Conversations Firmly but Cordially

Use the same ways for terminating phone conversations that you use in personal contacts. Use I-talk and legitimate reasons. Hang up without warning only as a last resort.

I've enjoyed talking to you, but I have to get back to work now.

I'd like to talk longer, but I'm due across town in twenty minutes.

I didn't intend to stay on the phone this long, but I've enjoyed it so much it's become later than I thought. I have to go.

I can't talk to you right now, but I'll call you back. When's a good time to reach you?

Advantages of Telephone Contacts

Use these advantages of the telephone to determine when you use the phone and when you make contacts in person.

◆ The phone saves time. You can contact more people and get more answers in less time than is possible with face-to-face contacts.

◆ The phone is effective. Oftentimes you can get through to people on the phone who would block you from a personal contact.

◆ The phone is commanding. When the phone rings, people stop what they're doing to answer it.

◆ The phone is versatile. You can carry on a warm personal conversation or you can purposefully maintain distance and aloofness. The phone affords privacy if your strategy involves not being seen with a particular person. It provides anonymity if you'd rather keep your identity unknown to the recipient of your call.

LIVE ACTION REPORTS

This weekend my neighbor came over and asked for some advice on planting his garden. Nearly every Saturday he bugs me with a request for help. I like him, but helping him cuts up my own weekend work. I told him, "Sure, but it'll probably be sometime Sunday afternoon. Listen, while you're here, I could use some help pruning these bushes. I'll get another pair of cutters from the garage."

My wife couldn't get over "Mitch the Mooch" helping me. But I think he actually enjoyed it.

I tried another new restaurant today. I was very friendly with the waitress and careful to ask for things assertively. I told her that I'd rather have cottage cheese than potatoes with my steak. She replied that the restaurant policy was "no substitutes." I told her to just leave the potatoes off, then, because my diet doesn't allow them. When she brought my meal, there were no potatoes, but there was a dish of cottage cheese. She didn't mention the substitution or bill me extra. I thanked her and left a larger-than-usual tip.

I had a lot of reference work to do in the library. My usual approach is to try to look things up for myself and then when I get totally frustrated and confused, I ask the librarian for help. This time I went straight to him and explained my problem. I went over in my mind first what I really needed to know, and then I asked in an assertive manner, starting with, "I've got a problem. I. . . ." He seemed to understand very quickly what I was after. I not only got the information in record time, I felt like a manager getting others to do my work.

At the Ice Show my boyfriend and I were sitting quite a ways back. The people in front of us had binoculars. I figured this was my chance to borrow something. I asked if I could look through the binoculars. I only kept them for a few minutes, and then I thanked them and I made a point of saying how much I enjoyed what I was seeing. Later I asked to use the binoculars again. Through the remainder of the show we passed the glasses back and forth freely. I enjoyed the show more and they seemed to be really glad to share.

I was really pressed for time this week so I decided to use the phone to advantage. From an ad in the paper that appealed to me, I ordered two shirts and a belt from a department store. When they were delivered, the belt was fine, but the color of the shirts wasn't what I wanted. I returned them to the store without feeling embarrassed. I didn't save any time because I ended up making a trip to the store anyway—but I discovered a new way to shop that I'll be using again in the future.

When I cashed my check at the bank today, I almost said, "Can I have two twenties and a ten as part of the change?" Instead I caught myself and said, "I'd like . . . , please." I'm just beginning to realize how often I beg for things. Every time I make an assertive request instead, I get a lift.

I hadn't seen my mom for a while. I called her up and said I'd like to come for supper. I asked her to make my favorite meal, meat pie. She was so excited you'd have thought I was doing her a big favor.

I chum around with a bunch of guys who usually get together on weekends. Last weekend I decided to go to a concert with a girl instead. When the guys called and said we were going to the beach, I said I wasn't going, because I had a date. They were surprised and ribbed me about it. I had a good time at the concert, and I felt good about doing something on my own and standing up to their ribbing.

I went with my girlfriend to her parents' house for Thanksgiving dinner. There were lots of other relatives of hers there, too. Usually I'm pretty quiet in a situation like that. But I decided to practice conversing with people. I listened and asked questions and volunteered information. I felt good that I seemed to make a positive impression on everyone. At the dinner table it was a little harder than talking to only one person at a time. But I managed to get my share of table conversation, too. I could tell that my girlfriend was pleased that I was making a good impression on her family. I felt a lot better for speaking up, and I learned a lot of interesting things about her family, too.

I got a call from a telephone solicitor. He started his sales pitch and I just said no and hung up. I thought I'd feel good about asserting myself, but I didn't. I guess I felt I was too abrupt. I was sorry I didn't use the opportunity to practice getting control of the conversation.

While I was in an art store a lady asked my opinion about a picture she was about to purchase. I told her that I really preferred another I'd seen her looking at earlier. She bought the one I suggested. I was surprised that she was so easily influenced, but it made me feel important.

I found a fascinating article in Business Week that was relevant to some problems we've been having at work. Normally I'd only mention it to my boss, since I know he takes the magazine himself. But I know he gets behind in his reading, too. So I made a nice clean copy of the article and put it on his desk with a note explaining that I thought it was pertinent to what we were doing. Later in the day he thanked me. He said he'd been to a meeting with his boss and staff and had already passed on some of the ideas and they were very well received. I told him I was happy it had helped him.

INSTANT REPLAY

You begin to concentrate on ends as well as means for the first time in this Round. The object is to get at least as much as you give in relationships. At the same time, you never lose sight of your long-term goals—the well-being of relationships you care about and your own personal and professional development. You deal in one-on-one contacts with strangers as well as with people you know. You continue to manage routine and mobility to your advantage, and use all the skills you've acquired in earlier Rounds.

Suggested Workouts are:

- Impose favors.

  Make offers others can't refuse.

  Do something unique and unexpected.

- Ask pleasant favors.

- Get your share of the conversation.

  Talk about your experiences.

  Practice giving opinions.

- Make more decisions.

  State your preference when asked.

  Stop letting others make decisions for you.

  Help others make up their minds.

  Take responsibility for outcomes.

- Say no.

  Delay action on a request.

  Make compliance conditional.

  Show others how to help themselves.

Refuse outright.

Refuse and counter with a request of your own.

- Suggest highly probable activities.

- Speak up for what you want.

- State your problem.

- Request full service.

- Insist on getting what's coming to you.

  Return unwanted merchandise.

  Get the services you were promised.

  Manage your personal appointments.

  Don't slam the door behind you.

- Do more things alone.

- Make the telephone serve you.

  Call for information.

  Transact personal business.

  Say no over the phone.

  Don't be a slave to a ringing phone.

ROUND 6:

MANAGING
THE BALANCE OF SOCIAL EXCHANGE
(TESTING LIMITS)

In this Round you're not satisfied with merely staying even. You move in to get ahead. In other words, you try to manage your personal and social interactions so that you have the advantage. That, after all, is what winners and leaders do.

For the first time in the program you intentionally tip the balance of give and take in your favor. Accomplishing your own ends becomes even more important than previously. Even so, you don't ruthlessly overpower other contenders you meet in the ring. You simply take assertive action to get what you want, even if it sometimes conflicts with what others want.

THE CHALLENGE

The challenge is to carry the "fight" to the other contenders. You trade punches and test the limits of those you interact with to see how much they'll willingly take. You test your own limits, too, to see how you handle dishing it out.

Your objectives are to shape circumstance to your advantage; to increase and extend your influence over others; to get others to accept your means of accomplishing ends; to appear attractive, confident, strong, and able; to accomplish immediate ends as well as to make it easier to win in the future.

THE STRATEGY

You use and reinforce all of the skills you've acquired to this point. You push past the point of equal balance in social exchanges and look for ways to get more than your "fair" share. You watch for situations that you can take over and control. You modify your standards of performance and conduct to become more aware of the new options that increased flexibility affords. You try new ways so you can experience both the pleasures and pains of varying your usual patterns of conduct.

You seek to take only that which is given up with comparative and apparent willingness. But you push to find where that limit lies—where resistance starts for both yourself and others—in a wide variety of situations. You adjust your own standards and behavior only to the point of your willingness to accept full responsibility for what you do. While you try to find out what acts you're capable of, you also push others only to the point of their stated or signaled resistance.

You continue to expand your arena of activity both with strangers and with people you know. You still stay clear of practicing on the job.

THE MOVES

Your moves in this Round include varying personal routines that affect others and intruding on others' routines; breaking in on others; directing conversations; changing others' minds; delegating; expanding relationships; pushing services to the limit; bucking lines; taking charge and maintaining control; modifying standards; deviating from propriety; using the telephone to advantage.

WINNING THE ROUND

You know you're having success when others yield to your influence; when you sense the extent of your influence and try to push to that limit; when you enjoy your new influence and control; when you welcome the challenge and manage the personal responsibility and the dissonance which is created by deviating from "standard practice"; when others look to you for guidance; when you're seen as a formidable contender by potential adversaries.

WHY TEST LIMITS

You test limits to discover how you handle CLOUT and to learn how to gain the advantage in social exchange.

DISCOVERING HOW YOU HANDLE CLOUT

To be an effective manager you have to be more than equal to those you manage. You have to wield more influence and take a bigger piece of the action. While this may not be your inalienable right, as is equality, it is an undeniable necessity if you are to influence people and shape circumstances to get what you want.

Whenever you get more from an exchange, others in the relationship may have to settle for less. This may or may not offend them. Not everyone enjoys being on top or wants to be a leader. And many times followers also receive legitimate benefits from leaders' actions that seem primarily self-serving.

The whole matter of leading and following is loaded with pros and cons which you must decide for yourself. Testing your own limits in this Round lets you discover from low-risk, real-life experience just how much mastery you want and can handle. You have a chance to learn firsthand how you really feel about the importance of means versus ends. You can see how you feel about controlling others. You can weigh your beliefs about propriety, fairness and equality against your need or desire to accomplish specific goals. You can find out if the ethical beliefs you articulate are based on genuine conviction—or if they're more a function of your previous inaction, through lack of either the opportunity or the necessity to act.

For the sake of both personal fulfillment and future career planning, it's important to at least try some testing limits Workouts. The authentic feedback you get from your practical experiences will help you decide whether or not you want to go full out for CLOUT.

Regardless of what degree of mastery you eventually decide is right for you, the Workouts in this Round help to make your choice a conscious, realistic, reasoned one based on knowledge about yourself and others. If you opt for the big win, you'll do so knowing that you can handle the responsibilities and pressures as well as the excitement of being on top. If you discover that a more even balance of give and take suits your needs and principles better, you'll be satisfied that it's the path you freely choose to take.

Here are two different reactions of program participants after trying some of the testing limits Workouts:

At first I felt that I was betraying people—plotting against them as I sought ways to push them one way or another. Then I saw how much I could get away with. I began to feel I was really challenging myself more than others. I kept being pleasant and assertive and I kept accomplishing what I had in mind. There's no question in my mind—people are more inclined to be followers than they are to be leaders. I found people would allow most anything I instigated—and not only without conflict, but without hesitation—particularly if they were treated pleasantly, politely, and with respect. I just had to act like I knew what I was doing.

This person's experiences in the exercises convinced her that there was room for her to "move in" without great resistance from others. The thought of more influence, more action—even more adventure—both pleased and challenged her. Undoubtedly she'll push in the future without hesitation and accept the responsibilities and consequences that CLOUT brings.

A second participant, a man, reacted like this:

I could do "pushy" exercises and was successful in executing them. It surprised me how easy it was to buck lines, change others' routines, interrupt people, get people to really give you extra services, change people's minds or make decisions for them. When I did these things I felt the "high" of added power and success. But it also made me extremely anxious and uncomfortable for long periods afterward. I kept thinking, "This isn't right. This isn't me." What's more, I really didn't want it to be me. I decided I could be satisfied with just staying equal. I got enough tastes of influence to realize that you need this kind of CLOUT to get the big jobs done. I just don't think it's for me. I'm willing to settle for less and I think I can be content, knowing the price I'd have to pay wouldn't be worth the rewards. I think my future lies in accounting and auditing, so that's the direction in which I'm steering my career. I'm glad I did some of the exercises. I think knowing how it works has made me less "pushable" than I'd be otherwise.

LEARNING TO GAIN THE ADVANTAGE IN SOCIAL RELATIONSHIPS

The testing-limits Workouts give you off-the-job training in many critical managerial skills. The nottims you practice in this Round include: *appearing credible and prestigious; seeking challenge, opportunity, responsibility, command, power, and influence; resisting the need for external support; maintaining a flexible concept of justice; sensing boundaries of situations, and defining and shaping them to advantage; putting things in "big picture" perspective, including objectives, ends and friends, rules and procedures, social propriety; setting implementable ends, performance standards, and time limits; keeping risks within reason; initiating change; compromising and adjusting to reality; striving for excellence; getting results; committing others to objectives; acting fast, decisively and assuredly; taking charge, influenc-*

ing and directing others, delegating duties; testing the power and independence of others; managing reciprocation; using others to advantage; negotiating.

GAINING VALUABLE INFORMATION ABOUT YOURSELF AND OTHERS

As you design and practice exercises to acquire these nottims you also gather valuable information about yourself and others.

You learn that if you lead, most others are inclined to follow. Not only do they not resist your leadership, many people much prefer to be led than to lead. Some freely state that they feel burdened rather than gratified by decision making and responsibility. Others won't admit it, but simply abdicate from any leadership position by nonaction or nondirection, leaving a void to be filled by others.

Your Workouts give you practice in spotting people and situations which are virtually begging for leadership. You discover how easy it is to step into a leadership vacuum. You experience firsthand the anxiety that accompanies taking assertive action for the novice— and the "high" from others' compliance that makes you eager to try again.

You learn that if you act with confidence, most others believe your actions are proper. Everyone has a degree of self-doubt and uncertainty, which varies in kind and degree according to the person and the situation. Con artists use this knowledge to influence their victims. They gain the trust and confidence of others partly because they themselves appear to be so sure of themselves.

Private investigators on TV programs (and in real life, too) use the technique all the time. They get information from people and gain entrance to forbidden places merely by looking and acting like they have a right to know or a right to be there.

While we don't advocate copying the behavior of either con artists or private investigators, you will find in your Workouts that an air of confidence gives you credibility and encourages others to follow your lead.

You learn that if you assume authority, most others become compliant. We've all been conditioned to yield to authority, both direct and implied. "Mind your parents," "listen to the teacher," "do what the doctor ordered," "follow the leader," "obey the rules" are familiar admonitions which create respect for authority figures and encourage compliance with their wishes. You'll see in your Workouts that this can be to your advantage. The strategy is to take control of situations with an air of confidence so that those who are easily influenced by authority will follow *your* lead. At the same time you resist unthinking compliance with authority yourself. This gives you greater flexibility to set your own course as a leader and to get the results you want.

You learn that if you push for advantage, most others cope by yielding or copping out. Most people don't assert themselves. They don't insist on their rights because it isn't worth the hassle. They're as reluctant to say no to imposition as you used to be. They put up and shut up.

The fact that about 80 percent of the people with whom you interact would rather switch their position than fight is to your advantage.[1] You learn from your Workouts when to push that advantage and when to back off. You learn to test for weak spots where inroads can be made to accomplish your goals. And you discover how willing you are to take advantage of soft spots when you find them.

HOW TESTING LIMITS HELPS YOU MANAGE

As manager and leader, you need to get the maximum that your environment and its resources can yield. You have to push and test all aspects of your surroundings to achieve this. You push the people with whom you work in order to gain the ultimate they have to offer. You push against the constraints in your environment to improve results. You test your own limits of commitment, talent, and energy.

TESTING OTHERS

To manage effectively you must push those who serve you to the limits of their capabilities. You hire the best, rather than fearing or avoiding competence in others. You guide them to achieve excellence. You try to get the best they're able to deliver. As a result they see you as a leader worthy of being served. Not only do they give you their loyalty, they also seek acceptance and strokes from you.

You also need to push for maximum support from those you serve—the higher-ups in your organization and profession. You try to portray yourself as a person who's able and willing to take on anything. At the same time you present yourself as a protégé rather than as a rival or aspirant to their jobs. As a result they're more willing to act as your mentor and sponsor your upward mobility.

Finally, you need to push for the upper hand over your peers. If you can show them that helping you accomplish your goals is to their advantage, you gain their cooperation.

TESTING CIRCUMSTANCE

To have CLOUT you need to test the strength of the various environmental factors you deal with: You try to make inroads into areas not properly covered or protected by others. You add new duties, responsibilities, and functions to your domain. You delegate less challenging duties to others. You create needs for yourself to fill.

Shirley Gettahedd climbed to the top of her division by making her own breaks. She started as a secretary, but soon shed the routine tasks first assigned her by passing them on to the secretarial pool. In turn she utilized the information flowing into the office to advantage. She prepared summary reports, analyzed statistics, set schedules, made up budgets. Her persistence soon made her appear indispensable. It was evident that she had literally created a new position for herself when her official title was changed from Secretary to Executive Assistant. She was on the track and on her way up the organizational ladder.

As an effective manager you also need to discover where the resistance is; how strong it is; what tactics will give you the edge. When you meet resistance, you act with persistence. When you face barriers, you find alternatives. When you encounter strength, you match it with an air of prestige, competence, and confidence. In this way you gain respect and compliance from others and keep them from chal-

SHAPE CIRCUMSTANCE TO YOUR ADVANTAGE

". . . and I'll take this side with the sun in my eyes."

lenging your actions or interfering with your goal.

Finally, as a manager you often need to shape circumstance to gain your ends by bending or adjusting restrictions imposed by others or by the system within which you operate. You use accepted methods when they help you, but you get around them when they get in your way. You cut corners and take short-cuts in established procedure. You see people informally to cut through the chain of command. You push to see someone right away instead of making a future appointment. You get things moving on the basis of verbal confirmation instead of waiting for triplicate copies of an order. If you need a part in a hurry, you sketch it on scratch paper and verbally explain your requirements to the capable employee involved instead of waiting for a blueprint to be carefully drawn up. In other words, instead of letting the building burn down because you don't have a requisition for a fire extinguisher, you deviate from the expected and accepted when you feel it's necessary to achieve an important end.

TESTING YOURSELF

To be a top manager you need to push yourself to excellence. You stretch your own limits of personal commitment by maximizing your talents and devoting whatever time and energy is necessary to accomplishing your goals. You work through the night if the job has to be done. You roll up your sleeves and pitch in to help find answers you need. You come up with unique solutions and have the courage to try new approaches. As a result you stand out as nonpareil among your associates.

Such actions leave a trail of successes and build an image which gives you a healthy respect from friend and foe alike. On the one side you develop a community of committed and able constituents. On the other, you signal

to those in your road to give you room. In short, you strive to weight the balance of social exchange in your favor on all fronts. It assures the big win.

Managers Who Tested Limits

John Wooden, former basketball coach of the UCLA Bruins is the epitome of this pressing style. Winning the NCAA Championship became a habit for UCLA under Wooden. He tested limits in every direction. He tested the limits of his players by demanding excellence regarding their physical condition, their execution of fundamentals in running, dribbling, passing, shooting, rebounding, ball handling, play making, discipline. He tested the limits of the opposition by a continual harassing, forcing defense countered by a driving, lightning-quick offense.

His exhausting training tempo and rotation system of practice play always provided him depth in manpower and variety in team makeup. That he was immune to player pressure is shown in this admonition to his players: "I can't tell you how to cut your hair, but I decide who plays."[2]

His team's ability to execute any strategy with precision made him immune from opponent surprise, too. In his capacity as coach Wooden said, "If we play our game as well as we can, we can beat an opponent no matter what he does. We let them adjust to us, rather than we to them."[3] This pretty well sums up his push-yourself, push-your-opponent approach. Excellence on every front is hard for the opposition to beat.

Harold S. Geneen, who guided ITT to its position of eminence in growth and profitability, was just as imposing on the business scene as Wooden was in sports. One close associate said of Geneen, "Hal somehow gets 110 percent out of everybody, not just in hours, but in every-

thing. He gets better performance out of most people than they know they have in them."[4] *Geneen also set almost unattainable standards. People would either stretch or break attaining them. Nor was it uncommon for Geneen to cut across established lines of conduct to get his way. For example, when ITT was threatened with antitrust prosecutions, he or his staff would approach administration leaders directly in the hopes of getting favorable treatment.*[5]

Managers like Wooden and Geneen put heavy pressure on themselves and accept it from others. Like well-trained athletes, they compete against themselves as well as against the opposition, searching for ways to better what they've already attained.

TESTING LIMITS INVOLVES RISKS AS WELL AS REWARDS

Testing limits, of course, is not without risk. Pushing within reason can be meritorious. Pushing beyond reason can be abusive. The consequences, whether benefits or penalties, have to be borne by the risk taker.

Earlier we mentioned that Royal Little pushed toward the limits of corporate propriety in using a unique strategy of acquisition expansion to accomplish growth at Textron. Similarly, John F. Kennedy used his office to push the limits of science, technology, and industry to effect man's landing on the moon in the decade of the '60s. The risks taken by these two men led to recognition and rewards for them. Little was selected as one of the first four living Americans nominated to the *Fortune* Hall of Fame for Business Leadership. Kennedy was ranked among the one hundred persons having the greatest all-time impact on world history.[6]

When limits are pushed too far, however, dire consequences may result:

Stanley Goldblum, head of Equity Funding Corporation of America, caused one of America's biggest business scandals when he pushed beyond corporate propriety in his strategy of creating hundreds of millions of dollars in fictitious insurance policies to achieve growth for Equity Funding Life Insurance Company. And President Richard M. Nixon used the power limits of his office to conceal the perpetrators of the Watergate crime. Goldblum was sent to prison for his actions, and Nixon was forced from office.

Managers need to both *test* the limits and *know* the limits to make their mark. They need to push relentlessly on all fronts, but know intuitively to stop short of the breaking point.

WORKOUTS

Although you should still try to leave others liking you as you practice testing limits in these Workouts, now you also become increasingly interested in making others respect you for the actions you take, for the prestige and power you emit, and for the control you sustain.

Don't test to put others down or to show them up. Try to maintain your dignity as well as show respect to others as you test.

Try to take only what others give up without a struggle—either through their willingness to be dominated or because they cope by copping out. In other words, take what others give up willingly as well as what they give up reluctantly—so long as they don't fight back. When your pushing doesn't result in yielding, stop pushing and back off. Effective managers stop short of conflict and attempt to negotiate impasses—a skill which will be dealt with in Round 8.

Practice testing limits with those who offer a reasonable challenge, not in relationships where you already have the upper hand. Bucking a line of little old ladies in a cafeteria is being a bully, not a master of circumstance. The same thing is true of an authoritarian husband who imposes his will on an already

GET YOUR WAY
AND LEAVE OTHERS GLAD THEY HELPED

"I'm taking them all, shorty . . . no hard feelings, of course."

submissive wife; a mother whose children have learned to hop when she speaks; or a colonel whose authority commands compliance from buck privates in or out of uniform. In other words, design your Workouts so you pick on someone your own size.

Vary Trivial Personal Routines that Affect Others

Change eating, sleeping, leisure, travel, spending, and other personal habits which directly involve others.

When you managed routines in Round 1 you deliberately avoided changing things that might bring resistance from others. Now that you've learned some new ways of dealing with people, go back and try some of the things you hesitated to do earlier.

Change "your" place at the dinner table and cause others to change theirs. Sleep on your bed partner's side of the bed. Change your means of transportation even though it causes others to change theirs, too. Dress differently and risk others' displeasure.

In other words, change what you do, when you do it, where you do it, how you do it, or whom you do it with. Manage interactions

and avoid conflicts, if they arise, by using I-talk or reflective listening.

Intrude on the Routines of Others

Try to change other people's rituals in some way.

Don't simply *tell* them to change. Rather, try to make your intrusion pleasant so that others are glad they allowed it. Use all the skills you've learned to improve relationships. Don't ask permission or offer options. Try to state preferences in ways that are difficult to challenge or refuse:

I feel like going for a walk tonight. I'd like to join you when you take your dog out. (Not: Can I go with you when you walk the dog tonight?)

On the walk: I'd like to cut over past the drugstore and buy a magazine before we go home. (Not: Could we stop by the drugstore and buy a magazine?)

Increase the difficulty of your exercises by tackling increasingly rigid routines or more seriously addicted people. Decide to break a particular routine and plan ways to do it.

[129]

Interrupt a household work routine by suggesting a more efficient method and more enjoyable use of the time or effort saved. Buy hard-to-get tickets to some entertainment for someone who "never misses" a particular Saturday night TV program. Invite Joe and Jane Plain to a dinner party on Friday night, one so appealing that they feel compelled to break their usual "date" at the Shanghai Palace.

Although your intent is to dominate, try not to appear dominating. Offer alternatives you're sure will tempt the other person to change—things that will make that person's life more enjoyable. Push and test only to the point of meeting unyielding resistance. Don't force the issue in this Round.

Be good company all the while so the experience is pleasant for everyone.

Break in on Others

Interrupt strangers to ask for help or information. On the street go up to someone and ask for the time, change for a parking meter, information, or directions.

Remember to ask expansive questions:

Where's the nearest drugstore? (Not: Do you know if there's a drug store near here?)

Or state problems:

I need to use a telephone—where can I find one? (Not: Can you tell me if there's a phone I can use?)

In stores, interrupt clerks who are serving others to ask a question:

Excuse me—I only want to ask a question. Which way is the men's clothing department?

Be sure that people you intrude on know that you're talking to them. Get their attention with a friendly "hello" or a polite "excuse me," and state your request loudly and clearly. Don't wait for them to acknowledge your salutation. Say, "excuse me" and continue right on with your question or request without hesitation. Say, "thank you" after the other person accommodates you.

Saying "excuse me" and "thank you" neither humbles nor degrades you when you're intruding. It's simply good manners that make others feel better about the interruption.

Direct Conversations

Try to influence conversations to serve your own purposes. Subtly impose your will on others by applying the appropriate skill that accomplishes your goal at the moment.

Try to distract people who bring up topics you don't want to discuss or ask questions you don't want to answer. Ask a question in return, be vague or noncommital or change the subject:

When are you going to lunch?
When are the others going? or *I don't know yet* or *Before we talk about that, there's something I want to ask your opinion about. . . .*

Give brief or distracting answers to expansive questions:

How do you feel about fuel rationing?
So-so or *I'd really rather hear your opinion on the subject.*

Or give expansive answers to restrictive questions:

Do you favor fuel rationing?
Yes, and I'll tell you why. First of all. . . .

With people you know well you can anticipate questions or topics of discussion that are apt to arise and plan and mentally rehearse your comments and responses in advance.

Set Specific Goals for Yourself

Decide you'll string out conversations or cut them short. Solicit information or opinions and don't give any of your own. Dominate the conversation and limit others' input. Interrupt what others are saying. Change the subject.

In other words, be the initiator, not a responder. With practice you can carry it off more and more spontaneously, doing whatever suits you and wearing whatever "hat" fits the occasion.

Use body language to help you. Look at your watch, stand up, move toward the door. Back someone into a corner or subtly cut off their escape.

Be straightforward and firm when necessary, but don't ever be rude or disrespectful. By now your self-esteem should be such that you think of yourself as a "good" person. Convey that to others in your interactions. Try to make them like you as you direct the conversation the way you want it to go.

Change Others' Minds

Try to reverse people's decisions or convince them to do something different from what they planned.

Give pertinent information:

If you don't leave here until seven-thirty you won't get there until a quarter to eight. The parking lot is usually full by that time.

Plant a seed of doubt:

I like the way you rearranged the furniture, but aren't you afraid the sun from that window will fade the upholstery on the chair?

State a different preference:

Hi, mom, I'd like to come over for dinner. What are you having? Macaroni? I'd rather have Swiss steak.

Refuse a suggestion and counter with another:

I'd enjoy going to a movie with you but I don't want to see the one at the drive-in. I'd rather go to the Orpheum.

The object is to try your hand at getting others to do what you prefer. Push only until you meet resistance. Don't argue if others refuse. Don't back down or feel guilty after you get your way when they give in reluctantly. Once they decide to do it your way, try to make them feel glad they did.

PLANT A SEED OF DOUBT

"I like it . . . I just hope the Paulson's dog doesn't mistake it for a cat."

Delegate Tasks to Others

Try to get others to help you with chores or to do them for you. This is similar to requesting favors in Round 5, except these may be things people don't ordinarily enjoy doing. Even so, try to get people to do them willingly.

Express your requests assertively or state your needs:

Here, take this sack out to the trash can on your way to the garage.

Bring me a cup of coffee when you come back.

Open the door for me, please. My arms are full.

Dry the dishes for me so I can be through in time to watch the start of the ball game with you.

Sometimes words aren't even necessary. Simply hand the dishtowel to a person standing by as you're washing dishes, for example. Hand your packages to someone to hold or carry, as if it were to be expected. Wait expectantly until the person you're with opens a door for you. Outwait your dinner companion and allow her or him to pick up the check.

Shift responsibility to others for some long-term task you usually do. Get someone else to mow the lawn, weed the garden, water the trees, pay the bills, wash the dishes, walk the dog, pick up the laundry or dry cleaning.

Offer to trade one responsibility for another if you can't get a one-sided agreement in your favor. Try to get a "division of labor" that's more to your liking: "I'll water the trees if you'll wash and iron my shirts." "I'll cook the meals if you'll wash the dishes."

Expand Your Circle of Acquaintances

Push yourself to meet new people or get to know casual acquaintances better.

Start with people you feel comfortable with socially, but try to make "upward" progress as your skills improve.

Increase casual contact with people you want to know better. Be where they are more often. Stay in their presence longer. Use the skills you learned in Rounds 3 and 4: Greet people with traditional openers, personalize greetings, find commonality, make favorable comments and give positive verbal strokes, ask appropriate questions, be a good listener—both substantively and reflectively—and use I-talk.

State invitations assertively. Be specific about times and activities:

Since we live so near to each other, I'd enjoy taking turns with you driving to these Tuesday night meetings or *I'd like you to be my guest for dinner and the benefit jazz concert at the stadium Friday night.*

Never: *I don't suppose you'd like to go out with me sometime* or *If you haven't got anything better to do, would you like to . . . ?*

To keep conversations going and show that you're a person of broad interests, share information about yourself and tell experiences you've had in your continuing exploring Workouts.

Try to maintain control of activities, people, and conversations.

Use these approaches with people of all ages, both sexes, various ethnic groups and economic classes. Merely vary your approach appropriately to deal with those who are more reserved, timid, defensive, fearful—or, at the other end of the scale, those who are assertive, bold, or even overbearing.

Push Services to the Limit

Try to get more than you have a "right" to in your personal commercial dealings.

Request services that aren't usually provided. Try to get faster service. Ask for demonstrations, special showings, or personal try-outs. Take things home on approval. Request pick-up and delivery when it's not a usual service.

Remember to state your problem and make assertive requests. Don't beg. Don't demand.

Don't let it bother you if you meet with refusals some of the time. Be courteous, back off, and try somewhere else. Your wins will more than balance your losses in the long run.

Buck Lines

Try to get served before others who are waiting at counters or in lines—in stores, at box offices, in restrooms, in libraries, or other public buildings.

In crowds, where there are no definite lines, edge forward politely but firmly. Fill a gap with your shoulder and pull the rest of you along behind. Spread your elbows to maintain your space. Lean forward just a little at a counter to get attention. You'll discover that if you act like you know what you're doing and act quickly, most people never question you. Even when they notice, more people are "into" glaring their annoyance than are "into" confrontation. Nevertheless, don't push or force. Stop—even apologize if you're challenged.

Where there are short lines, try asking assertively:

I'm in a hurry and I have the exact change. I'd really appreciate it if I could go ahead of you.

The best place to buck a long line is at the very front. Be prepared for a quick transaction so you can take others by surprise. Don't ask permission. Have exact change. Walk up quickly and confidently. Don't hesitate or look around at anyone. Act as if you don't know there is a line. Move away quickly as soon as you're served.

That's how Sherwood Hornin got himself and his wife, Neva, into a popular movie. When they arrived at the theater half an hour before show time, the line at the box office already curled around the corner of the building. As he took his place at the end of the line, Sherwood asked an attendant what the chances were of them getting in. The usher said it would be close—they were near the cut-off point in the line. Sherwood told his wife to hold his place in line while he went up front to check with the cashier. Seconds later he was back. "C'mon," he said. "Let's go." As they left the line Neva asked, "We were too far back to get in, huh?" "No," said Sherwood. "I got the tickets." Inside the theater he explained how he walked up to the front of the line, exact change in hand, slid into place at the counter as the previous customer moved away and before the next one in line moved forward. He placed the money on the counter and said, confidently, "Two adults, please." The cashier took the money and handed him the tickets without hesitation. As he walked quickly away he heard the next person in line ask, "Where'd he come from?"

Someone answered, "Beats me." But no one challenged him as he disappeared into the crowd, and their attention turned to buying their own tickets.

Neva asked if he was scared, and Sherwood admitted, "Yeah, I was a little nervous. But I was prepared to back down if anyone challenged me."

"Well, don't you at least feel guilty that you might have kept someone else out who was in front of us in line?" Neva persisted.

"Naahh," said Sherwood. "I feel too good about carrying it off to feel guilty."

A little while later he said, "That girl just coming in was three places behind us in line outside. We didn't keep anyone out after all. I'm glad."

So am I," said Neva as the movie started.

Appropriately, Sherwood went up to buck the line alone because he was less conspicuous that way, and he could carry out his plan without possible distraction or interference from his wife. If he had failed, he confessed later, he wouldn't have told her that he tried.

Keep your own testing limits plans to yourself. Until you're very sure of yourself, only try things when you're alone among strangers. That way no explanations will be required. Although the temptation is great to share your enthusiasm with others when you succeed, be discreet. Not only will you have a tactical advantage, you'll also get valuable practice in managing information output.

Try Unsolicited Selling

Influence a fellow customer's purchase in a store when you see an opportunity. An outsider expressing a preference is very persuasive. Recommend a brand of packaged food in a grocery store, or a kind of fruit or vegetable.

These are my favorite cookies. I recommend them to anyone who likes chocolate.

I bought some of these peaches a few days ago, and they were so good that I'm coming back for more.

The following example shows how this Workout gives you a chance to combine a variety of skills:

During some free time on a business trip to Miami, I "explored" a Nieman-Marcus store in nearby Bal Harbour. As I stood admiring a casual sport shoe in the women's shoe department, a well-groomed, energetic, older woman stopped beside me. She picked up the shoe, examined it, replaced it on the display pedestal, and started to turn away. I caught her eye, smiled, and said, "I really like the lines of this shoe. What do you think of it?"

"It's very attractive," she answered, "but it's too heavy for what I want."

"What do you want it for?" I asked.

"For walking on deck," she answered. "We're going on a cruise."

"That sounds like fun. Where are you going?"

"It's a world cruise. We'll be gone for quite a while."

"I guess you'll walk a lot of deck before the cruise is over. I can see why you want to get the right shoe."

"Yes, indeed. These are too heavy."

"They look heavy all right," I said, "but here, lift it again." I handed her the shoe. "They're deceiving—they're really quite light. And feel this soft inner sole and this soft roll around the opening and the soft tongue. They remind me of my jogging shoes, and my jogging shoes feel so good they're almost a part of me."

"Maybe you're right, I'll try them," she said.

"I'm glad you're going to try them," I replied. "I think you'll love the feel on your foot. What size do you wear?"

She told me her size. I offered her a chair and told her I'd get someone to help her as soon as possible. I took the shoe to a clerk and told him her shoe size.

Later I saw the woman in another part of the store. She was wearing the shoes. I walked up to her and said that I noticed she'd bought the shoes.

"Yes," she answered, "and they're the most comfortable shoes I've ever worn. I insisted on wearing them right away. I'm so glad you sold them to me."

This pleasant woman never realized that I wasn't an employee of Nieman-Marcus, and Nieman-Marcus never realized that I made a sale for them that day. It was fun. I was pleased that I could carry it off so spontaneously. It felt good to know that I influenced someone in a happy choice.

The person in this anecdote never represented himself as a store employee, although his business suit and air of cordiality might have given that impression. He was friendly, poised, showed interest and understanding, listened reflectively, asked pertinent questions, expressed his own feelings, and gave a subtle endorsement of the shoes. You can do this same sort of thing, even when it's obvious that you're *not* a salesperson. Most people who are faced with indecision welcome attention and opinions from friendly interested people.

Take Charge and Keep Control for a Prolonged Time

Sustain your influence over someone else for a day, evening, or weekend.

Take someone on a daylong outing. Decide when to go, how to get there. Suggest what to wear. Guide your guest to the activities you want to participate in or observe. Eat when and where you prefer. If you take a picnic lunch, have the other person prepare it. Even specify what to bring. If you buy your meals, try to influence what the other person orders.

Start with those who are most compliant or easiest to direct. Proceed gradually to those you feel are your equals. Tackle those who are hard to lead last. Give yourself an advantage by getting them on ground that's familiar to you but unfamiliar to them.

Take a novice to an activity you're an old hand at—a horse race, auction, concert, competition or show, ethnic or community celebration. Take a "stranger" to a place where you know your way around.

If necessary, brush up on some area of expertise first. If you know that someone prestigious who's unfamiliar with your area likes seafood, for instance, personally check out the seafood restaurants in your community. Find the best one, invite the person to go to dinner there with you, address the service personnel by name, and recommend the entree of your choice. Being "in the know" gives you both advantage and prestige. It makes you look like you're in command—which, indeed, you are.

TAKE A NOVICE TO AN ACTIVITY YOU'RE AN OLD HAND AT

"Fellas . . . meet Bixley. He wants us to teach him the game."

[135]

Modify Standards of Personal Performance

Modify your habits and standards of personal performance to accomplish specific ends, instead of varying trivial routines mainly for the sake of change itself as you did in Round 1.

Cut down the time you spend on some task but try to maintain or improve the quality. Or settle for just "good enough." Mow and trim the lawn, read the paper or your favorite magazine, or clean your house in half the time you usually take.

Increase the time you usually take to do a task and upgrade your results significantly. Wash the car and also clean the interior, dash, and door frames. Prepare a meal where the ingredients or the setting have an extra touch of class.

Try to put your time, talents, and resources into new combinations for greater efficiency. Cook double portions and freeze part for an easy meal later on. Use the solitude of jogging to plan a project or solve a problem. Accumulate errands and do them all at one time; map out an itinerary so that you use your time and energy effectively instead of zigzagging or retracing your steps.

Value your time and take pride in your accomplishments. Set goals—deadlines, output, quality—and put pressure on yourself to accomplish them.

If you usually procrastinate, do it right away. If you're usually prompt, put it off (if it can wait). If you don't enjoy doing it, try to delegate it or omit it. If it has to be done and you're the one to do it, get at it. If you usually strive for perfection, do it so it's passable. If a lot of your performance is borderline, clean up your act. If you usually concentrate on one thing, put several other irons in the fire. If you've got a lot of things going, try to concentrate and finish up one first. If you're deliberate, act on impulse. If you're impetuous, try weighing decisions carefully.

Reconcile your checkbook and bank statement to the nearest five dollars instead of to the penny. Leave some food on your plate if you're full. Pick up your clothes if you leave them lying around. Read that stack of magazines you've been saving, or throw them out. Put off returning a friend's call right away if you have other plans. Don't put off inviting your rich uncle over for dinner.

In other words, try alternative ways of doing things. Learn to be comfortable with significant changes. Learn to be flexible in making tradeoffs of time, resources, quality, quantity, and specific ends. Practice doing what your major goals and the particular situation call for.

Deviate from Propriety

Disobey standards of socially acceptable conduct. Many of the testing limits exercises fit this description. Here are some other suggestions: Arrive early or late. Jog clockwise on a running track and greet those who come toward you in the traditional counterclockwise direction. Go nude in the privacy of your own home.

Disregard directions. Don't "cut on the dotted line" or "open here." Go up a stairway marked "down." Go out a door marked "in"—*very* carefully! Try to get two of something that's offered "one to a customer."

Question authority. Ask a doctor to thoroughly explain a treatment or medication prescribed. Ask a lawyer to explain procedures or give you an itemized bill. Discuss or question established policies with teachers, store managers, public agencies.

If you decide to disobey signs like "Parking for Guests Only," "Keep off the Grass," "Private Road," "No Solicitors," or "No Dogs Allowed," be both willing and able to face the consequences if you get caught:

QUESTION AUTHORITY

Mike Itthappen and his family arrived at the Shady Rest Motel at the end of a hot afternoon drive. After registering, the whole family donned their swimsuits and headed for the motel swimming pool. The two children, Hope and Will, ran ahead and were confronted by a big sign that read, "Adults only after 5:00 P.M." It was just after five and both children began to cloud up with disappointment at the thought of not being able to swim. As Mike approached, he looked at the sign and looked at the pool. No one was in or around it. He looked also at the faces of his children and his wife, Elsie. He said, "The sign is there for a reason, either to allow adults to swim without being bothered by children or because the management doesn't want kids making noise around the pool from cocktail time on. But there are no other adults here right now and I'm sure we can enjoy the pool without making a lot of noise. C'mon— last one in's a rotten egg."

Mike didn't allow himself to be intimidated by the authority of a sign that had no relevance at the moment. He set an example for his children that rules need to be interpreted sensibly, not ignored. If adults or the motel manager had arrived on the scene, Mike would have played it as he saw it—seeking their concurrence with his decision, backing off, or hanging firm—depending on the circumstances. Meanwhile, the Itthappen family could enjoy the pool without infringing on anyone else's rights.

Don't deliberately break the law. But know your legal rights and don't hesitate to respectfully question procedures or ask for clarification of issues involving police or law-enforcement agencies.

Don't unthinkingly follow irrelevant, unreasonable, or unjustified authority, whether it's personal or implied in rules or printed signs. Try to establish for yourself a balance of conformity and noncompliance that you can live with comfortably.

Use the Telephone to Advantage

Test limits on the phone the same way you do in person:

- Intrude on routines of others, shape conversations, delegate, ask for special services, try to change people's minds.

- Put others on hold, but don't let others put you on hold.

- Preempt customers in business establishments or service bureaus by phoning in orders or requests.

- Use the phone to give yourself the edge—to save you time, effort, or money; for the sake of comfort, convenience, or pleasure.

GENERAL STRATEGY

The Workouts in this Round involve more personal challenge as well as greater risk to relationships than those in earlier Rounds. The way to successfully meet the challenge and minimize the risk is through effective management—of self, others, and circumstance.

To "win" this Round you need to selectively use, improve, vary, and expand the basic managerial skills you now have in your repertoire through practice—lots of it. Don't be surprised if some of the sample exercises seem contrary to those in earlier Rounds. Now you interrupt and monopolize conversations, for example, instead of practicing smart listening. Remember that the object is to accumulate a collection of as many different skills as possible and to be able to spontaneously draw out and use whichever ones will best accomplish the particular goal or goals you choose at any given time.

Remember, too, that the specific moves you try in this Round are not necessarily meant to become a way of life. You won't, for example, buck every line you see from now on. Instead, the Workouts are meant to teach you skills you may need to get what you want *when* circumstances and your own priorities warrant it. Thus the same skill that it takes to buck a line successfully may come in handy to slip your order ahead of others for critical delivery.

Trying the Workouts will help you personally reconcile the benefits and costs of getting more than your "fair" share in social ex-change. Through firsthand experience you can weigh both the intrinsic satisfactions and extrinsic rewards of getting what *you* want against the discomfort of sometimes displeasing others or deviating from previously held values and standards.

Proceed gradually. Push yourself and others only to the point where you believe your ability and others' lack of resistance will make success likely.

Remember that the *appearance* of authority *gives* you authority. Dress appropriately. Act like you know what you're doing. Look like you belong.

Carefully plan out what you'll do and with whom you'll do it. Decide in advance what limits are acceptable to you so you maintain control at all times. Don't allow the pressure of others (direct or unconscious) or the "heat" of circumstance to push you past your preset limits.

Don't do anything that endangers the health and safety of yourself and others. Be sensitive to the feelings of others. Look for signs that tell you to back off and seek alternative ways to your goal instead of expanding energy uselessly, getting battered unnecessarily by willfully pursuing a collision course, or alienating others who can retaliate later.

Be especially careful with people you don't know well. Your perceived "affront" may be the last straw for some overdefensive, disturbed person and cause an aggressive reaction.

News stories tell of fistfights along the freeway caused by one car cutting in on another. In San Diego a man was stabbed in an argument over a car blocking a street. In New York a passerby shot a man who bumped him on the sidewalk. In Los Angeles a student shot up a classroom because someone took "his" seat in class.

The object is not to get your own way *at any cost*. It's to get what you want *at a cost you're willing and able to pay.*

GIVE THE APPEARANCE OF AUTHORITY

"Sometimes I think the boss overplays his role."

Good managers keep control of the situation. People who are convinced of their own superiority aren't compelled to prove it by *always* besting others, regardless of the consequences.

Maintain your own dignity and self-control, and treat others respectfully at all times. Your self-esteem is now high enough so that you don't need to put yourself down to gain favor from others, nor put others down to build yourself up in your own eyes. You can afford to treat the helpless kindly and face the powerful with self-confidence.

LIVE ACTION REPORTS

I was shopping with my brother. At the counter he bought some gum. I talked him into buying a different flavor. It's the first time I've consciously tried to change someone's mind like that. I was really excited at my success.

I asked my boyfriend over for dinner. He eats with me a lot—always my groceries. When we go out, it's usually dutch. After he accepted I asked him to pick up my dry cleaning. I also asked him to stop for groceries and wine. I told him exactly what to buy. When he arrived, I asked him how much I owed him for the cleaning and ignored the cost of the food and wine. I put him to work helping to make the dinner, and when we were through eating I asked him to help me clean up, instead of watching TV as usual. As he was putting the pans away, I slipped into the living room and turned on the stereo, with soft "background" music. I was determined to spend the evening talking, not gawking at the TV. I like Al, but I've decided that if this relationship is to survive, it's got to do more for me in the future than it has in the past.

Suggested to my wife that we take turns paying the monthly bills, so we'd both have a better understanding of where the money goes. She agreed. I hope later I can get her to do it all the time. I hate to pay bills.

I was making an appointment over the phone, talking to a receptionist. She asked if she could put me on hold. I said, "No, I'd like you to finish with me first." She did.

I was in a disco the other night. I don't ordinarily dance much and in the past haven't enjoyed it too much. This night I decided to really move. I asked the prettiest girl in the place to dance. The thought of rejection never entered my mind. She said she'd love to. We hit it off great and talked and danced for over an hour and a half. Before I left I asked her out for Saturday night. She accepted. Formerly I wouldn't have had the confidence.

I called up a friend and was talking to him on the phone. Then I said, "I'm going to hang up. I'll call you back in twenty minutes. Don't go away." I called back later and never had to explain why I interrupted the call.

I was at a baseball game. There was a line that seemed a mile long in front of the men's room entrance. After a quick look at the situation I walked in the exit. No one said a thing. It was so simple—and so satisfying.

After playing poker until three-thirty in the morning, a friend and I went to an all-night diner I like for an early breakfast. My friend said he was going to have steak and eggs. I told him that the place specialized in buttermilk waffles and got him to order them. I then ordered steak and eggs. He accepted the situation, but I felt he resented the intrusion. I think I went past the limit. I think if I could do it over again, I'd join him in having waffles. The way I did it seemed too much like tricking him. As it was I lost some credibility, which was pointless.

The sign in a coffee shop said, "Please wait to be seated." There was only one empty table and no one else waiting to be seated, so I walked in and sat down. The hostess brought me a menu and greeted me cordially.

Told my boyfriend that the garbage had to be taken out before we could leave for our date—and it would save me time if he'd do it for me. I made it a point to tell him how much I appreciated it.

In the grocery store I saw a man looking at English muffins. I saw a brand advertised widely on TV. I put a package in my cart and told him how great they were. He said he'd heard of them but had never tried them. He put some in his cart. I noticed an elderly lady close by. She had heard our conversation and she also went over and put a package of muffins in her cart. When they were gone I put my package back on the shelf.

I've started to spray my car off with water from the garden hose twice a week instead of washing it thoroughly with soap every week. It looks nearly as good and saves a lot of time.

Set a limit of twenty minutes to read the morning paper. Skimmed some articles and skipped others completely. Spent the time I saved eating a better breakfast and washing up the dishes before I went to work.

I've had long blond hair for several years. My girlfriend liked it that way and always got upset when I talked about cutting it. To get a more professional image, I decided to cut it short anyway. I thought it was going to cut our romance short, too, when she saw it. But she laughed when I told her my hair would grow on her.

INSTANT REPLAY

You're out to get more than your share in this Round, so you put a higher priority on results than previously.

You don't force your will on others or put them down. You test for willingness—or lack of resistance, at least—on the part of others. You try to size up situations, become aware of opportunities, and find alternate ways of reaching goals you set for yourself. You discover how far you're willing to go to get results as well as how far others are willing to let you go. You back off gracefully rather than argue or fight.

You try to leave those you encounter feeling better for having the contact.

The suggested Workouts are:

◆ Vary trivial personal routines that affect others.

- Intrude on the routines of others.
- Break in on others.
- Direct conversations.
- Change others' minds.

  Give pertinent information.

  Plant a seed of doubt.

  State a different preference.

  Refuse a suggestion and counter with another.
- Delegate tasks to others.

  Express requests assertively or state needs.

  Shift responsibility for long-term tasks.

  Trade one responsibility for another.
- Expand your circle of acquaintances.
- Push services to the limit.

- Buck lines.
- Try unsolicited selling.
- Take charge and keep control for a prolonged time.

  Take someone on a daylong outing.

  Take a novice to an activity you're an old hand at.
- Modify standards of personal performance.
- Deviate from propriety.

  Disobey standards of socially acceptable conduct.

  Disregard directions.

  Question authority.
- Use the telephone to advantage.

ROUND 7:

MANAGING
COMPLEX SOCIAL RELATIONSHIPS
(DEALING WITH GROUPS)

You begin to work with groups in this Round. You try to achieve with two or more other people all that you've accomplished up to now in one-on-one relationships.

The larger number of people itself makes the interactions more complex than those in previous workouts. You have to deal with interrelationships among the others in the group as well as those between yourself and others.

For the first time you work out with an "audience." You play to the crowd as well as to individual members of the group. You play to impress your audience, to make them like you and to get them on your side—so you'll get the results you want.

THE CHALLENGE

The challenge of this Round, quite simply, is to "cut it" with groups. The object is to gain entry into groups which you see as beneficial; to display yourself and your abilities in front of others and to win the appreciation of the group; to shape groups to get results and to keep them functioning effectively; to restructure old groups and form new ones.

In effect, you try to manage the balance of social exchange in your favor in more complex group relationships, just as you did earlier in simple social relationships.

THE STRATEGY

You work out with both formal and informal groups of different size, makeup, and purpose. You learn to vary the roles you play within the same groups as well as among different groups.

You apply everything you learned in individual Workouts to group relationships.

You make your presence in groups seen, heard, and felt and you begin to get used to being the center of attention.

You use groups to make profitable contacts and influential connections.

You use groups to accomplish your own goals, at the same time maintaining the group as an ongoing, effective working body.

You continue to build self-esteem by realizing success in what are now tougher social situations.

Finally—and this is especially important since you're outnumbered now—you try to get others to willingly follow your lead and to leave them feeling glad that they did.

THE MOVES

The maneuvers in this Round call for redoing some earlier Workouts, this time with groups. In addition, you draw attention to yourself, practice being more outgoing in gatherings, talk to groups, join new groups, and participate actively in groups and meetings. You try to influence group decisions, establish a following, start new groups, realign groups, and gain personal ends through group influence.

WINNING THE ROUND

You know you're a winner when you can enter groups with ease and move about in them freely; when groups invite your participation, seek your counsel and leadership, and automatically endorse your suggestions; when you enjoy the glare of the limelight; when you can function freely as your own agent in the presence of others; when you can easily switch roles to affect results or group continuity, whichever a situation calls for; when you can manage the action in groups—bringing out the best in some members, subduing others, mixing and blending individual contributions to gain both harmony and strength—to make things go your way.

WHY WORK OUT WITH GROUPS

To have CLOUT you obviously need to be able to deal effectively with more than one person at a time. Not only do you need to avoid blindly following group dictates for the sake of self-management, you also need to get the group to follow you.

Group participation of some kind is inescapable in normal everyday living. There are countless off-the-job groups that you're a part of—your family, circle of friends, neighborhood cliques, church, clubs, athletic teams, and political action groups, for example. Some groups are so short-lived that you may not even think of them as such—people waiting in the same line, riding on the same elevator, watching the same sports events or theater performance, or the three others you join to make a foursome for bridge or for golf.

COMING TO GRIPS WITH AN AUDIENCE

These are the kinds of groups you practice with in this Round. In so doing, you gradually come to grips with a factor you've deliberately tried to avoid previously—an audience.

An important goal of the group exercises is to help you get used to being watched as you take action. Even though you've banked enough successes now so that you can handle "mistakes" without undue self-blame or serious damage to your self-esteem, the idea of being watched by even one extra person still creates a new challenge. Fear that others will ridicule you or think less of you if you "fail" may make it harder to try. You might be tempted to overextend yourself to show off to others. A desire for group acceptance could sidetrack you from your goal.

Even if you escape all that emotional static, others in the group might try to interfere with your goal. This could be either someone accompanying you or members of the group you're trying to influence. A companion might try to stop you from taking action. Members of the group might simply ignore you. A member of the group might oppose your goal and persuade others to join in resisting your leadership.

Here are two experiences that show how merely changing from two to three participants can result in greater challenge to the would-be group manager.

Kent Sustane decided to join two coworkers who were having lunch together in the cafeteria. He interrupted them successfully and exchanged greetings and some good-natured bantering as he pulled up a chair to join them. In a matter of seconds the other two men were again almost totally absorbed in talk about a golf tournament in which Kent had not participated. Kent found himself totally left out of the group interaction, an observer at best. He felt trapped—he couldn't break into the ongoing conversation, but he didn't feel he could get up and leave, either. He sat it out until he finished his lunch, then he excused himself and left, feeling disappointed with the outcome of his group exercise.

Carrie Throo was with a friend in a coffee shop, talking about a forthcoming backpacking trip, when she noticed an old school friend enter and she decided to "make a group." Carrie introduced her two friends and told something about each to the other to help them establish commonality. She shifted her attention back and forth, including first one friend and then the other in the conversation that followed, like a director bringing in players on cue. The experience made her realize the added challenge involved in trying to manage a conversation with more than one other person. "But," she said, "having decided in advance that I would take control helped. I liked the way I handled it."

Although these two experiences differ in one respect—Kent tried to *intrude* into a group of two and Carrie *invited* a third person in—both were an attempt to form and influence a three-member group.

Carrie succeeded partly because she saw herself as the "take-charge" person and directed the interaction so that all three members of the group felt that they had a share of the action.

Kent's experience was disappointing partly because he didn't preplan and anticipate what he would do after he said, "hello." He'd have fared better if he'd been prepared to take charge with a new topic of conversation that was of interest to all three group members. And rather than totally commit himself to the group by sitting down, he might have remained standing until he was sure of his control over the group. In leaving himself an easy option to move on if the task proved too difficult, he'd at least be practicing independence and self-management.

APPLYING OLD SKILLS TO NEW CHALLENGES

By applying the skills you've accumulated in one-on-one training to group situations, you meet the challenge of complex social relationships.

Even though you've made many of the moves before, working in groups is just enough different that you need this practice with off-the-job groups before you try the same things in the workplace. This increases your competence and confidence and safeguards your professional image.

LEARNING COMPLEX GROUP MANAGEMENT SKILLS

The nottims you acquire as you practice with groups are: *appearing attractive, credible, and competent; maintaining high visibility; drawing positive attention to yourself; dealing directly with groups, formally and informally; daring to be distinctive; sensing and resisting external pressures; managing information; arranging new and better combinations of existing elements; seeking power and influence for their utility; getting results; starting and sustaining others; committing others to objectives; nurturing relationships; moving in and about people, meeting and talking with them, and terminating conversations with ease; maintaining independence; resisting socialization; influencing others; seeking command and extending control; making and using contacts and connections; gathering and assimilating information; taking charge; attracting and committing followers; using others to advantage; making and breaking alliances; dealing with individual group members; dealing with the total group.*

USING GROUP SKILLS IN MANAGEMENT

Groups are an unavoidable part of the managerial experience. Managers deal with the more structured groups like the organization, firm, division, section or department, commit-

tees, and boards. They take part in more loosely formed groups like those in the executive dining room or in the corner of the company cafeteria, bull sessions at the coffee breaks, informal work groups, and other casual associations at the workplace. They're also involved in quick-forming and quick-dissolving business relationships which take place both on and off the business premises. These include groups like problem-solving conferences, client or constituent entertainment, instructional or promotional meetings, and negotiation sessions.

The groups in which managers participate may vary in size from a few people to a hundred or more. Their associations with them may be brief or long-term. Their individual roles will differ from group to group and from time to time, too. Their participation may be formal or casual; they may be leaders or constituents; they may be peace makers or task masters. Regardless of the group or the particular managerial role at the time, the manager's object is always the same—to work in and through groups to get results or to further the cause.

DEALING WITH GROUPS

"Now there's a cat with clout!"

GETTING RESULTS
THROUGH GROUPS

Managers use groups when they can accomplish more *with* them than they can *without* them. The group serves as a pool of human resources that can be harnessed to help a cause. The cause can be as uncomplicated as promoting sociability among members or as complex as solving a major diplomatic crisis:

When President John F. Kennedy discovered in October 1962 that the Russians had established missile bases in Cuba, he called together not only his close body of regular advisors, but also outsiders like experienced international troubleshooters Dean Acheson and Adlai Stevenson to provide fresh input. He intentionally absented himself from meetings to avoid influencing or restricting group discussions. He intentionally withheld his own point of view to prevent the group from focusing on his thinking rather than searching for viable options. The result was the development of the Cuba naval blockade strategy which sent the Russians packing and resulted in what is regarded as one of the most brilliantly executed diplomatic confrontations ever undertaken by the United States government.[1] Its success was due in part to Kennedy's ability to make the most of the available resources.

By the same token, your function as manager is to tap the total talent of group members and keep the group functioning smoothly and effectively. By such joint action, you accomplish more and better results than you could alone.

USING AND INFLUENCING GROUPS

As a manager you call groups of people together and use meetings to pool resources, make announcements, disseminate information, issue directives or lay down the law, explain issues and procedures, clarify internal or external problems, seek support, or reach consensus.

Since meetings are used for so many different purposes, the immediate and current end sought may not always be apparent nor agreed upon among others present. It's your job to make the purpose clear and unify group sentiments concerning it. Your title as manager helps. But mainly it's the strength that comes from your relationships with individual group members that enables you to get what you want and overcome group sentiment when it's contrary to your own point of view. Consequently, much of what you do as a manager in groups involves one-on-one interactions. Some of these interactions take place privately. Others take place in the presence of one or more additional people. Through such individual relationships you create an image of competence, consideration, confidence, credibility, and CLOUT. You also gain information and input that give you advanced knowledge of what the group sentiment is apt to be and how you can shape it to your advantage.

You also need to be able to deal effectively with the total group. Charismatic, total-group appeal can be attained by being seen as an attractive person—one who has concerns in common with the group, conforms to group sentiments and standards, and inspires confidence. This appeal, once achieved, makes it easier for you to obtain group support.

John Connally, who has been successful in both business and politics, has this charismatic ability to sway people to his way of thinking. He has served on the boards of some of the nation's most prestigious corporations as well as in numerous agencies and committees serving national interests.

Connally is known to be quick and thorough in his study of any situation in which he partici-

pates. He also makes it a point to learn from the other people involved—studying them, watching them, and listening to what they say. It seems to pay off. A trustee from U.S. Trust has commented about his presence at board meetings, "no one would make a move without turning toward Connally's end of the table and saying, 'What do you think, John?' "[2]

Similarly, W. W. Clements, the Chairman of the Board of Dr. Pepper, with whom Connally also served, characterized him as follows: "I don't know what it was, but there were twelve men in the room and then there was John Connally."[3]

Connally's influence is particularly impressive because in many cases he functions as "just another member" with no special title or formal position of leadership.

Whether or not you achieve this level of charisma, to have CLOUT you need to be able to sway the thinking of group members as well as bring out the best they have to offer. This kind of managerial skill allows you to influence group direction, decision, and achievement. It provides easy entry into other groups. It extends your influence, increases your contacts and connections, and provides a wider arena for displaying your competence.

GROUP WORKOUTS

The Workouts in this Round aren't a comprehensive course in group processes and behavior. They serve as a practical introduction to managing groups. They show you specific moves you can make to feel more comfortable in groups. And they suggest ways you can improve your image in groups and enlist group support to gain your ends.

Do the suggested Workouts in whatever order seems easiest for you. But read through all of the suggestions first. Then go back and plan your own approach according to your personal style and preference.

Redo Earlier Workouts

Repeat Workouts from earlier Rounds with groups of two or more people besides yourself:

Take others along when you explore new places, and try to maintain control of the action.

Greet and talk to groups of transient strangers and waiting people. Approach several people who are "together," and make positive comments or ask for the time, directions, or help.

Smart-listen with groups of people and reflect back understanding of group and individual sentiments: "It looks to me like we're agreed that we should go on a picnic, but Jack wants to go to the country and hike and Mary would rather go to the lake and swim."

Give positive verbal strokes to groups: "I like the way we all pulled together in an emergency."

Express your own feelings in I-talk to two or more people at a time. "I'm disappointed to hear you making accusations and counter-accusations instead of dealing with the basic issue of whether this neighborhood needs a park or an apartment complex."

Impose favors on groups. Take your family on an outing you know they'd enjoy. Bring candy or send flowers to the secretarial pool or to the personnel at your favorite restaurant.

Resist or refuse requests from groups. Decline a nomination or committee assignment you don't want.

Make your wants known. Try to get the group to accommodate you: "I really want to serve on this committee, but I can't meet on Tuesdays. Any other day of the week is fine."

As you gain group confidence and competence, gradually try to intrude on group routines, direct group conversations, and change group consensus.

Draw Attention to Yourself in Public

Arrive at a meeting or gathering after everyone is seated and take a front-row center seat.

Get up and leave during a performance or speech. Return a few minutes later.

Have yourself paged over a public-address system in an airport, hotel lobby, or other public place.

Arrange to have a birthday cake presented to you at a restaurant (whether or not it's your birthday).

Be the first to ask a question after a speech or demonstration.

TRAINING TIPS

Work into this gradually by starting with whatever you're sure you can pull off. Try to draw positive—or at least not unfavorable—attention to yourself.

At first success may be simply discovering that you can live through being noticed. Later, after many experiences in the limelight, you

DRAW ATTENTION TO YOURSELF IN PUBLIC

find that you can take attention, expected or otherwise, in stride. (Some previously shy people even learn to enjoy being the center of attention!)

Pat Reeotic volunteered to lead the pledge of allegiance to the flag at his lodge meeting. He figured that after he said the first word or two to start the group out in unison, his voice would be drowned out by the crowd and everybody would be looking at the flag, not at him. He was a little nervous anyway at first, but soon got over it when he saw the group follow him so matter-of-factly. He decided to volunteer at every meeting until he felt no nervousness about it at all.

Be Sociable at Informal Get-Togethers and Parties

Enter with a flair.

Acknowledge the group as a whole or greet individuals by name.

Symbolically reinforce greetings.

Get group attention with a startling announcement or interesting anecdote.

Move around. Show genuine interest in individuals, but don't get stuck with one person or small group.

Talk to a balanced "mix" of people, including those you feel apprehensive about and those you see as "above" or "beneath" you.

Volunteer to participate in games or performances. (Give a speech, tell a joke or anecdote, sing or play a musical number, do a trick or stunt, start the dancing.)

TRAINING TIPS

Try to appear attractive and likeable. Practice consideration and good manners by conforming to standards of dress, attitude, and conduct of the group you're dealing with.

Anticipate who will be present, and do your "homework": refresh your memory on names and personal interests you can ask about.

Find out what activities are planned and brush up on the needed skills—rules for card games, words of songs, technique for bobbing for apples. Be a good sport and a good guest by joining in activities.

Play jokes on yourself, not on others, to get a laugh. When you "perform" in front of a group, try to make it look spontaneous. Don't force it, and don't make others coax you. If necessary, develop a few new simple skills, like juggling or card tricks:

Miles Offkee was no match for his wife or their musically talented friends when they got together to entertain each other. But he could always be counted on for a laugh when he performed "Yankee Doodle" or "Three Blind Mice" with the flair of a concert recitalist— on his comb and tissue paper "musical instrument."

Address the Total Group

◆ In informal groups

Call attention to something: "Look, everybody! It's stopped raining. The sun's coming out!"

Relate an incident: "The mayor stopped by the office yesterday and gave us a donation."

Share information: "Bill just called and said the polls show Victor ahead by seven points."

Tell a joke.

◆ In more formal meetings

Ask questions about proceedings.

Make or second motions.

Volunteer information or viewpoints.

Volunteer to be a spokesperson.

Give positive group strokes: "I enjoy this group. We seem to have fun, but we accomplish a lot, too."

DEVELOP A FEW NEW SIMPLE SKILLS

TRAINING TIPS

Again, do your homework. Plan and mentally rehearse what you can say that will interest groups of people you know.

Look for and seize opportunities (unique knowledge or an observation about your surroundings) to speak spontaneously to small groups of transient strangers.

Be sure your attempts at humor are in good taste. Don't make fun of others or tell offensive jokes (ethnic, sexist, or off-color).

For meetings, brush up ahead of time on parliamentary procedure if it's used. Learn special terminology. Learn about the objectives and past performance or experience of the group. Observe group members—their strengths, weaknesses, sentiments—for future reference.

Della Gate's first experience with talking to the total group was to volunteer as spokeswoman for her club at intercity council meetings. She explained, "I knew I'd learn everything both groups stood for, and it was a chance to meet and talk to people outside my local club. I wasn't afraid of criticism, because I was only relaying the club's viewpoint, not my own."

Take an Active Role in the Group

Talk more to the total group.

Ask more questions.

Bone up on the issues or alternatives and contribute unique ideas or clear explanations.

Volunteer your services.

Offer your special expertise or take a job nobody else wants and do it well.

Run for office.

TRAINING TIPS

One of your goals is to be seen as a valued member of the group. Simply drawing positive attention to yourself and being more active in the group helps you gain that goal. In fact, there's evidence that leaders are often chosen more because of how often they speak than because of the quality of their contribution.

Nevertheless, performing your duties responsibly and well also helps you to be valued by the group. Don't allow yourself to be typecast by always taking the same job. Vary the roles you play: questioner, advocate, clarifier, summarizer, peacemaker, joker—whatever serves individual and group needs and helps gain the group's objectives.

Before you run for office, give the group members time to know you and accept you as one of them. Learn how the group works—qualifications for office, progression from lower to higher positions, current influential members, and cliques. Watch for opportunities to expand your functions, fill leadership vacuums, and become indispensable to the group.

Hope Toogayne volunteered for the job of program coordinator even though she knew it would be a big responsibility. She saw it as a challenging opportunity for personal growth as well as a chance to meet a lot of interesting and prominent people. She knew she'd be noticed by the group each month as she introduced the speakers and she felt that it would open the door to greater influence in the group.

Influence Group Decisions

Anticipate the obvious and make suggestions the group is apt to accept.

At dinnertime: *Hey, everybody, let's start eating.*

At the end of a long night's work: *Let's celebrate when we're through with this job. I know a place about ten minutes away from here that serves pastrami sandwiches and Irish coffee. We can go in my car.*

After a meeting: *I couldn't help noticing during the meeting that I felt the same way as you three did— but we seem to be a minority. I think our position is valid and needs to be explained fully to the principal. Let's go down and tell him our viewpoint right now.*

"Sell" your position to other members, both in and out of the group meeting.

Establish a shared interest: *We both ride bikes so I know you agree on how dangerous a street is without a bike lane.*

Pinpoint the action's importance: *Every day that we delay taking action invites another injury or death on that busy thoroughfare.*

Establish relevance: *With the current emphasis on conserving energy, adequate bicycle lanes would serve to encourage more people to leave their cars at home.*

TRAINING TIPS

Get to know individual group members and be aware of the ongoing "big picture" so that you'll know what suggested actions are likely to be accepted by the group. Start with pleasant activities like social get-togethers. Suggest unique ventures that spark enthusiasm. Have your suggestions well thought out and present

SELL YOUR POSITION TO OTHER MEMBERS

"It's agreed, then . . . you'll vote my way."

them clearly to avoid misunderstanding. Try to keep control of the activity after it's accepted and while it's being carried out.

Establish and Maintain a Following

Contact more individual group members more often and spend a longer time with them, both in and away from group meetings.

Establish commonality of viewpoints and objectives between yourself and others.

Show understanding.

Smart-listen for facts and feelings.

Express your own opinions and feelings without you-ing anyone out.

Give your advice freely to those who seek it.

Try to maintain a "personal" relationship even when issues predominate.

Assign tasks and delegate duties to your followers in line with their abilities.

Make contacts with individuals seen as influential in the group.

TRAINING TIPS

Making assignments that individuals want and can do makes them feel that you have their best interest in mind at the same time that it improves total group effectiveness. Being in the company of the prestigious or influential makes you appear more attractive to the group in general. Appearing attractive and getting others to identify with you and feel that your views and objectives are the same as their own is the essence of charisma.

Continue to treat people with respect after you're in a position of influence. The same people whose support put you on top may be in a position to topple you by withdrawing their support. The best policy is to treat subordinates with the same respect as superiors.

Kissing up to those above and kicking down those below is very unattractive and only invites contempt from observers, superiors and subordinates alike.

Join New Groups and Organizations

▶ *Intrude on groups of transient strangers:*

Join a threesome teeing off for a golf game.

Suggest playing doubles in table tennis.

Join informal groups at a bar or at a table in a restaurant.

Invite yourself into informal activities at the beach or park (volleyball, frisbee, baseball, sand sculpturing). Try to get others in the group to take joint action (get refreshments, meet again).

Suggest an action or activity to a group of allied spectators at a sports event (lead a cheer, share the cost of refreshments).

▶ *Intrude on groups with more structure and stability:*

Join a "usual" threesome for lunch.

Join a bowling team, hobby club, interest group, discussion group, class, political organization, church group, charitable agency.

TRAINING TIPS

It's important to employ Gradualism here. Decide for yourself what's easiest for you personally, and design your workouts accordingly.

We recommend that you start with those who appear to be most like yourself. Try small informal groups first. Find the captive audience. Corner waiting people or those in situations where circumstances will terminate the contact naturally before long.

Give legitimate reasons for intruding: *I don't have a golf partner today. I'd enjoy joining your threesome* or *I heard you say you're going to the new Greek restaurant for lunch. I've never been there. I'd like to go along* or *I've always been interested in model trains. I'd like to become a member of your club. I'd be glad to stop by and pick you up for the next meeting.*

In the group establish commonality quickly. Learn and use names. Assert yourself, but don't be pushy.

If your intrusion is rejected, don't worry about it. Try again in a group more likely to accept you. Overall you'll find you have more acceptances than rejections.

In this Workout you can also join classes or other groups where you expand and improve social and personal skills. Learn to play bridge or poker; learn to ski, play tennis, golf; take dancing lessons, cooking lessons, public speaking lessons.

Start a Group from Scratch

Get strangers to take some joint action: In a lobby or depot, bring several strangers together to share a cab with you.

In a waiting room, involve the whole group in a discussion on a subject of your choice.

Get a group to have dinner together (three couples to share a table for six instead of waiting for three tables for two).

Cora Sleeder decided that a busload of State University football fans shouldn't just ride in satisfied silence following a big victory. She stood up in the aisle in front of several friends, and together they yelled, "Yay-y-y-y Tigers!" Everyone clapped and shouted. While she still had their attention she urged the crowd on: "Okay, everyone! Let's sing the fight song." She started and everyone joined in. Then she asked for "requests" and they sang the songs of other schools and colleges, too. They were still going strong as they pulled into the lot where their cars were parked. Everyone's spirits were high, especially Cora's for having pulled off her plan successfully.

Have a party. Take personal charge from start to finish. Make the plans, invite the guests, prepare the entertainment and refreshments, greet and introduce guests, sustain interest, terminate gracefully, clean up afterward.

If you often give parties, change the usual procedure in some way (more, fewer, or different guests; different purpose or procedure—talk, games, dinner, cocktails).

Form new social groups. Bring together previously nonaligned people into a more permanent, semiformal organization based on common interests or experience (hobbies, skills, same home town or state, same make of sports car, same favorite team, player or performer). Plan the time, place, activity. Delegate tasks to others.

Form special-purpose groups. Put together a team of talent to further some cause (raise money, elect a candidate, promote social or political action, eliminate a social injustice, establish a community service). Develop the membership and strategies to make a functioning organization.

TRAINING TIPS

To start a group you have to establish a purpose, recruit members, and provide the motivation and leadership to create a functioning body.

The purpose can vary from purely social to a very specific interest or cause. The membership may consist of as few as two others besides yourself. They may be strangers or people you know. The group's "life" may last a few minutes, several months, or many years.

Some groups will be harder to lead and control than others. Start with what's easiest for you and work up to the more difficult ones.

It's your job as organizer to initiate the action, introduce members, find commonality with and among members, and tap the group resources to accomplish your goal.

When organizing permanent groups or special-interest groups, be realistic about how much of your time and energy will be required to do a good job and set your goals accordingly. (Don't bite off more than you can chew.)

As your skills increase and your involvement in the community expands, you discover that you can build a bank account of talented people to draw from—people upon whom you can rely and with whom you have a good working relationship to accomplish almost any goal.

Realign Existing Groups

Form subgroups or splinter groups from the larger group membership:

Start a theater group from the membership of a dinner club, or vice versa.

Establish a fund-raising committee from the membership of an agency.

Try to reassign tasks or roles in a group.

Try to modify group standards or change basic group objectives.

TRAINING TIPS

These Workouts *force* change on others. They may go against expectations and firmly rooted ideas about individual roles, group standards, and allegiances. Since they also deal with groups rather than with individuals, this places them among the more difficult tasks to accomplish. For this reason you should delay making any moves to realign or reorganize until you've established good relationships with individual group members and built your reputation as an attractive, worthy person to follow.

To form a successful splinter group, you

need a common purpose which potential members see as important to themselves or to the concerns of the larger group or community. Search for real but unmet needs in the larger organization through personal contacts. Enlist support from others who are seen as prestigious.

In organizing the new group, help members adjust to different roles and relationships through proper delegation. Recognize individual wants and needs. Maintaining goodwill between yourself and members and among the various members themselves is essential to group survival and effectiveness.

Use Groups to Gain Personal Ends or Maintain Your Control

Get the group to sponsor a social event you'd like to attend, to pay expenses for a trip you'd like to take, or to make a purchase you'd like to use or control (camera, projector, car, club or lodge membership.)

Get the group to "spontaneously" advance your candidacy for an award, recognition, office, or position in the public, professional, or social arena.

Get the group to back a particular project you favor (which the group would not undertake without your intervention, and which you could not achieve without group support).

TRAINING TIPS

Adopt an attitude that the group owes you and should serve your ends, just as you as a member owe the group and should serve its ends. Both functions play a part in successful managing, and to lean lopsidedly to one or the other leads to long-term dissonance. On the one hand, the group suffers if you don't tend to its needs and goals. On the other hand, you suffer if the group doesn't return intrinsic or material satisfactions to you.

The ultimate challenge, of course, is to weld the group goals to yours.

Many famous men in business have shaped organizations to fit their personal needs, goals, and ambitions. John D. Rockefeller, J. P. Morgan, and Revlon's Charles Revson are examples. They accomplished more through their burning personal ambition than they ever could have by merely serving an impersonal, though worthwhile, end.

This kind of purposeful zeal applied to your own organizational world has a functional utility. It serves to strengthen your commitment to a self-defined cause, ideal, or end—and is essential to bring about dramatic organizational movement. On a smaller scale in your own group workouts, try to make a group the instrument of your ends by getting them to identify with you and your cause.

Try the Workouts in Triads (A Pair Plus One)

Most of the exercises in this Round can be done effectively in triads—groups of two other people besides yourself.

Since the three-member group's simple structure includes many of the features of any size group, dealing with it helps you to gain insight into more complex groups.

However, although the triad seems to be the easiest step up from one-on-one relationships, experience shows that this is not always the case.

Perhaps the main reason why triads are difficult is because of the two's-company-three's-a-crowd syndrome. Rather than remain a group of three people sharing a relationship equally, three-member groups tend to separate into a pair with one dominant member plus a third party. If nowhere else, you're familiar with that kind of relationship among childhood playmates:

[154]

Susie and Gordie both like to play with Bobby. When Susie gets to Bobby's house first, they gang up to ditch or taunt Gordie. When Gordie gets there first, he and Bobby do the same thing to Susie. Bobby's always the ringleader, and whoever is in his favor for the day willingly does his bidding.

A lot of insecurity and a little bit of childish malice probably account for this kind of behavior. Insecurity and a need for acceptance may contribute to it even at the adult level. Certainly competent, confident managers can afford to include more than one other person in a benevolent relationship, knowing that they can still control the action.

Whatever the reason for it, the three's-a-crowd syndrome can't operate in groups of four or more members where the "third party" has opportunity to form alliances of his or her own. For this reason, some people find it easier to begin their group Workouts in larger groups and tackle triads after their skills and confidence have risen to a higher level.

TRAINING TIPS

Here are some tips to help you with triads whether you try them before or after larger groups:

Set up situations like Carrie Throo did in the earlier example. Compose your threesome of two people who both know you better than they know each other, and consciously direct each member's participation.

As a listener, listen smart—showing both interest and understanding, so attention and conversation come your way. Then take advantage of the attention to make an impact on the others.

Be sensitive to which of the other two in the group appears most responsive to you and specifically direct your comments to that person to get a foothold in a relationship.

Build a supply of interesting topics or information (gathered in your geographical or mental mobility searches) to draw upon when you want to enter and get attention in twosomes.

If you're usually a passive member in a regularly meeting threesome, try to see each other member separately to build rapport and establish greater commonality to share when all three are together.

GENERAL STRATEGY

Do lots of Workouts at each stage of difficulty. Do the same things frequently with different kinds of people and different size groups. You can be actively involved in several groups at the same time. For instance, while you're the mainstay in a small, informal group of friends who meet once a month for dinner, join a community cultural or service group and begin to work your way up in the hierarchy of command.

Use all the skills you've learned in earlier Workouts to improve relationships and get your way with individuals.

Try to leave people glad about your leadership role in the group. There are more of them now to hold grudges and retaliate in organized fashion if they believe they've been treated badly.

Try to achieve harmony in groups but remember that harmony plays a two-sided role in group relationships. While harmony is an end in itself in purely social groups, it's an important means to ends in special-purpose groups. It helps to keep the group operating smoothly and efficiently, which in turn helps to get results.

At the same time, it's seldom possible to please everybody, and the larger the group, the more difficult it often is to reach consensus. To dwell on trying to please everyone leads to stalemates and sidetracking of goals.

Certainly where the group has the power to retain or remove you as leader, you must get the support of the majority—then try to make compromises with dissatisfied members to restore group equilibrium. Try to reach a satisfactory balance of group objectives somewhere between maintaining harmony at all cost and achieving goals regardless of consequences to individual group members and group solidarity. In other words, try to effect a proper balance between means and ends.

Finally, keep in mind that a group is made up of individuals. Continue to touch bases with individuals to establish rapport between yourself and the group and to hold your following together. The most charismatic leaders never talk to a *group* of people. They always talk to people who are *in a group.* Even when their listeners number in the millions, it's the speaker's ability to make individuals in the group feel that they and their sentiments are being addressed directly and personally that gains followers' support to the speaker's cause.

LIVE ACTION REPORTS

At a hockey game the announcer asked the crowd to join in singing the national anthem. What my voice lacks in quality I can easily make up for in loudness. I decided to really belt it out—they asked for it. My wife was embarrassed, but when people turned to me afterward and smiled and said, "All right!" and "That's some voice you've got," I just nodded and said, "Thanks!"

I moved to the front row in all my classes. Seems like a little thing, but the prof looks at me more. It's easier to hear comments from the class and much easier to get involved in class discussion. Both the prof and the class know me better because of it.

I arrived at a party late. Everyone was clustered in little conversation groups. As the hostess steered me to the table of practically untouched hors d'oeuvres, she remarked that nobody was paying much attention to the food. I saw my opportunity to please her and intrude on groups at the same time. I picked up a tray of food and headed into the crowd. It was easy to break into the groups with an offer of food, chat with each one for a minute, and then move on.

Waiting in a line to buy tickets, I started to talk to the person in front of me about ticket prices. Then I turned around and brought the person behind into the conversation. We talked for about fifteen minutes while we waited. It was a very pleasant conversation.

While talking to a girl I've dated occasionally, my good friend Scott walked up. I introduced them and tried to manage the conversation. I mentioned that they both grew up in Beverly Hills, and that Scott has friends that lived less than a block away from her. This commonality got to be too much, because they started talking about things that left me out. But I hung in there. By listening attentively and asking each one questions about Beverly Hills, I got my share of the action. After about ten minutes I broke it off by telling Scott that we were going to lunch.

I'd never thought much about it before, but I realize now that I have never been the one to initiate the moves when I'm with friends. I'm consciously trying to assert myself more. I was at a beach barbecue on the weekend and after we lit the charcoal we got involved in a volleyball game. Later I noticed that the coals were ready—even past their peak. At first I was hesitant to say anything. I guess I thought if I said, "Let's eat," and someone else said, "No, let's wait awhile," I'd feel put down. I thought for just a second about how to phrase it; then I said, "I'm hungry. The coals look ready— I'd like to eat now." Everyone seemed to say at once, "Me, too," and took off for the fire ring. I felt so high I got goosebumps.

I went to the local dinner meeting of the Personnel Managers' Association. The speaker's topic was one that I knew a lot about, so I anticipated what he was going to say and mentally rehearsed a question to ask. This was a big first for me, because I'm normally quiet at meetings. I was a little anxious all through dinner and I really felt my heart pounding when he finished speaking. When the discussion was opened up to the audience, my hand was the first one up. I felt my anxiety lessen as I asked the question, and I could actually see from the audience reaction that they approved of the question. It started a general discussion, and several people asked me questions, too. I was amazed that the nervousness completely disappeared once I got going. I was pleased with my showing, and really felt great when people came up to me after the meeting to talk more.

My softball team had a practice game. It's an informal group with no real leader. Today I handled the team as if I were the manager. After practice, some of the members mentioned to me how great a practice it was and how they liked being on the team.

My oldest sister has always planned family festivities like birthdays, Christmas, and Thanksgiving and held the get-togethers at her house or at my parents'. Mom and Dad's thirtieth anniversary is coming up, so instead of playing my usual "gofer" role, I took the initiative and made plans to have the surprise event at my house. I've made all the decisions, delegated the cooking to my sisters, and put their husbands in charge of getting extra chairs and tables. I put myself in charge of the fun things like decorating the house and buying the gift. I've enjoyed taking over. My sister can't get over my ambitiousness.

As I waited for my luggage at the airport in New York, I walked along the conveyor and asked if there was anyone who'd like to share a cab into Manhattan. I got three takers right away. We got into the city faster and it was cheaper to share a cab than if I'd taken the bus like I usually do. It was more convenient, too, to be dropped right at the hotel entrance. I was pleased that I could lead the conversation during the entire cab ride. I exchanged cards with one man who worked in the corporate offices of Rockwell International. He said he'd call me to get some information I referred to. It may prove to be a useful contact.

I was able to get the city's most popular TV news anchorman as a speaker for a group I belong to. Instead of telling the president ahead of time, or even at our planning committee meeting, I held onto my news until the regular monthly meeting. I got to the meeting just as it started, burst in, and made my announcements to everyone. Besides being pleased I could tell they were impressed. People crowded around me for the details, and I savored every last bit of the prestige and attention.

Marge, the leader of our church quintet, called me to tell me that she wanted us to do a special Christmas number, "The Twelve Days of Christmas." I just listened reflectively, even though I didn't like the idea at all. I know she's headstrong, particularly if I buck her, so after she hung up I called Betty, Irene, and Joan, the other members of the group. I told them that I didn't think it would work out for five of us to sing a song designed for at least a dozen people. Each one agreed with me. In addition, Irene said she'd really like to do "Here We Go A-Caroling." I agreed it would be a good choice. I mentioned this when I talked to Joan. She knew about Irene's preference, but neither had planned to say anything. I called Betty back, and she agreed with Irene's choice, too, so I suggested that she bring it *up at our next practice. She's more vocal than the other girls and I thought it would be better if the suggestion didn't come from me.*

At our next meeting, before Marge could raise the issue, Betty suggested that we sing "Here We Go A-Caroling," and we all "spontaneously" agreed. Marge never mentioned her choice. I got a lot of satisfaction out of getting my way without arousing any suspicion of manipulation.

INSTANT REPLAY

You learn to manage people and circumstance to get results in complex group relationships in this Round.

By appearing attractive and prestigious—by displaying competence, confidence, and consideration—and by expressing common concerns with group members in your interactions both in and out of meetings, you enlist loyal, enthusiastic support for your causes. This kind of charisma helps you accomplish the important goals of gaining willing followers and leaving the people you deal with satisfied with the interaction.

The suggested Workouts are:

- Redo earlier workouts.

  Take others along when you explore new places.

  Greet and talk to groups of transient strangers.

  Smart-listen with groups of people.

  Give positive verbal strokes to groups.

  Express feelings with I-talk in groups.

  Impose favors on groups.

Resist or refuse requests from groups.

Make your wants known.

- Draw attention to yourself in public.

- Be sociable at informal get-togethers and parties.

- Address the total group.

- Take an active role in the group.

- Influence group decisions.

  Anticipate the obvious and make suggestions the group is apt to accept.

  "Sell" your position to other members, both in and out of the group meeting.

- Establish and maintain a following.

- Join new groups and organizations.

  Intrude on groups of transient strangers.

  Intrude on more structured and stable groups.

- Start a group from scratch.

  Have a party.

  Form new social groups.

  Form special-purpose groups.

- Realign existing groups.

  Form subgroups or splinter groups.

  Reassign tasks or roles.

  Modify group standards or change group objectives.

- Use groups to gain personal ends or maintain your control.

- Try the Workouts in triads.

ROUND 8:

MANAGING
TOUGH TRANSACTIONS
AND TERRITORIES

You're ready now to pit yourself against top contenders. These are people who are as determined to win as you are. Some are already at the top, maintaining their position through expertise and an aura of prestige and inaccessibility. Others are on their way up, boldly employing their legitimate strengths or getting results by resorting to whatever devious means they can get away with.

We could call this Round "Testing Limits II," because it's a sequel to Round 6 in many respects, except that it's harder. It promises greater winnings, involves higher risk, and requires tougher action. The stakes are high and neither you nor those you challenge can afford to pull punches in the tough transactions and territories that you face here.

THE CHALLENGE

The challenge is to take on all contenders and come out on top, enjoying your victory and the position you win. Your objectives are to handle confrontation and overcome resistance; to manage information to your advantage; to recognize and resolve preconflict and conflict situations; to learn to negotiate; to use whatever bargaining tactics work best against your opponents to keep your control—talking them into things, trading favors, bluffing them out, or even backing down, if it's to your advantage.

The ultimate goal is to win and leave your opponents feeling that they've won, too. But if someone has to lose, you make sure it isn't you!

THE STRATEGY

In Round 6 you backed off when you met with resistance. Now you keep pushing to get your way. You get what you can with cordiality. You get what others won't give willingly by bargaining or by outdoing your opponents in the match.

You deal with inner toughness and determination, although you don't necessarily act tough. While you never act superior, you never allow yourself to feel or appear inferior. You refuse to take no for an answer as you try for a win, but you retreat gracefully when you recognize that you're in a "no-win" situation—to seek alternatives or save your strength for a later skirmish.

You take the action to your opponents' corners or lure them to your home ground as you deal with both individuals and groups. Although you practice with easy people in minor confrontations to start, you eventually take on the most prestigious, inaccessible people in hard-to-enter places that you considered off limits in the past.

THE MOVES

Again in this Round your moves involve redoing some earlier exercises, particularly those like intruding, controlling conversations and activities, imposing on others, and exploring your surroundings. But now you push a little harder in the direction you want to go and tackle more difficult challenges.

In addition you practice information management—seeking facts, shunning advice, and

withholding information; fraternizing with those who are distasteful to you; getting through to inaccessible people and getting into inaccessible places; associating with prestigious people; and negotiating and bargaining.

WINNING THE ROUND

You know you're winning when you can deal successfully and comfortably with people in high places; when you automatically separate fact from advice or opinion and use the input to properly interpret and resolve problems and conflicts; when you can handle and dismiss bold people who act bold and tell bold lies that sound like truth; when you welcome the opportunity to bargain and match your skills against a worthy opponent; when others see you as a winner; when you can live comfortably with winning, knowing that others have to lose.

WHY PRACTICE TOUGH TRANSACTIONS

When you're out to win you're bound to meet people who won't willingly do things your way. Whether it's because they want the victory for themselves or simply because they don't want you to have it, confrontation often becomes unavoidable. To get what you want in such situations requires skillful maneuvering. You have to be prepared to do whatever works—persuade, compromise or collaborate, move others aside, go around or go over them.

You also need to be able to go beyond the boundaries of your usual domain, into unfamiliar or even inhospitable territories, to get people and resources to help you get the results you want.

LEARNING WITH MINIMUM RISK

Practicing maneuvers such as negotiating, managing information, dealing with inaccessi-

WIN AND ENJOY IT

WHOOPEE

"Looks like D.J. won another big one."

[160]

ble and prestigious people, and balancing ends and personal relationships in the Workouts shows you the importance of such skills and develops your ability to use them. In low-risk situations you learn what works and you build confidence and competence in handling tough transactions and territories.

COPING WITH DEVIOUS MEANS

You also learn to recognize and anticipate what other skilled contenders will do—from appearing honest and straightforward at one end of the scale to using trickery and bold lies at the other. You discover how devious others can be to get what they want and you find out how far you're willing to go to get what you want in competition with them— or what you must do to avoid being deceived by them.

By perfecting your ability to size up situations and see through to the "real" person, you learn to act spontaneously and appropriately—treating the straightforward with fairness and sensitivity, and beating the cunning and ruthless at their own game.

FEELING AT EASE EVERYWHERE

You learn to neither be awed by authority, power, prestige, or wealth nor unsettled by strange or awesome surroundings. You come to feel equally at home in the castle with the king and in the quarters of the commoner.

GETTING YOUR OWN WAY

Besides preparing you for winning tough transactions in the workplace, skills like these are useful any time you want to get your own way—whether you're dealing with strangers, with friends and family, with community organizations, or with people in high places:

Ed Gin only wanted to buy a quart of milk, so he asked to cut in front of a man with a loaded shopping cart in the supermarket check-out line.

"I've got the exact change," Ed explained, "and I'm in a real hurry."

"Nothing doing," the man answered. "I'm in a hurry myself, and I still have to buy a six-pack in the liquor department. I'll barely make it home for the start of the ball game as it is."

"Hey, now that's a coincidence," Ed answered good-naturedly. "I'm trying to make the start of the game myself, and I just happen to need a six-pack, too. I'll make a deal. Here's the money for my milk. If you'll ring it through with your order and bag it separately, I'll buy your six-pack and you can pay me when I come back to get the milk. That way we'll both be ahead of the game."

Percy Veering had called every public meeting place in town and failed to find a place to hold the lodge banquet. Finally he remembered the Reserve Officers Club facilities. The problem was that only one lodge member was a reservist—Malcolm Tent—and he was so negative about everything that Percy made it a point to avoid him whenever possible. Still, the RO Club was the ideal place for the banquet. Percy decided that he could stand one evening of Tent's company for the sake of the lodge banquet and gave him a call. Tent agreed and the conversation was almost not disagreeable.

Bea Discreet checked the interview notices in the placement office every Wednesday on her way to class. She usually shared the information with her roommate, Aldys Playsieu, because the placement office was out of Aldys's way. After interviewing all the same companies, Aldys had two job offers and Bea had none. When Bea saw that Just Rite Enterprises was coming on campus to interview, she signed up for an appointment, but she didn't tell Aldys about it. She really liked the firm and felt she had an excellent chance for a job offer without Aldys's competition.

In the first example, Ed Gin turned a flat refusal into a gain for both himself and his adversary. He took the information that he was supplied and demonstrated that negotiation doesn't have to end up with a winner and a loser. Both can come out ahead if the conditions are right and they're willing to collaborate.

In the second case Percy Veering found a solution where the advantages of having a successful banquet far outweighed the disadvantages of fraternizing briefly with the offensive Tent. He decided he could tolerate the temporary unpleasantness in return for getting the results he wanted.

Finally, Bea Discreet wanted a clear shot at what she saw as a very desirable career opportunity, so she simply kept the interview information to herself to reduce competition. In so doing she gave priority to her career goal and risked the relationship with her roommate.

NOTTIMS FOR MEETING TOUGH OPPONENTS

This is the ultimate off-the-job training Round. In it you use and improve all the nottims. Certain nottims receive special emphasis, however. They are: *managing appearance— especially displaying ambiguity, clouding intent, and presenting a goal-serving posture; seeking audience with the prestigious; circumventing accessibility barriers of others; keeping aspirations high; thinking highly of yourself; seeing the "big picture"; shaping situations; managing information; making and breaking alliances; compromising and adjusting to reality; making and using contacts and connections; managing reciprocation; influencing others; seeking and extending control; using others to advantage; negotiating—introducing new ways of looking at issues, seeing ways of integrating benefits to all partners, testing opponents' skill and power, managing the climate of transactions, managing the mode of transactions.*

These nottims make you a viable contender in tough transactions. They are the keys to making any transaction come out the way you want it to. With these skills you're able to take on tough transactions and win.

HOW MANAGERS USE TOUGH TRANSACTIONS SKILLS

The skills you learn in this Round give you CLOUT when you need it most. They enable you to cut it when the results you're after are blocked in some way: You don't have the information you need for planning strategy or implementing operations; you lack the resources you need to manage the program task as planned; you're unable to get the necessary cooperation from others to put your energies, information, and resources together.

SURMOUNTING OBSTACLES

To get the results you want, you have to surmount the obstacles in your path. Sometimes that means contacting hard-to-reach people who can provide information and leads, release resources, or deliver cooperation. Sometimes it involves getting the better of enterprising and energetic counterparts—people who disrupt your pursuits as they push for goals of their own. Perhaps they're after the same privileged or elusive information. Or they're maneuvering for the same scarce resource or are partly responsible for its scarcity. And sometimes you need to outwit less scrupulous rivals—people who deliberately intercept, withhold, or distort information, intentionally divert or hold up critical resources, or undermine your efforts and whittle away at your credibility.

NEGOTIATING SKILLFULLY

Whether you're dealing with friends or foes—and whether they're on your back or out of reach—the secret to getting your way is to negotiate.

In Everyday Contacts

Negotiation occurs everywhere in management. Generally speaking, every contact you have with another person in the conduct of your business can be viewed as a process of give and take. Usually it's a subtle process. You cultivate cordiality to get or keep people in your corner or on your side. You probe to understand the total meaning and feeling of the exchange. You structure conversation to focus on the information and concessions you need. You try to distract others' attention so they won't notice that they aren't getting an equal share.

You negotiate in this subtle manner to reach simple accord between your own self-interest and the self-interest of others. You get information, resources, and cooperation from superiors, subordinates, and staff; from counterparts, customers, suppliers, community and government representatives; from people who serve as gateways to other people who are hard to sell.

To Resolve Controversies

When the cordial appeals and subtle pushes fail to yield the results you want, negotiation as we usually think of it comes into play. Then *issues* become of uppermost importance. You negotiate issues of personal salary, promotions, and limits of authority or responsibility with superiors, for example. You bargain over issues like wages, benefits, job content, and jurisdictional matters with subordinates. You try to reach agreement on issues concerning priorities or jurisdiction with staff; priority or allocation problems with counterparts; price, quality, delivery, terms, and service problems with customers and suppliers. You try to come to terms with community and government over issues of compliance, jurisdiction, and support.

In such cases the lines of contention are apt to be clearly drawn and the opposition is likely to get tough. You strive for resolution

TOUGH TRANSACTION SKILLS
HELP RESOLVE CONTROVERSY

"Ladies and gentlemen . . . there seems to be a slight difference of opinion."

[163]

of differences in your favor—to win what you want through collaborative arrangements, if possible, but to win at the expense of the others if there is no other way.

To come out on top in tough negotiations, you think and act quickly. You put your horse-trading ability into play spontaneously, just as soon as you meet resistance. You give a little to get a little—or a lot. You don't waste time licking wounds, saving face, or serving ego. You focus on getting the job done the way you want it. Immediate, fast action gives you the advantage of surprise. A quick settlement eliminates haggling and bad-mouthing and leaves the climate more amicable for the next round. It also allows you to keep your best blockbuster punches secret, saving them for times when the fight is so hard or the prize is so important that ordinary moves won't suffice.

MAKING AND USING CONTACTS

To come out on top you get CLOUT in your corner. You make and use contacts and connections—people inside or outside the organization who are in the know; people who—through prestige, power, or position—can provide you with guidance as well as pull strings and get other people to see things differently in a hurry.

Here's an example of how being on good terms with the "right" people can overcome obstacles:

Herb Bane's success as a sales rep for Top-nawch Industries was only partly due to his suave and affable manner. He was also a master at making cordial contacts and using connections effectively, from receptionist right on up to chairman of the board.

While making the rounds at Uppin Aircraft, Bane learned that, because of a misunderstanding, Topnawch's qualifying proposal had

not arrived in time to be included on the bidding list for the UA99 package that was to be released at the end of the day. Furthermore, a new materials manager had ruled against accepting late proposals from anyone, despite the fact that Topnawch had an excellent reputation for such work in the aerospace industry and had always delivered top-quality results to Uppin.

Bane decided to try to pull some strings. Years earlier, when he played baseball for State U., he had worked as a "go-fer" in the Uppin executive offices. Arden Fan, current chairman of the board of Uppin, loved baseball and each year had sponsored a job with the firm for a State U. team member.

From a contact in the executive offices, Bane learned that Fan was lunching in the Paragon Room at twelve-thirty. Bane arrived at the exclusive restaurant at one-fifteen and spotted Fan's table. As the table was being cleared, Bane strode in and "accidentally" went by Fan's table. "Hello, Mr. Fan," he said warmly. "I'm your old mail boy extraordinaire, Herb Bane."

Fan invited him to have a drink. They reminisced briefly and then Fan turned back to conclude his discussion with the two others at the table. As they all got up to leave, Fan turned his attention back to Bane. Fan's question, "How are things going with you?" was the only opening Bane needed to explain his problem.

"I'm on my way to the airport," Fan said. "Tell me about it as we go."

When Bane had finished his story, Fan said, "Sounds like a reasonable request to me." He turned to an aide and said, "Call in and tell them to hold the UA99 bid and consider late proposals for inclusion on the list." Then as he boarded the company jet he turned to Bane and said, "Come on along with me for the ride. We'll have a few drinks and talk about baseball."

Six hours later, Bane reported in to his boss. "I've got good news," he said. "Uppin Aircraft has agreed to consider our UA99 proposal. I'd have called you sooner but I've been tied up with Arden Fan on the company jet until now." Then Bane continued, "I've got bad news, too. I won't be able to make the sales meeting tomorrow. I thought we were making a short hop to the upstate plant when I got on the plane. How the hell did I know he was going to Washington, D.C.?"

DEVELOPING AN INFORMATION NETWORK

To come out on top you enter the fray well armed with information. You develop a network of sources that can supply you with information. This includes people from all levels, both inside and outside the organization; people whose cooperation you gain and whose talent and input you use; people who can tell you what is going on, what is coming up, whether your sources are reliable, how the system works, or who you have to see to get things done. You also develop an understanding of the total system to know where to go for special information you need.

An incident early in the career of Ernest R. Breech, former chairman of the board of Ford Motor Company, illustrates an effective use of information gathering which resulted in personal benefit to Breech as well as substantial gain to the firm for which he worked.

In 1931, when he was a young employee of General Motors, Breech's knowledge of foreign exchange led him to the firm conviction that the British pound sterling was about to be devalued—contrary to the prevailing opinions in the firm. To verify his belief, he sought out Dr. Warren Persons, GM's consulting economist, in addition to getting information on Wall Street from the managers of the foreign departments of all New York's large banks.

He took the information he'd gathered to Donaldson Brown, chairman of GM's Finance Committee. Brown, in turn, consulted with George Whitney of J. P. Morgan and Company. Finally, he reluctantly gave his OK to Breech's plan to withdraw half of GM's $30 million from Europe and protect the rest by selling the pound sterling short. Within two weeks, the pound sterling was devalued by 30 percent. By taking the initiative as he did, Breech saved the firm $10 million. Needless to say, he also centered attention on himself as a promising candidate for future challenging assignments.[1]

Your information must, of course, be accurate and reliable. It's to your advantage to have a variety of information sources so you can cross-check instead of accepting input at face value. You put bits and pieces of information together to make a complete picture. You look for ulterior motives to protect yourself and your winnings. Blind faith, even in friends and business partners, can lead to dire consequences.

George Zerber, Isaac Singer's partner in the Singer Sewing Machine Company, found that out the hard way. After the company began to make it and while Zerber was ill with a fever, Singer convinced him that the doctor had said he was dying. Singer got Zerber to sell his interest in the company to him for six thousand dollars. Zerber recovered his health, but not his fair piece of the action. He'd been duped—despite the fact that he had literally kept Singer from starving when he first came to New York. Meanwhile the transaction put Singer on the road to becoming a millionaire.[2]

DEALING FROM STRENGTH

To come out on top you negotiate through strength and resourcefulness. You form alliances to improve your leverage if going it alone won't hack it. You offer new approaches to avoid a deadlock. You search for collaborative outcomes so both sides can win. You shape the encounter to your own advantage (setting time, place, agenda, procedures, for example). You keep your attention on the goal, refusing to be drawn off course by emotional factors in the ongoing process. You set high aspirations—to win and win big. If you know what you want and you're willing to live with the consequences, you can get it all.

Tony Dorsett, the explosive running back of the University of Pittsburgh, went this route when he turned professional. Dorsett was dead set against going with the Seattle Seahawks, even though it appeared inevitable that they would have the right to draft him. Mike Trope, Dorsett's agent, knew he could put Seattle in a bind. The Seahawks were in no position to chance a wipeout in the draft if Dorsett refused them. Trope had his attorney send a curt letter to Seattle, informing them that Dorsett didn't want to play with them, that he wouldn't sign if they drafted him, and that neither Dorsett nor his agent intended to discuss it further.

Seattle knew a stone wall when they saw one. They traded their draft rights to Dorsett to the Dallas Cowboys in return for a handful of high draft choices. Dallas got a "million dollar player" and Dorsett got a club more to his liking.

Dorsett took an extremely high-demand stand, a strategy that's possible if you have power and determination. In this case Dorsett was prepared to sit it out for a year if he had to—and his superior competence was his power.

There are, of course, other negotiation strategies besides the extreme-demand approach. Lemuel Boulware, vice-president of employee relations for General Electric, for example, was known for starting his labor negotiations at a moderate position and stubbornly sticking to it. His opposition often realized that they'd lose more than they'd gain by a deadlock and strike, since his original offer was close to where they might end up anyway after compromising extreme positions.

Whatever strategy you use in your own negotiations as a manager, the tough transaction skills you learn in this Round will help you get what you want.

ADOPTING WINNING STRATEGIES

Effective management requires a variety of other tough transactions skills and strategies besides those specifically discussed here. Among them are things like withholding information, fraternizing and forming alliances with people you regard with distaste, putting ends ahead of friends, and forgoing immediate gratification or enduring temporary discomfort—all for the sake of long-term gains.

While these may be distasteful or offensive behaviors to some, they are nevertheless commonly used, frequently effective, sometimes necessary strategies for winning when the competition gets tough and the stakes are high. They work. The extent to which you use such strategies depends, of course, on how you resolve your own feelings about means and ends. If nothing else, as an effective manager you have to be aware of and on the lookout for such strategies as they're practiced by others who are both willing and able to use them effectively on you.

The Workouts will give you a chance both to try such strategies yourself and to observe their use by others.

THE WORKOUTS

The suggested Workouts in this Round are more general than those of previous Rounds. This allows you maximum flexibility in planning exercises that fit your particular level of development, your individual life style, and your special needs.

In addition—and especially important from now on—they require you to practice self-reliance in deciding what you'll do and how you'll carry them out.

Practice Gradualism as you design and do some Workouts that meet the purpose of each category of suggestions. Repeat the Workouts until you achieve a sense of mastery and feel comfortable doing them. Be sure to try increasingly harder challenges, because the false sense of accomplishment that you gain from being an expert at the easy things won't get you through when the going gets tough.

Seek Facts

Practice asking questions so that you get facts, not advice or opinions. Ask questions like "What happened?" *not* "What do you think?" Ask, "When is it needed?" *not* "When should I have it done?"

Practice distinguishing between fact and opinion or conjecture in the answers people give you:

Opinion

It was an expensively decorated room.

Fact

The furnishings were antiques and the floors were covered with Oriental rugs.

Conjecture

It looks like the neighbors have visitors from out of town.

Fact

There's a car with an out-of-town license parked in front of the neighbors' house.

Subtly probe for complete, honest answers by asking for elaboration or explanation. Try to get answers to who, what, when, where, why, and how. Cross-check the validity of information by asking the same questions of different sources. Don't accuse people of deliberately withholding or falsifying information.

TRAINING TIPS

Use your rapport-building skills as well as listening techniques to draw people out and keep the avenues of communication open.

SEEKS FACTS, REJECT ADVICE

"Just give me the facts! When I want your opinion I'll ask for it . . . Now, what do you think about . . .?"

Don't come on too strong. Remember that some people are threatened by too direct a question. Insecure people may be suspicious of your motives and wonder, defensively, "Why do you want to know?" Some assume that any question contains a veiled accusation.

To put people at ease try prefacing your inquiry with a reason:

I heard a frightening crash in there—what happened? (Not: *What's going on in there?*)

I'd like to have a watch like that—where did you get it? (Not: *Where did you get that watch you're wearing?*)

Finally, you're more apt to get the whole story if you conceal emotions such as anger, disapproval, and disgust. Children learn early not to volunteer information that will bring parental wrath down upon them, and wise parents learn to withhold judgment to encourage complete revelation. The same strategy works with adults.

The purpose of the exercise is to practice eliciting facts from others and to learn to quickly distinguish fact from opinion, advice, or even fabrication. As manager, the buck stops with you. It's to your advantage to get the raw information you need to make valid decisions, not the edited versions someone else wants you to have.

Reject Advice

Don't solicit advice, and don't promise to follow it when it's offered.

Avoid saying things like "I don't need any advice," or "Don't try to tell me what to do."

- Make noncommittal acknowledgments: "I appreciate your input."

- Say you've already made your decision: "I've already made my decision, but I'm glad to know how you feel."

- Reveal your decision only if it's to your own advantage: "I've made my decision, and that's all I'm going to say right now," or "I'll have an announcement to make at a later time."

TRAINING TIPS

The object is not to tell other people that you don't value or appreciate their advice, but rather to avoid committing yourself to following advice from them.

Actually, it's to your advantage to consider all the input available, advice included. The trick is, first, to recognize the difference between advice and factual information; and second, to make it appear to others that the decision is your own, not something someone else recommended. Asking for advice creates an image of dependence, but appearing to make independent decisions makes you look strong, capable, and commanding.

Withhold Information

Don't volunteer information that nobody has asked for. If you hear a rumor or some interesting news, keep it to yourself. If someone tells you something you already know, act like it's new to you. If it's told in confidence, don't pass it on. Your sources of information are more likely to continue confiding in you if you show appreciation for their contributions and keep their confidence.

Politely but firmly decline to answer. This works best when the inquirer has no particular "right" to the information and you do have a right to privacy. Give your reasons briefly, in fact and feelings form.

What caused your divorce?
It's a personal matter that I'd rather not discuss.

What were you and Bob talking about in his office this morning?

We agreed not to discuss the conversation with anyone else.

What's the ingredient in this punch that gives it that refreshing tang?

It's a secret family recipe I promised not to divulge.

Be evasive. Some people are better at evasiveness than others. At least try your hand at it, if for no other reason than to become aware of the ways others try to avoid answering *your* questions. You may discover you're better at it than you think.

Answer a question with a question:
What are you doing on the weekend?
Why do you want to know?

Change the subject:
How do you like your new boss?
Speaking of bosses, did you hear that Jack was made district manager?

Be noncommittal:
How much did you have to pay for that watch?
Not enough! It loses ten minutes a week.

Where do you stand on women's rights?
Now there's a question that requires a careful answer.

TRAINING TIPS

Remember that any refusal to divulge information, justified or not, may offend the inquirers, because they're not getting what they want. Take this into account when you design your exercises, and practice with people in situations where the risk to relationships you care about is low.

Your object in these Workouts is to get into the habit of managing information input and output. The strategy is to encourage others to share information with you freely—while you share information with others on a strictly "need-to-know" basis. You lend your ear—but not your mouth—to rumor and other verbal communication. You soak up information like a sponge, but squeeze it out sparingly, only on surfaces that you feel need wetting.

Obviously every situation you encounter doesn't require withholding information. To build rapport and improve relationships you share some information about yourself and your activities. In other words, you're after a two-sided skill here: to know when, how, with whom, and what kind of information to either share or withhold in specific dealings with others. The ultimate goal is to be able to spontaneously use whichever side of the skill is to your advantage in getting the results you want.

Do Something with Someone You Don't Like

Plan an activity with someone whose company you don't especially enjoy.

> Sit next to someone who turns you off when you're in a meeting or at mealtime.
>
> Call on someone who's hard to get along with.
>
> Offer a ride to someone you usually avoid.
>
> Invite someone you'd usually exclude to a party or other group event.

TRAINING TIPS

To carry this off successfully you have to decide ahead of time that your *only* goal is to improve relationships and make the disliked person like you. Then you must keep that end clearly in mind at all times and not allow your ego needs to get in the way. Your satisfaction

[169]

comes from knowing that *you* managed the interaction, not from having had a meeting of the minds or from enjoying the time spent together.

After you've perfected this ability, try it on someone who considers you an adversary, or on someone with whom you've had a run-in previously.

There's an interesting side effect to this exercise. Applying the skills that build rapport and improve relationships in contacts with nonfriends sometimes makes you dislike the people less, or at least understand and tolerate them better.

In any case, it's an advantage to have as many friends and as few enemies as possible. More important, this Workout gives you a chance to experience dealing with people you dislike or oppose—in order to practice coping with your feelings, minimizing your emotions, controlling your actions. It also helps you realize the advantages of appearing cordial and likable as compared to the drawbacks of showing antagonism and malice when you're out to win.

Gain Entry to Inaccessible Places

Go places you previously considered awesome, inaccessible, or threatening.

Go backstage at a theatrical or musical presentation.

Explore behind the scenes in public facilities or places of business—a laundry or dry-cleaning plant, radio or television station, pottery factory, hospital, post office, garment factory, printing plant.

Look over the rooms at the ritziest hotel in town. Inspect the banquet facilities and kitchen at the best restaurant in town.

Enjoy the pool or sauna at a motel or hotel without registering.

Gain entry to VIP lounges in clubs, convention centers, travel facilities.

Get special showings of designer clothes, furs, luxury items.

Go to receptions or social events to which you weren't invited.

Try to get into private clubs.

TRAINING TIPS

The object is to find what's hard for you to do—whether it's attending a formal ball or going to a pool hall—and push yourself to do it. What you consider awesome or inaccessible naturally depends on personal factors as well as your range of experience and level of expertise. An automobile repair shop might be a challenge for a woman, while a visit to a women's beauty salon might be difficult for a man. By the same token, the marble and gold fixtures, mirrored walls, crystal chandeliers, and plush carpeting in the restroom of an elegant hotel would intimidate one person—while it would take no less than Buckingham Palace to faze another.

Whatever you decide to do, plan your approach carefully. Do your homework: check the place out ahead of time; learn names of staff members; telephone for pertinent information; dress appropriately; mentally rehearse alternative things to say or do if you meet resistance.

Remember that crashing a large gathering of strangers is easier than intruding on a small group or a group where some of those present might recognize you and know that you're uninvited.

Try to emit a cordial self-confidence that makes it look like you "belong." Smile, nod, say hello—but don't linger, look confused, or ask questions that will give you away. Make your way to your destination without hesitation.

Once you're in the door, try to sustain whatever image is necessary to accomplish your goal. Manage your behavior and contacts so that you keep control of the situation, even if that means leaving voluntarily before you get thrown out.

Increase the difficulty of the exercises gradually, and try lots of different things. In this way you learn to deal with the emotional static of unfamiliar or threatening situations. You learn to at least look like you "belong." And you gradually find yourself feeling comfortable in a great many different circumstances.

Gain Access to Prestigious or Hard-to-See People

Try to see people who are outside your normal circle of contacts. Some possibilities are school officials, city council members, judges, religious leaders, labor union officials, people in the military, community leaders, heads of social agencies, government officeholders, local radio and television personalities, store managers, people with special skills or talents, heads of companies, prominent socialites, successful businesspeople.

TRAINING TIPS

Here again, as with inaccessible places, there's a great deal of variation in who different people view as inaccessible or prestigious. Tackle whatever kind suits you and try to gradually increase the challenge.

Have a reason for wanting to see people and something to talk about when you do. Try to find out about backgrounds, interests, accomplishments, and associates. Be pleasant but persistent to get through the door.

In your conversation, establish commonality—place of birth, schools, military service, mutual acquaintances, interests, goals.

Give positive strokes about their contributions or accomplishments. Discuss issues that are important to *them* and how the issues relate to you. Get them to give their opinions and points of view.

These are usually people who value their time and give it sparingly to someone who can't do anything for them in return. Therefore, try to make them feel that they are benefiting from the contact in some way—gaining information, support, or ego satisfaction, if nothing else.

The purpose of the Workout is to discover and practice what works to gain access to hard-to-see people, to overcome any hesitation you have about contacting prestigious people, and to learn to deal with prestigious people effectively and comfortably.

Practice Observing Body "Language"

Notice facial expressions—blank, set, frowning, twitching, smiling—for evidence of people's feelings and moods.

Watch people's eyes—blinking, staring, shifting, drooping—for evidence of nervousness, embarrassment, openness, boredom, vulnerability.

Observe body movements—fingers tapping, clutching or wringing hands, fidgeting, stillness, heavy or short breathing, erectness of posture, the direction people face—for evidence of confidence or doubt, sincerity or evasiveness, relaxation or tenseness.

TRAINING TIPS

The main purpose of this Workout is to practice using your skills of observation, particularly to catch actions that betray or contradict words. The obvious example is shaking one's head "no" while saying "yes."

In tough transactions, any subtle behavior on the part of others that gives away feelings like uncertainty, insincerity, or rigidity is helpful in adjusting your own approaches. On the other hand, if you know your own objectives and limits and think highly of yourself, *your* body language will take care of itself.

[171]

Negotiate for Material Gain

Look for opportunities to bargain for personal advantage in dealings for goods or services.

Barter with Friends

Trade something you've grown tired of—personal accessories, clothing, furniture, sports equipment, tools, cars. Try to get something you like that a friend owns.

Answer Want Ads

Call and inquire about items advertised for sale. Get as many facts as you can. Use information you gain anonymously to decide whether or not to follow up in person—and to improve your bargaining position if you do.

Go to Garage Sales

Establish rapport with the sellers. Try to get them to lower prices or throw in bonus items.

Go to Swap Meets

These salespeople are apt to be more experienced, so beware of their hard sell. Watch them deal with others and try to figure a way to penetrate their system.

Bargain with High-Pressure Salespeople

After you've polished your negotiating skills, take on the pros—people who sell cars, insurance, and real estate, for example. Observe the way they arouse previously nonexistent interest in their products, how they close a sale, how they ease you into signing on the dotted line. Practice bargaining for terms. Discover how little or how much sales resistance you have. Practice refusing the purchase politely but firmly and sticking to your decision despite apparent anger or disappointment from the salesperson.

Try Selling

Help sell for a friend who is having a garage sale. Volunteer to sell at a charity bazaar, auction, or rummage sale. Place a want ad to sell personal belongings.

TRAINING TIPS

The object is to practice bargaining in as many different kinds of situations as possible—for small, insignificant items as well as for big-ticket purchases, with friends or

GO TO GARAGE SALES

"and every Saturday he brings home another one."

strangers, and with naïve beginners as well as with smooth, high-pressure salespeople.

You can learn a great deal in these Workouts by careful observation of those you deal with, both in person and over the phone. Some people are sincere; others are evasive. Some literally want to give things away; others would rob you blind. Some people are warm, friendly, and interested while others are cold, aloof, and couldn't care less. Some melt easily under pressure; some freeze and hold their position; some have a knack for putting pressure on you. Some tell you everything; others hide it all. Some are overly honest and open; others are outright deceitful. Try to spot differences and sense what is real and what is camouflage. Discover what your own reaction is to these various behaviors. Practice dealing as coolly with the deceitful as with the trustworthy.

Remember that the challenge is to test your skills and not the size of your pocketbook. Make up your mind ahead of time that you're not going to buy—regardless! Otherwise you may end up broke, with a back yard full of "really great" used cars and maple dresser sets.

Persist Past the First Refusal

Don't take no for an answer the first time. Persist in commercial transactions where there's a difference of opinion about what you have coming regarding things like advertised items, prices, or guarantees. Push for what you want in terms of special services or preferential treatment. Similarly, when you meet resistance in personal transactions hold out past the first refusals to get people to change their minds.

TRAINING TIPS

When you meet resistance, reflect understanding. Then restate your case or add new information. State your needs and expectations in I-talk.

Explain consequences as they affect you as well as how they affect the other person. Use an emotional appeal or sob story if you can do it convincingly.

Avoid you-ing people out for ego satisfaction or to "show them." Keep your cool, even when you feel that others are unjust.

Concentrate on your goal and avoid being drawn off course by emotions. Get your satisfaction from getting what you want, not from getting even.

Here's an approach that worked:

Stan Fast wanted to avoid paying the twenty-five-dollar registration fee for a seminar sponsored by local business firms. At the door he asked to see the seminar manager. He introduced himself, shook hands, and said that he admired their setup and was impressed by their list of topics and speakers. He said he was a student and wanted a complimentary pass. The manager refused.

The title "Performance Appraisal" had caught Stan's eye as he glanced over the program listing, so he told the manager he was thinking of doing a paper on performance reviews and he'd really like to hear the speaker's approach to the matter. The manager refused again.

Stan pointed out that the appraisal method the speaker advocated was unique; that he felt it would be the chance of a lifetime to discuss it personally with the speaker; that it was just what he needed to convince his professor that he was a serious student; and that he'd give the seminar and its manager full credit for making the contact possible when he presented the paper to the class. The manager suddenly reconsidered. He offered Stan a pass only for the morning sessions, which covered the performance appraisal session. Stan accepted, thanked the manager graciously, and asked him for his business card so he'd be sure to

*get his name correct when he commended him
to others.*

Resolve Interpersonal Conflicts through Negotiation

Whatever disagreements crop up in your life, try to resolve them by negotiating so that you get your way but your adversaries feel that they haven't lost it all. Practice with friends or relatives concerning differences over things like personal habits, use of money, or leisure time.

TRAINING TIPS

When you believe resistance to something you want is inevitable, try to avoid "setting the other person's opposition in concrete." Reflective listen to show understanding of the other position *first.* Then state facts, needs, and feelings in I-talk. Emphasize how it's to the *other person's* advantage to do it your way.

Try out various negotiating positions. Start with a high demand and lower it to what you've already decided you can accept: You want a Volkswagen, for example, so you start by asking for a Mercedes and finally "settle" for a Volkswagen.

Try for a compromise in which each side makes mutual concessions:

Will Settle accepted a student's invitation for cocktails and dinner without consulting his wife, Hedda. When he told Hedda, she reminded him that it conflicted with their standing cocktail-dinner date with the faculty social club. Will said he'd feel embarrassed to call his student and decline after giving such a firm acceptance. Hedda suggested that they each go to their own affair alone. Will said he'd promised that she'd attend the student party with him. Hedda refused to give up the faculty affair. Finally they agreed to go early and have cocktails only with the students—and arrive late and have dinner only with the faculty.

Try to collaborate by working jointly with adversaries for mutual gains:

The Days and the Knights were next-door neighbors who both owned dogs that barked incessantly whenever they were left home alone. The Days had eight-to-five jobs and the Knights owned a nightclub, which meant they were away from home from late afternoon until two or three in the morning.

AIM HIGH

"Buddy, can you spare a C-note?"

The Knights' dog kept the Days awake at night and the Days' dog interfered with the Knights' daytime sleeping.

Finally, at the urging of other neighbors whose sleep was also disturbed at night, Day confronted Knight and asked him to keep his dog shut up in the house at night. Knight countered that he would do so only if Day locked his dog in the house while they were away during the day.

As they talked, their two dogs romped together contentedly. This gave Day an idea. "Let's cut a gate in the fence between our yards," he said. "When you're home during the day we'll let both dogs play together in your yard. At night your dog can stay in our yard until you get home from work."

Knight agreed to collaborate and the difference between Knight and Day was resolved to the advantage of both.

GENERAL NEGOTIATION STRATEGY

Negotiation is a complex skill, all aspects of which are impossible to deal with here. Nevertheless, here are some general suggestions to help you with your bargaining exercises, followed by a list of specific rules for negotiating.

Try Different Strategies

Find out what works for you and what works best in various situations by trying a variety of negotiation strategies:

▶ Make extreme opening demands and follow up with small concessions to get what you want when you think you have the edge.

▶ Make moderate opening demands and hold firm to your position when you think your opposition has the edge.

▶ Let the other side reveal their position by making the first offer if you don't know much about your adversary or the deal in question.

Practice Getting Out of Deals

Realistically speaking, even though you need to practice bargaining in the real world, you can't buy up everything you negotiate over simply to learn the skills of trading. For that reason you need to be able to extricate yourself gracefully from situations where you don't want to carry through on a deal.

This is a good place to try out techniques like displaying ambiguity, clouding intent, and backing out of promises—tactics which are often part of successful negotiating.

One approach is to act as an agent for someone else whose approval is needed before you can close the deal. Don't say that you're "only looking" for someone else, however, or the salesperson won't negotiate with you seriously. Set the stage by saying something like, "My brother would really like this, but I don't know if he'd approve of my buying it. The price would have to be just right, because he can't afford to pay much." Then when you've reached a satisfactory price, say something like, "I think this is a really good deal, but I still feel I should check with my brother before I buy it." This tactic is not unlike what happens when you buy a car from a dealer. The salesperson makes the deal, then seeks an OK from the sales manager—thereby maintaining the bargaining advantage.

Use tactics like these only if they don't create internal conflict for you. Notice, nevertheless, that others do use such less-than-straightforward ploys in their bargaining encounters. Find out for yourself if your tolerance for your own chicanery increases when stakes are high and winning is a top priority, and decide for yourself how far you're willing to go to get results.

RULES FOR NEGOTIATING

1. Aim high. This is the single most important point in winning big.

2. Think highly of yourself. Your own confidence is your best bargaining strength.

3. Serve your end, not your ego. Keep your eye on your goal. Don't get caught up in the interaction process or get distracted by personal emotional involvement.

4. Appear cooperative and friendly. Avoid abrasiveness which often triggers irrational responses.

5. Appear open to your opponent's offers or suggestions, but remain noncommittal.

6. Appear uncompromisingly dedicated and immovable in your convictions.

7. Make "unreasonable" demands politely but firmly to trigger major concessions.

8. Offer your opponent emotionally appealing, immediate satisfactions which are relatively unimportant to you in return for larger, goal-oriented, long-term gains.

9. Deal from strength if you can—but create an *appearance* of strength, regardless.

10. Form an alliance if you can't get what you want alone.

11. Collaborate. Search for ways you can both win big.

12. Don't underestimate your adversaries. To plan an appropriate bargaining strategy learn about their motives, emotions, attitudes, ethics, objectives, strengths, and weaknesses—as well as what they have to gain or lose by negotiating.

13. Find out what your opponents want. Don't assume their objectives are the same as yours.

14. Keep your opponents in the dark about your strategy and your stake in the deal. Put them at a disadvantage by making them deal blind.

15. Push for a quick settlement if you feel you have the advantage.

16. Test your opponents' skills early in trivial exchanges before serious negotiations begin.

17. Shape the bargaining situation to your advantage. Determine place, physical setting, time, limits, agenda.

18. Covertly practice your offensive and defensive arguments prior to negotiation to avoid surprises and to appear in control.

19. Ask for clarification if you don't know what is going on. Don't let the opposition deliberately confuse you.

20. Determine whether those you're dealing with have final authority. *Get* concessions from delegates but *make* concessions to the final authority. Introduce ambiguity of a final authority beyond you if you want a last chance to reconsider the final agreement.

21. Make general commitments which sound firm, yet leave some room for adjustment.

22. Try to prevent your opponents from becoming irrevocably committed to a position. Introduce new approaches and directions to keep the interchange moving toward your goal.

23. Try to get your opponents to lower their aspiration level.

24. Try to make your opponents' goals appear less valuable or desirable to them.

25. Verify anything you're told that you don't know for a fact.

26. Document or legitimate what you agree upon, if it's to your advantage to do so.

27. Display ambiguity regarding demands, concessions, and agreements reached.

This gives you leeway in finalizing deals, especially with those who don't ask for clarification.

Some of these rules may seem to contradict one another. This is to be expected, since various people and circumstances require different tactics. The object is to be *able* to use them all—and to spontaneously choose and use the ones that fit your need at the time.

RULES FOR RESOLVING INTERPERSONAL CONFLICT

1. Start with what you *can* agree on.

2. Keep a lot of options open.

3. Keep both ends *and* relationships in mind.

4. Deal with both feelings and facts.

5. Avoid making judgments.

6. Speak for yourself—and avoid interpreting the meaning of what others say.

7. Keep to the issues rather than "choosing up sides."

8. Reach amicable accord rather than browbeating others into submission.

9. Emphasize the joint benefits of agreement.

10. Use collaboration or compromise rather than win-lose strategies.

11. Avoid deadlocks by not taking "stands" or making extreme demands.

12. Get help from a third party if necessary.

13. Get a personal commitment to the resolution from others involved in the conflict.

LIVE ACTION REPORTS

I walked into a restaurant about three in the afternoon and said, "I'm here to inspect your restaurant." The manager was called and I was treated with great courtesy. He showed me their complete operation—kitchen, dining room, bar. He never questioned my authority. I'm sure I could have had a meal and drinks on him as well. This was a sort of impulse thing on my part. I'm not sure I yet have the guts to plan such a caper in detail. I was prepared to tell him I was a curious prospective customer if I was challenged.

I have a neighbor in the next apartment whom I don't much care for. He avoids me, too. I know from the music I hear him play that he likes jazz. I had two tickets to a jazz concert, so I asked him to go with me. We had a pretty good time together. Our common interest in jazz helped. I don't think we'll ever be close friends, but I'm sure we'll be better neighbors, now. It was a good experience for me.

My brother-in-law quite often sells things at swap meets. I asked to go along and help. He laid out all his stuff and priced it, but he said the prices were high, because people expect you to come down. He said to try to get at least half the tagged price. I got off to a good start. The first fellow who came up to me picked up an old car distributor priced at three-fifty. He asked me how much it cost, and I confirmed the price as marked. He said, "Too much," and walked away, without giving me a chance to let him have it for less. In ten minutes he was back with his brother. He asked if the price was still three-fifty. I said, "yes," and they both left. A few minutes later they were back, and the brother said, "I'll give you two-fifty." I said, "No, the price is three-fifty." He offered three dollars. I refused. He said, "OK, three-fifty," and called me a crook. I figured they wouldn't have come back unless they really wanted it and were willing to pay my price. My brother-in-law was impressed.

A friend of mine in the office snagged her cashmere sweater on her bracelet. She said, "That does it! Who'll give me five dollars for this [expletive deleted] bracelet?" I've admired the bracelet many times and really wanted it. I started to think about how I could bargain for it, but before I could say anything, someone else said, "I will!" I was disappointed to miss out on the bracelet, but it showed me the advantage of moving fast if the deal looks good.

In Anchorage, Alaska, I wanted to see a view of the city and the mountains from a high point. I took an elevator to the top floor of a hotel, looking for an observation balcony. I couldn't find one, but I did see a maid making up rooms. I told her that I'd like to inspect one of the rooms. She opened the door and let me in. I commented on how nice it looked and then I walked to the window and enjoyed the view. Then I asked to see a room on the other side of the hotel. She took me around and opened a door for me again, and I saw the view on the other side. We had a pleasant conversation as I looked at the view. She never asked me who I was or why I wanted to see the rooms. I was "suited up" and looked prestigious, and I think she saw me as an authority figure she should obey without question.

My new girlfriend belongs to a rather elite social club. They're having a semiformal dance on Saturday. I needed a new suit anyway, so I took this occasion to buy one. I selected an expensive vested suit and said I needed it by Saturday. The salesman said it usually took a week for alterations, but I could have it Saturday at an extra charge. I said, "no," that I expected alterations and the suit at its advertised price by Saturday or it was no deal. The clerk agreed to my terms. Then I told him to hold the suit for a few hours while I looked elsewhere. I found one I liked better at another store. They gave me no static at all about alterations by Saturday. At first I felt a twinge of guilt about getting my way at the first store and then not buying there, but then I thought,

"What the hell—when you pay a good price for something you have a right to expect quality, service, and freedom from hassle."

I was talking to a friend of mine who was looking for a camera lens. He said he'd located one he liked through an ad in the paper, but the guy wanted seventy dollars for it, and he thought that was about fifteen dollars too much.

The ad was on the table, so I jotted down the number and called the next day. The lens was still for sale, and since the ad was five days old, I thought the owner might be willing to bargain. I went over to see the guy. I asked him if he'd had many calls on his ad. He said there'd only been a couple. That made me think he was probably honest and might be eager to make a sale. I asked him about his photography interests, and he showed me some of his pictures. I told him I was just getting started and a friend had recommended the kind of lens he had for sale. I told him I could only pay thirty-five dollars and reached for my wallet as I said it. He was reluctant, but he said, "OK."

I felt really good about my deal. On the way over to Jim's I found myself thinking, "Maybe I should charge Jim fifty-five dollars for the lens—and make myself a quick twenty bucks!"

I went to a border city in Mexico, where all the shopkeepers are prepared to bargain. I saw a jacket I admired for seventy dollars. I offered the salesman forty dollars and stood firm. He came down to fifty dollars and wouldn't budge. I walked out and he came after me and let me have the jacket for forty dollars. I felt really great. Then I went into a store down the block. Their beginning price for the same jacket was forty dollars.

My father-in-law is a baseball nut and prides himself on knowing World Series statistics.

Last Sunday at dinner he made a statement I knew was in error. When I said, "That's not the way I remember it," he stiffened for a split second and an angry look flitted through his eyes as he said with apparent good nature, "Well, then, you'd *better check your sources.*"

I did and found out I was right. I could hardly wait to set him straight. Yesterday when the family was together again and he started quoting baseball figures, I saw my chance to beat him at his own game. But just as I was about to unload on him I remembered the way his eyes betrayed his feelings when I doubted him before. I thought to myself, "Whoa! What am I going to gain by showing up my father-in-law. I've had enough trouble convincing him that I'm not a jerk. Sure, it would give my ego a boost to win this skirmish—but I'd be back at war with him." I decided it was more to my advantage to have him as a friend. I kept my mouth shut about his mistake and took satisfaction from knowing I was right. If I know him, he'll check the figures out himself—and then he'll know I was right, too.

I was in the manager's office right after he'd fired the assistant manager for stealing. The manager felt compelled to tell me what had happened. I kept the information to myself. I didn't let on that I knew even when others told me. This was really hard to do, but I gained a real sense of satisfaction from knowing that I could carry it off.

A friend of mine called me to tell about a house for rent near her. She told me about how nice it was. As I listened I felt that all of her description was subjective and pointed toward convincing me that the house was right. When I could break in I asked for facts—number of rooms, room size, layout, carpeting and color, windows and view, appliances, landscaping. I felt awkward doing it, but at the same time I felt more self-confident and in control. I found myself really wanting to make the decision on my own, free from her influence. Asking for facts and tuning out advice seemed to give me confidence and make me want to take charge of the matter myself.

I was writing a report on consumer fraud and decided to get some information from the consumer advocate reporter of the local TV station. I was somewhat hesitant to call, because I've always considered public people like that beyond reach. When I called and asked for her I got through right away, which surprised me. She was cordial and very willing to see me.

I had a good interview. She answered my questions freely and was equally curious about what I had learned in my research. I noticed how effectively she questioned me to get facts and information. I decided to try the same approach when I ask for information.

My girlfriend's friend asked me to get a date for her to a dinner dance, because her date had to cancel. I knew that my best friend, Frank, would like to go, but he's not really tall enough for the girl, and I didn't think he was quite right for her anyway. A less close friend, Tom, is 6'2", and I thought he'd hit it off better with the girl. Knowing that Frank is tight with a dollar, I told him about the date, but I also told him that the bids cost fifty dollars. He lost interest in a hurry. Then I asked Tom, but I didn't mention the bid price to him, since I knew that the girl had already paid it. My "information management" worked. I was able to exclude my friend without offending him.

I went to a motorcycle dealership to try my hand at bargaining. I spotted a model that really appealed to me. After asking the salesman all the questions I could think of, I took it out for a test drive. Then I told him that if the deal was right I might *buy* it. I told him my time was short and to make up the *best deal he could. When he was through figuring, I asked for every extra I could think of, plus a hundred-dollar price reduction. He countered that he'd already cut it to the bone. He brought over his manager, who said he'd throw in a few of the lesser extras at the salesman's price. I refused and left, feeling satisfied with my effort.*

Next morning the salesman called me with another deal and more concessions. I held firm. Later that morning the manager called me, making still more concessions. He said it was this or nothing. I thought it was a really good deal, and if I'd been a real buyer I'd have snapped at it. But I refused again and started feeling guilty about putting them through all this trouble.

The following day the owner called me. He told me how good the manager's offer was. I held firm. Then he cut the price to where we were only twenty-five dollars apart. I knew I'd have trouble refusing my own offer, and it looked like it was coming to that, so I said, "Let's cool it for a while. I'll keep in touch."

I felt I did pretty well. I held fast to an extreme offer and they made all the concessions. I learned that their last deal isn't really their last.

INSTANT REPLAY

You find out if you can cut it in this Round. Ends are uppermost, so you keep pushing to overcome obstacles or resistance to get what you want.

You use all the means at your disposal to arrive at "no-lose" outcomes which maintain cordiality. But you also discover how far you're willing to go when your victory means someone else's defeat, possibly at the expense of congenial relationships.

If you find some tactics too devious for your taste, at least you'll learn to recognize subterfuge and be able to prevent others from duping you.

Whatever you decide to do should be freely chosen with complete willingness to accept the consequences to yourself and others.

The suggested Workouts are:

- Seek facts.
- Reject advice.
- Withhold information.
  Don't volunteer information.
  Politely decline to answer.
- Do something with someone you don't like.
- Gain entry to inaccessible places.
- Gain access to prestigious or hard-to-see people.
- Practice observing body language.
- Negotiate for material gain.
  Barter with friends.
  Answer want ads.
  Go to garage sales.
  Go to swap meets.
  Bargain with high-pressure salespeople.
  Try selling.
- Persist past the first refusal.
- Resolve interpersonal conflicts through negotiation.

ROUND 9:

MANAGING PROFESSIONAL CHALLENGE

This Round is the main event. All your incremental training comes together now. You have a large repertoire of skills. You know your own interests, capabilities, and limitations. You've wrestled with personal values and resolved ethical considerations.

Now as you apply your expertise on the job, you begin to order your activities so that everything you do improves your ability to accomplish "big picture" goals. As you reassess your own fitness and size up both adversaries and circumstances in the work "ring," you gradually move from self-development to career development.

THE CHALLENGE

The challenge in this Round is to cut it on the job. The object is to manage effectively and advance your managerial career. In other words, you use resources and information in unique ways to get results, for *your* gain as well as for the benefit of the organization.

You take on the mantle of the professional in demeanor and in action. You try to spot problems and initiate actions that effect change, avert crises, resolve difficulties, surmount obstacles, and make significant positive contributions to outcome in general.

THE STRATEGY

The strategy is to apply all the skills you learned in earlier Rounds to job-related situations, both to maintain advantage and to gain the ends you want.

While you now redo all of the earlier Workouts on the job, you don't necessarily do them in the order in which you originally learned them. Instead you try to size up situations and spontaneously use the skill or combination of skills the situation calls for. In this way you become accustomed to using the skills in the professional environment. As your competence and confidence increase, you gradually apply them to serve your ends or the ends of the organization—whenever, wherever, and with whomever it's appropriate.

The objective is to see the big picture, establish long-term goals, keep ends constantly in mind, reassess and redesign your job, take a positive approach to annoyances that are an inevitable part of your job, manage resources as well as operations, show that you're both eager and able to move upward, and actively pursue your career.

In this Round you utilize all the nottims to open your own personal door to managerial CLOUT.

THE MOVES

Besides redoing exercises from previous Rounds, you tour your professional territory, communicate with the people in it, and assess your organization in dollar terms.

You set career goals and job objectives. You try to simplify your job, avoid isolation, set priorities, develop sources of information and support.

You try to see annoyances as challenges and turn problems into opportunities.

You seek various uses, arrangements, and combinations of resources to get the best possible results.

To get things done you make and implement decisions, direct others, and delegate tasks to others as well as take action yourself; you influence others to your advantage and negotiate differences—all the time zeroing in toward results, gaining endorsement of your actions, and establishing a reputation as a doer.

To advance your career, you identify with superiors, seek a senior sponsor, and act as mentor for others.

WINNING THE ROUND

Winning the main event means getting the results you want and enjoying intrinsic satisfactions in the process.

You know you're winning on the job when your presence is sought and your influence is felt; when you're making contributions of consequence; when you're seen as indispensable to the organization.

Your career and total life style are headed for victory when you feel that you're moving in the direction you want to go at a rate you feel is acceptable.

WORKOUTS

Your Workouts in this Round fit into two general categories—polishing appropriate managerial skills in the workplace and taking purposeful action to accomplish career and job goals.

Redo Exercises from Earlier Rounds

Start out by redoing in the job environment some of the exercises from previous Rounds. Vary insignificant routines, increase mobility, manage simple social relationships, change the balance of social exchange, influence groups, and practice tough transactions—all in work-related situations.

TRAINING TIPS

Use judgment in designing Workouts, always adapting the exercise to fit your own ability and circumstances.

Take small steps before you take big ones on the job. Practice on a broad front, but proceed at a rate that both you and those in the organization can handle.

Take into account that you and those you deal with on the job have established role relationships that may have to be adjusted. Such preestablished patterns may be harder to manage than casual relationships. To avoid becoming discouraged in this Round and to maintain your confidence and enthusiasm for change, continue to practice "easier" off-the-job exercises at the same time that you begin to apply your skills on the job.

At first make changes that affect only you. Gradually make changes that have impact on others. As you sense the acceptance of your actions, step up your tempo and broaden the base of your activities.

Seek a "Big Picture" Perspective

Try to gain a "big picture" perspective from which you can better manage your work and guide your career.

Tour Your Professional Territory

Move about and find out what goes on both inside and outside your organization.

Within your own jurisdiction, observe the facilities, people, and flow of materials, information, and work. Learn the same things about the areas above, below, and parallel to you in the total organizational hierarchy, including both line and staff functions.

Outside the organization, become familiar with suppliers, customers, competitors, and community, including their people, facilities, and procedures.

Interact with People in Your Professional Territory

Talk to both strangers and people you know. Broaden your circle of contacts and connections. Gain access to those who are prestigious or less accessible.

Make it a point to know receptionists, secretaries, managers, staff personnel, counterparts, executives, key employees, salespeople, maintenance and security people, supply and service people, competitors, customers. Establish rapport and build a network of people you can call upon to get the information and help you need.

Make a point of being seen by others. Show yourself as an interested, confident, competent, energetic, goal-oriented person.

Count the House

In the days of vaudeville, theater owners often peeked through the curtain to count the house. A few quick mental calculations told them if they had enough paying customers to cover the costs of the acts, the wages of the stagehands and ticket takers, the expense of the heat and lights—and how much they could expect to pocket themselves.

In this exercise, do the same kind of thing in your organization. Get the big picture in dollar terms. Make ballpark estimates of major cost and revenue components. Rough out the costs of payroll; material, energy, and utilities input; physical space and facilities. Rough out the revenue contribution of the various products and services produced.

If possible, get your information from appropriate documents such as reports, budgets, and audits. If specific data are unavailable, estimate things like salaries and wage rates; prevailing cost of space per square foot; usage and price of materials, energy, and utilities; debt and depreciation costs.

Convert what you know about production volumes, services delivered, and marketing pricing to determine the revenue side. Balance costs against revenue to determine the profit or loss of the total operation.

Try to discover which factors in the operation contribute to desired ends and which ones cause drag. Assess the effect of individual components and consider how changes would improve the operation of the overall results: Should the resources you use be of a different kind or mix, for example? Should you produce more of one product and less of another?

Should you concentrate on some customers and not on others? Do you need more or fewer workers, researchers, or administrators? Can you substitute equipment for workers? In other words, try to get a picture of what's happening and what makes it happen that way.

Roy Ash, former president of Litton Industries who created and directed the Office of Management and Budget for the Nixon administration, is an executive who uses the "big picture" approach to advantage.

In 1977, Ash took over troubled Addressograph-Multigraph (now AM International) as chief executive. Before joining the firm, he used only publicly available information such as AM's annual report to make calculations which showed that the company had potential as well as troubles.

After joining the firm he spent months touring the widely scattered operation to get a handle on what was going on and to assess the people who were in charge. He made no changes right away. He established cordial relations with the people he contacted, continually asking searching questions. For the most part he went to others instead of summoning them to him. "He left his office door open, placed his own intercom calls to arrange meetings, and always questioned people in person, not in writing. By casually asking office secretaries to suggest ways to 'de-bureaucratize' the company, he received some clues about which executives were heavily engaged in paper shuffling."[1]

When the firm received a complaint from an important customer, he quickly flew off to visit him to gain firsthand understanding of the problem, to show concern, and to get the word out that he knew what was going on.

One of Ash's early discoveries as he explored AM's operation was that no one in the corporation knew exactly which products were profitable, nor the sales effort devoted to each prod-

uct. He asked for and got this kind of analysis.

From his observations, contacts, and assessments Ash was able to assemble a "brickpile" of issues which needed to be resolved to redesign the firm and turn the company around. The problems included such things as profitability or acceptance of products, archaic organization structure, bureaucratic drag, and unneeded personnel.

Fifteen weeks after taking over, with the big picture in mind, Ash was able to spell out his broader objectives to five of his key executives. Together they reviewed and refined the issues and problems, made assignments, and established deadlines for action. With this base they set about making what Ash called "a deliberate attempt to change a corporate culture."[2]

Whether you're the chief executive or a worker on the line, getting the big picture is essential. Grasping broad concepts enables you to fit strategy, action, and excellence into place on the job. It also helps you to integrate job, career, and personal life goals.

The old story of the three bricklayers who were asked what they were doing sums it up neatly. The first bricklayer answered, "I'm earning my pay." The second replied, "I'm laying bricks and doing a damned good job." The third one said with pride, "I'm building a cathedral."

TRAINING TIPS

As you practice mobility on the job, actively *see* what you look at. Observe procedures and attitudes: What's going on? What's used? Why is it used? Why are things done the way they are? Who does what? Why do they do it? How well do they do it? Why are the facilities and procedures as they are?

As you tour, use whatever social exchange skills are useful to establish a friendly working relationship with people. Establish commonal-

MANAGING PROFESSIONAL CHALLENGE

"Smith can really cut it . . . increased sales, reduced costs, improved corporate structure . . . and next week she's marrying the boss's son."

ity, give positive strokes, ask appropriate questions, smart-listen and reflect understanding, express feelings, state problems, ask favors.

Talk to people you deal with in your organization wherever you encounter them—at your desk or theirs, in the cafeteria or parking lot, at the water cooler or on the production floor. Do the same with people in your industry and profession outside the organization.

Use the contacts to find out what others know as well as to size them up. Discover who can give you information and insight as to what's really going on. Appraise people's competence—do they run a tight ship or merely shuffle paper?

Use your contacts, too, to get past barriers and to gain access to less accessible areas and people.

All the while, keep your goal in mind— to gather information that will give you a big picture view of your sphere of operations; to understand the general mission, goals, philosophy, and character of the organization and determine how well they agree with your own values; to find out how the system is supposed to work and how it does, in fact, work; to know where the power lies and what buttons to push to get things done.

Establish Long-Term Objectives

Set long-range career goals and job objectives.

Set Career Goals

In line with your interests, competence, and inclinations, determine a career pattern for yourself that you perceive as challenging, enjoyable, and attainable. Use information and contacts to help refine your intentions and set your strategy. Avoid letting immediate job success deter you from examining long-term career objectives:

It was Henry Ford's long-term goal to put America on wheels with a low-cost automobile that shaped his career and contributed to his success in industry.

Ford's work with the Edison Illuminating Company was characterized by success and achievement. He rose from night engineer in 1891 to chief engineer and engineering superintendent in 1899. Recognizing Ford's ability, president of the firm Alexander Dow offered Ford the general superintendency of the company when a major expansion was in the works. The thirty-six-year-old Ford could have regarded this as a prize opportunity. Instead, because of his insatiable hobby and long-range plan involving automobiles, Ford turned Dow down and left Edison to become a small stockholder and superintendent in the newly formed Detroit Automobile Company. This was the challenging stepping-stone which led him to form the Ford Motor Company in 1903, which in turn eventually made his career dream a reality.[3]

Set Job Objectives

Decide what you want to accomplish in your job arena. Consider whether you have the available information and resources to do it. Determine who the users or potential users of your goods or services are. Find out, too, what their needs are and how you can give them what they want—whether you supply parts for assembly, provide market research to sales, screen personnel for staffing needs, or produce consumer goods for external customers. Search for ways to deliver an end product that's even better than what the users asked for.

Continually reassess circumstances and modify goals to fit changing capabilities and users' needs. Make sure that you're doing right things, not merely doing things right.

Henry Ford's career also illustrates this strategy, showing both what to do and what not to do.

Ford's career objective was to work with automobiles. His job objective was to build a standardized, cheap car, which he accomplished through mass production of the Model T. His notion of what the public wanted actually was a projection of his own enthusiasm for a new form of transportation. He happened to be right, and he was labeled a man of vision. By 1926 he had produced 15 million cars and had controlled 60 percent of the market.

But times changed, and the American public's attitude toward cars changed, too. Once people were accustomed to the new form of travel they wanted better styling, more comfort, more convenience—and they were willing to pay higher prices to get them.

Meanwhile Ford remained a private thinker and an autocrat. He was not a good conversationalist and he claimed that he got little out of talking with others. As his fame made him retreat even more into isolation, he not only lost touch with what the public really wanted, he spent less and less time with his own people in design and engineering.[4]

Ford's failure to explore what was going on around him and adjust his job goals accordingly caused fifteen straight years of operating loss and shrank his market share to 20 percent by 1941. If he hadn't built up astronomical reserves previously, the firm would have been bankrupt.

Keep Your Eye on the Goal

Don't become so involved in methods that the end you seek is neglected or forgotten. Remember that *ends* are what you're after. Things like organization form, employee motivation, job design, and control systems are means used to accomplish ends and should not become ends in themselves. Learn to recognize the difference.

Make it a point to critically examine whatever you're doing and identify the bottom-line objective. Then keep your goal constantly in sight as you direct your energies, capabilities, and resources toward accomplishing that goal.

Here's a case where losing sight of ends nearly led to corporate disaster:

Andy Kay founded Non-Linear Systems to manufacture and sell electronic instrumentation. His equipment featured digital display systems at a time when they were virtually unknown, and his firm enjoyed success and growth.

When consultants interested him in psychological theories about employee participation and motivation, Kay embarked on studies that have become classic for successfully applying the motivational theories of Abraham Maslow, Douglas McGregor, and others to a business situation.

Kay's attention to the motivational research was so complete that he lost touch with what was happening in his company and in the industry. His top and middle managers were also preoccupied with trying out new participative techniques. Competitors sprang up and got a larger piece of the action than they might have if Kay and his executives had paid more attention to product research, the market, and marketing strategy. To make matters worse, the whole industry went into a slump, which caught Kay by surprise. Suddenly he found himself with a year's supply of inventory and few new orders. He cut back drastically to keep afloat and started rebuilding, using more conventional methods.

In retrospect Kay recognized that you can't assume that operations will take care of themselves just because the workers are smiling. In fact, the employee excitement that occurred proved to be more a product of rapid growth than application of well-intentioned theory. He also realized that he'd inadvertently let means become ends in his organization. In summing up the experience Kay reflected, "I may have lost sight of the purpose of business, which is not to develop theories of management."[5]

Reassess and Redesign Your Job

Restructure your job so that everything you do leads toward goal-oriented results.

Simplify Your Job
Streamline your job by reducing it to basic essentials.

Cut out rituals that keep you busy and tie up your time. Eliminate small talk that only wastes time. Take action on your mail the first time you go through it.

Set up routines that economize your time. Cluster similar tasks together—phoning, answering mail, seeing people. Set aside discretionary "no calls" time. Combine functions when you travel. Arrange your itinerary to accomplish multiple goals. En route to your destination or in nearby locations see customers, tour facilities, do public relations work, lobby for your interests.

Vary routines to increase your versatility and find what works best for you. Try different ways of communicating with others—dictate, write short memos, phone, let your secretary handle it according to your instructions. Seek out others or ask them to come to you. Phone or see people in person. Vary the order or time of performing job activities—touring facilities, handling correspondence, holding meetings, going out to see others or seeing them in your office.

Reduce paperwork. Make assignments verbally. Get verbal reports. Gear systems for results, not to "cover" yourself. Create paperwork only when it helps you get results. Make it short, simple, and easy to understand. Don't waste time with or circulate incoming printed material which has proved useless.

Avoid Isolation
Move around and talk to a variety of people. Observe what's going on and be seen by others. Make and use contacts and connections.

Do First Things First
Set priorities. List projects according to bottom-line importance. Spend your time and effort on the important things.

List the tasks required to carry out the projects. Don't get caught in the trap of cleaning up trivia before tackling consequential matters.

DO FIRST THINGS FIRST

"Can't you see I'm working on my tan? Have the White House call back in half an hour."

Put off less important tasks, delegate them to others, or transfer them to ritualists outside your jurisdiction.

If there's trivia you can't escape, do it between—not instead of—important things, letting it serve as a change of pace.

Develop Support Sources

Build a support system of people throughout the organization, industry, and profession to supply you with timely and relevant information, provide you with adequate help, and furnish support when you need it.

Analyze situations to discover what you need to know. Seek analytical and technical assistance, making sure that it's of a quality and quantity you can use. At the same time, work toward becoming your own best advisor by absorbing relevant information, acquiring know-how, and learning where to go to get quick answers.

J. P. Morgan, the financier, knew the importance of establishing reliable information sources. He was well aware, for example, that the brother of George Whitney, his partner, was in deep trouble from overextending himself financially. Nevertheless, when junior partner Frances Barton told him the news, Morgan acted surprised and listened with appreciation.[6]

By so doing, Morgan accomplished two things: He was able to check Barton's accuracy in reporting the facts. And he encouraged Barton to bring him other information in the future.

Take a Positive Approach to Annoyances and Problems

Don't let petty annoyances on the job interfere with your goal of getting results. Build a reputation as an "in charge" person.

Regard Annoyances as Challenges

Take satisfaction and pride in managing interruptions, resolving conflict, ending crises, handling difficult people. See such things as an inevitable part of your job requiring managerial expertise, instead of regarding them as interferences.

The advantage of a positive approach is illustrated in the following examples of two managers with different attitudes toward interruptions:

The first thing Wanda B. Leftalone does when she arrives at her office is to make a list of "important things to do" for the day. The list literally rules her. She refers to it constantly and painstakingly checks off each item as she deals with it.

She resents requests for help from subordinates, and she hates unexpected problems that arise, even though they fall within her jurisdiction. She sees such things as hindrances that keep her from getting "her work" done. At the end of the day, when she evaluates her day's work by how many items have been checked off on her list, she often feels frustrated and disappointed.

Bess Efferts also makes lists of jobs to be done, but Bess doesn't let the lists control her business day. Instead she uses them as guides to keep her on track toward major objectives. "I accept interruptions as par for the course," explains Bess. "I don't judge my effectiveness as a manager by how well I avoid interruptions of work I've planned to do. I see success in terms of how well I handle interruptions when they occur. I feel I've had a good day when I've correctly distinguished trivia from matters of importance and dealt with each appropriately— ignoring some, delegating some, and attending to some personally. I think the ability to handle the unexpected is what management's all about. I feel I'm having a good day whenever I successfully solve problems and overcome obstacles that are in the way of getting the results I want."

See Problems as Opportunities

Try to turn problems into opportunities. See setbacks or mistakes as challenges, not as calamities. Bounce and roll with the punches and come up with fresh thinking and a new approach to accomplish your end:

In the 1978 primary election in California, Democratic incumbent Governor Jerry Brown went on record as opposing Proposition 13, a ballot referendum which cut property taxes drastically. The referendum won by a landslide, and while Brown won his party's nomination, he quickly realized that he had a problem: If he remained out of step with popular senti-

ment on tax relief, he could lose the general election. Thus his first action after the primary was to announce his office's intention to wholeheartedly implement the spending cuts the voters had decreed. His enthusiastic compliance was so complete that many voters thought he had always been in favor of the referendum. The strategy worked and Brown easily won reelection. Thus Brown was able to see the problem as an opportunity and handle it both to his advantage and to the voters' liking.

Manage Resources

Use the assets that you have where they will do the most good to accomplish the ends you want. Strategically plan to do right things with your resources.

See Alternate Uses

Use assets to gain the greatest possible payoff:

Recently some executives in the tobacco industry have diverted assets out of cigarette production and into other activities because of concern that future cigarette sales might be affected by research linking cancer to smoking. The Liggett group acquired liquor and pet food interests; Reynolds Industries bought into food and transportation; Philip Morris made major inroads in the brewing and soft drink markets.

Arrange Resources Differently

Rearrange your organization with respect to activities, products, functions, or people in order to effect greater results:

In the early days of the automobile industry, Henry Ford made dramatic improvement in the use of resources by moving the product past the materials rather than moving the materials to the product in the traditional way.

Alfred Sloan of General Motors followed Ford's lead by adopting the assembly line idea and then went him one better by setting up autonomous product divisions (Buick, Oldsmobile, Chevrolet) which could easily be made accountable for their own profit and loss.

Use Imagination in Controlling Assets

Own outright, lease, or borrow to get the assets you need. Base your decisions on cost of money, projected rates of return, and availability of funds. Look for ways to extend your control through liquidity or leveraging.

Here's an example of how imaginative thinking about holding assets profited one group of businessmen:

In 1977, the Irvine Company, a giant southern California land developer, was purchased by a group of eleven investors known as the Taubman group. Among others the group included Alfred Taubman, Henry Ford II, and Joan Irvine Smith, a descendant of Irvine Company's founder. Mobile Corporation had also bid for the firm, but lost out. The Taubman group incurred a five-year, $240 million debt in the purchase and many outsiders thought the debt could not be repaid short of wholesale land selloff.

A year later only $50 million of the debt remained outstanding. Irvine's thirty-three-year-old president, Peter C. Kremer, had lined up a $100 million mortgage with Prudential Insurance Company of America. This covered land Irvine leased for industrial and commercial buildings owned by others. The lease income more than covered the mortgage payments. Kremer also nearly doubled the price of the choice acreage that lies in California's top growth area, yet sold nearly 75 percent more sites than the previous year. He also made housing tract builders put full cash up front rather than lease the construction sites until the houses were sold. All this resulted in a dramatic cash flow increase, which provided the means for paying off the debt. Mobil and Taubman had bid fiercely for Irvine, yet Taubman reflects,

"We bought it well under market value."[7] *The fast debt payoff has been no surprise to him. He conjectures that Mobile's mistake was that they "bid based on profits, as though Irvine were an industrial company."*[8]

Vary the Mix of Assets

Find the best combination of resources to maximize results.

A gardener, for example, can expand his income by employing and supervising labor that is less skilled and less costly than his own time and by using labor-saving equipment to speed and improve the quality of his work. Similarly, managers can vary the quality or quantity of resources they employ or vary the ratio of capital to labor they utilize.

Howard Hughes, functioning in his prime, was a shrewd resource manager, even though he was notorious for his bad operations management. Despite the corporate chaos he left in his trail, Hughes amassed a fortune estimated at $2 billion at the height of his career by means of astute management of resources.

Using his Hughes Aircraft Company as a base, he seized the opportunity to develop the electronics and missile fields after World War II. He assembled a most impressive and capable administrative and scientific staff: General Harold L. George, former chief of the Air Transport Command; Charles B. Thornton and Roy Ash, who later founded Litton Industries; Dr. Simon Ramo of the California Institute of Technology and Dr. Dean Wooldridge of the Bell Telephone Research Department, who later merged their talents to form a company which eventually became TRW; and hundreds of other first-rate scientists.

Hughes also foresaw the eventual boom in aviation travel and designed TWA accordingly. His pioneer work in world flight patterns enabled him to build a worldwide commercial airline route and the logistics to support it. He chose to borrow the massive capital required to equip

TWA with jet aircraft instead of using equity capital.

Hughes's handling of resources paid off. Despite his operational incompetence and personal idiosyncracies, Hughes Aircraft remains nonpareil in guidance systems and satellite and space probe control. TWA is the third largest domestic airline in the United States. Its competitive strength still lies in its route structure, and its unique, high-leverage position from borrowed funds promises a large profit potential if the upward trend in aviation travel continues.

Continually bear in mind that the greatest gains toward goals are made by proper use of resources. Be alert to ways of moving and adapting your resources in order to take advantage of opportunity and change.

In other words, *do right things.*

Manage Operations

Maximize the productivity of the resources you use to get things done. *Do things right.*

Make and implement decisions. Decide what needs to be done and quickly initiate definitive action to make your decisions a reality.

Direct those who work for you. Take unmistakable command. Present an air of authority which shows that you're in charge. Make assertive requests. Accept responsibility for all actions under your command.

Take personal action. Do those things yourself that require your personal attention and expertise.

Delegate. Assign appropriate tasks to others. Clarify assignments; establish relevent objectives; set performance standards. Release personal control over the actual execution and live with the consequences.

Know your subordinates' jobs. Learn what your people do. Make sure their work contributes to the results you want. Be familiar with their procedures and their people.

FIRST DO RIGHT THINGS

"Wait a minute! Maybe there's a better way . . ."

DELEGATE

"I've got it worked out so nothing ever reaches my desk."

John deButts, former Chairman of the American Telephone and Telegraph Company, maintained a curiosity about all phases of the telephone business. Even after he had risen well up in the hierarchy, he occasionally joined a work crew on their rounds. He installed phones and helped repair cable to get a feel for what was involved.

Donald H. Sharp, a vice-president under deButts at Illinois Bell, tells of walking with him through a corridor of the company's huge headquarters in Chicago. As they passed a room of seventy or eighty people working at desks, Sharp commented, "John, I wonder what all those people are doing." Debutts replied pointedly, "Donald, I know what they're doing."[9]

Influence others. Affect the behavior of those above you, below you, and on the same level with you, both inside and outside the organization. Sway them by persuasion or pressure; by giving, withholding, or promising information, support, or rewards. Keep motivation and interest high by making projects and work exciting and challenging.

Negotiate. Resolve differences through collaboration or compromise when mutual accord is beneficial. Win over others through hard bargaining when it's to your advantage.

Charles Schwab, founder and chairman of Bethlehem Steel, had a great deal of faith in the negotiating skill of his first vice-president, Archibald Johnson. In 1906, he sent Johnson abroad to see if he could get an increase in the European market share allocated to Bethlehem in exchange for their promise not to undercut the European pool price. When Johnson met with the foreign representatives, he demanded a sixfold increase over their previous share in the market. "That is our lowest figure," he stated firmly. "We're not here to haggle and engage in any undignified bargaining. If we don't get it, we're not going to make any compromise. We shall merely withdraw."[10] *After a moment of hesitation, the spokesman for the Europeans agreed to the ultimatum.*

The settlement surprised even Schwab. The increase was so unexpected that he thought Johnson's cable telling him the news had been garbled.[11]

Stay on target. Set tough but realistic goals and strive to meet them. Monitor your operations to keep on course.

David J. Mahoney, chairman of Norton Simon, is known as a tough taskmaster in this respect, as shown in the following encounter:

Richard Beeson, president of Norton Simon's Canada Dry, had been on the job only a few weeks when he talked to Mahoney about goals. Here's how he recalls the conversation.

"I said to Mahoney, 'Dave, we're a little bit below budget now, and I think we can hold that for the rest of the year. It won't get any worse.'

"Dave looked at me, smiled, and said: 'Be on budget by the six-month mark; be on budget by the year.'

"'But Dave,' I said, 'there isn't enough time to get on by the half. I inherited this situation after all.'

"Still smiling, Dave looked at me and said: 'Do I pay you a lot of money? Do I argue with you over what you want to spend? Do I bother you? Then don't tell me what the goals should be. Be on by the half; be on by the end of the year.'

"'What if I can't, Dave?' I asked.

"'Then clean out your desk and go home.'"

Beeson argued why he couldn't meet the goals. Mahoney replied, "Not interested. My board and my stockholders want me to make my numbers. The way I make my numbers is for you guys to make your *numbers. Make your numbers!"*[12]

Get results. Work hard and smart. Concentrate on outcome. Seek ends, not acceptance.

Persist. Commit yourself and others to the objective. Find alternatives and overcome obstacles.

Win endorsement of your actions. Be subtle, but make it clear to those above you that the action was yours. To those who helped, give credit where credit is due. Win endorsement of your actions and gain a reputation as a doer.

Donald F. Nyrop, chief operating officer of Northwest Airlines for twenty-two years, illustrates what good operations management can do. While nowhere near the biggest United States carrier, Northwest has repeatedly been first in profits and boasts an impressive record of nearly a quarter of a century of uninterrupted dividend payments.

Nyrop's style was to watch operations on all fronts. He maintained a lean management structure, with fewer vice-presidents than other trunk lines and no executive vice-presidents at all. He didn't believe in committees, and foremen reported directly to the V.P.'s.

His ground crews were as slim as his executive ranks. He bargained hard with unions to keep crew size down, to get favorable work rules, and to juggle workers' schedules to get maximum utilization of their time and skills. He was just as tough in his bargaining with pilots, who worked more hours than those of any other trunk. He strictly interpreted union contracts to maintain operating conditions in his favor. Nyrop also used 10 percent fewer pilots, thereby getting maximum service from the standby pilot reserve that airlines are required to maintain. The overall result was employee productivity 50 percent above the industry average.

Unlike other airlines, when Northwest bought their DC-10s, Nyrop had them equipped with the same engine as their 747s. This cut the necessary inventory of spare engines, utilized his mechanics' skill to advantage, cut down on tools and training time, and reduced his spare parts inventory to half the industry average. In addition, he simplified pilot training by standardizing cockpit interiors and flight procedures. Even the seats on the various aircraft are interchangeable for greater flexibility and control.

In spite of Northwest's concern for costs, they've had a good safety and comfort record. They've also been industry leaders in meteorological study, airport noise abatement, and navigational backup systems.

Although Nyrop and his executives shared in planning and thinking through the ramifications of decisions, it was Nyrop himself who personally made the decisions of consequence. And while he was a shrewd, tough competitor and a ruthless, tightfisted cost cutter, he was also known for his cordial demeanor.[13]

Essentially, Nyrop knew how to work hard and smart. And he was able to get others to use their talents as adroitly as he used his own.

Demonstrate an Upward Mobility

Be energetic and strive for excellence. Show unmistakable competence by getting results. Show that you're eager to advance.

Identify with Superiors

Establish and maintain amicable relationships with those above you. Make sure your superiors see you as an ally, not as a threat.

George L. Clements, president of Jewel Tea Company from 1953 to 1965, reflects back to his fledgling days with the company. He and Franklin J. Lunding, Jewel's president before him, enjoyed a complementary relationship through which they tapped each other's creativity. "Anything that I thought was worth talking about, he thought was worth listening to. Needless to say, anything that he thought was worth

talking about, I thought was worth listening to."[14]

Avoid being closely identified with non-movers, ritualists, and people in dead-end jobs. Be cordial in your associations with subordinates, but maintain a social distance that clearly sets you apart in the eyes of superiors.

Find a Mentor

Search for a senior power to take a personal interest in your future.

John deButts of American Telephone and Telegraph Company was helped up the corporate ladder by patrons in the higher echelon. At one point in his career he was offered the job of traffic manager for Northwestern Bell Telephone Company. After he enthusiastically accepted it, the offer was apologetically withdrawn, because his boss, George Best, had objected. A short time later deButts was offered a similar position as traffic manager at Chesapeake and Potomac Telephone in Virginia. This time Best described the job as a great opportunity and advised him to take it. Nine months later deButts was made general commercial manager of Chesapeake and Potomac. When he called to tell Best the good news, Best laughed, "Yeah, I knew they were gonna do that."[15]

Still later in his career, when he was in charge of AT&T's government relations office in Washington, D.C., he was offered the position of general manager of New York Telephone's Westchester office. He considered this a demotion and was going to turn it down—until his friend, Joe Morrison, who was president of Chesapeake and Potomac, told him: "Don't ask any more questions! Take the job!"[16]

Years later deButts learned that Frederick Kappel, who was then chief executive of AT&T, was responsible for his going to Westchester. Kappel had taken a liking to him and wanted to keep the promising young executive in the *running for the company's top job. However, deButts had only had departmental experience up to this point. At Westchester he would be responsible for everything—plant, engineering, commercial, traffic, accounting. The fact that the job was a demotion was totally irrelevant to Kappel. He simply wanted to see if deButts could handle it all.[17]*

Whereas men on their way up have traditionally had mentors, women in management have only recently recognized their need for guidance from other women who are successful in the field.

Paula L. Gottschalk, director of corporate relations at CBS, says this about the advantage of mentors to women, especially: "There are a lot of bright women out there who are very good at their tasks but not good at politicking. . . . You need to use political and diplomatic skills in your career as much as the functional skills."[18]

Gottschalk says she attempts to show women the way things really are. She's also specific in her advice. For example, she steered a young woman with two promotional offers toward an executive she knew was solidly entrenched, rather than toward one whose job was hanging in the balance, who could easily pull his subordinates down with him if he fell.[19]

Be a Mentor

Play the mentor role yourself. Come up with bright prospects and develop their future value to the organization.

The role of mentor brings favorable attention from those who are both above and below you. Those above are impressed with your ability to develop talent. Those below are more apt to court your favor.

Increase Your Exposure

Move about to be seen. Volunteer to serve on committees. Be a spokesperson or representative. Speak or make presentations at meetings. Join and serve actively in civic, volunteer, and social groups.

Look Like a Winner

Upgrade your personal appearance and dress. Create an image that will help you achieve upward mobility.

Work toward establishing a basic, quality wardrobe, consistent with your personal budget and working conditions. Achieve the

FIND A MENTOR, BE A MENTOR

"Now that I've taken over your job, what can I do to help you?"

illusion of a larger wardrobe with a variety of ties, shirts, and shoes (for men) or scarves, blouses, accessories, and shoes (for women). Match colors and styles for pleasing effects.

Keep your stockings up and your shoes neat. Keep your clothes and your person unmistakably clean and neat.

If you wear glasses keep the frames and lenses clean. Get them fitted so they stay up on the bridge of your nose.

Act alive. Be brisk and energetic in your bearing and speech.

Know Your Boss's Job

Learn your superior's job. See the big picture as well as specific procedures. Contemplate what you'd do if you held the job.

Surround Yourself with Competent People

Attract and hire competent people. Don't fear competence in others. Use it to advantage.

Develop competence in your subordinates. Encourage learning and excellence by setting a positive climate. Provide unique opportunities to learn. Dispense the kinds of information subordinates need for progress and growth. Monitor their progress.

Train a ready replacement for your job, so you can move on and up.

Extend Your Control and Influence

Aim to broaden your job experience and background. Choose jobs for power and influence rather than pay and status.

Assess and test the power, authority, competence, and independence of others. Seek power and take it when you find it. Seek more authority and responsibility and use the competence of others to your advantage.

Mary Joan Glynn, general manager and operating head of the Borghese Division of Revlon, painstakingly taught herself new skills at each step up as she progressed. She recalls, "I was vice-president for product development at Doyle Dane Bernbach [the New York advertising agency] before I learned how to prepare a budget. I sat down with the accountant and studied how."[20] Eager for new responsibilities, she became a successful vice-president at Bloomingdale's and then president of Simplicity Pattern Company, a job she quit when the responsibilities she perceived as hers were retained by Simplicity's chairman. Her next job as operations head of Borghese better matched her ambitions and desire for greater responsibility.[21]

Actively Pursue Your Career

Put your career above your job. Don't sacrifice yourself for the good of the organization.

When Al Leegiance was offered a lateral transfer to be assistant superintendent at the plant in Metro City, he didn't take it. "I really would have liked to get that broader experience in operations, but I felt I was badly needed at the Middletown branch to make their critical purchases for the big government job they'd just received. They'd have been in the soup without me—and they begged me to stay. I've never had an offer like that since. That was three years ago. It looks like I'm stuck in materials control for good, now."

Consider both long- and short-term consequences of professional decisions. Yielding to short-term concerns may bring immediate satisfaction but often results in regret in the long run.

GENERAL STRATEGY

As you conduct your affairs look for challenge, opportunities, broader assignments. Do things that lead to results, not things that merely fill time.

Take advantage of every opportunity to demonstrate your competence. Show your ability to take on anything. Make every effort to be cordial, yet be tough when you have to be tough.

Do more than you need to do, faster than you need to do it. Use others to your advantage and help your allies to help themselves.

Don't complain or share the complaint of others. Use the information and insight you gain from unpleasant experiences to help you plan future action: to improve your relationship with others, to change the way things are done or the way things are going, to free yourself from situations that are beyond your ability or power to change.

Know how the system works and how to work the system. Be able to cut corners, bend rules, and suspend protocol where important goals are at stake.

Increase contacts and connections to secure information, resources, and support. Establish rapport and manage exchange patterns so you get what you want from relationships, whether it's your fair share or a substantial edge over others.

Find out the strengths and weaknesses of others. Ally and use strengths when it's to your advantage. Respect the strong who oppose you. Take advantage of the incompetence and weakness of those who oppose you.

Establish your own image of strength and competence, so that others give you room or seek your help.

Join groups, establish yourself as a valued member, and move to influence group direction and outcome. Determine the nature of group sentiment and use it to advantage.

Deal to get information, special treatment, cooperation.

Above all, in the heat of the fight serve your ends, not your ego.

LIVE ACTION REPORTS

Rumors were flying yesterday that the president's secretary was going to get the axe. People were openly cutting her down since they thought she was on the way out. I don't particularly care for her, but I decided to keep my mouth shut about it. At four-thirty the president called her in. Everyone smiled as the rumor seemed confirmed. But at four-fifty-five she walked out again, still the president's secretary. I was glad I'd stayed out of it.

Today I talked Mary into switching jobs with me for the day. I did payroll and she did payables. I learned the procedure of another job and broke up my own routine.

I practiced putting off a request today. Our personnel representative came into my office to ask me to telephone several people for her. Usually I would stop my own work and then end up staying late to finish. Today I just said, "As you can see, Jan, I'm really up to my ears. If you don't finish today, I'll be glad to help you when I finish my budget." It worked! She was happy with my response and I didn't feel imposed upon.

In my personnel job I communicate with a lot of people, usually by telephone or memo. This week I decided to meet this faceless society I deal with, so I set out to talk to people in person. It was a real shot in the arm for me. Everyone seemed delighted to know who I was. I got a lot of compliments on the clarity of my messages and many said they liked my sense of humor in the memos I sent. It was nice to meet people who were only voices to me before. I think, too, that my communications, whatever the form, will be even more effective from now on.

The advertising manager stormed into my office raising hell about some bills he'd incurred in his work that hadn't been paid. I reflected that I could understand how that would be upsetting. Then I asked for the facts. It turned out that he'd never forwarded the bills to me.

Instead of rubbing it in or making counteraccusations, I said that I'd take care of the matter immediately. Although he didn't apologize for his rough treatment of me, I could tell he knew he was in the wrong. I think the fact that I didn't tell him off or say he should have brought them to me earlier will improve our relationship in the future.

I learned the value of the telephone today when I discovered that I could gather data I need much faster by phone. I found out the name of our lawyer's secretary and phoned her personally. I asked her to look up the fees record for our department. She was happy to do it for me and it took her only fifteen minutes. It would have taken me at least two hours to go to the accounting department and look up the records of the fees, separate them by departments, and determine the amount to allocate to each account.

I used the phone again when projecting insurance premiums. Instead of digging through plant documents, I called our insurance agents and asked them for the figures I needed. Since they work with the figures daily, it took less time and provided me with a few valuable contacts.

About one-thirty Friday afternoon the divisional manager stopped by my office to say that he wanted me to gather and analyze some data from the seven subdivisions in the area. He said it was a top-priority job—and he'd like the report by Wednesday morning, if possible. I didn't say so, but I figured with luck and ingenuity I could get it done that afternoon.

As soon as he left I made some quick calls to alert people to what I needed. I dictated a report format to my secretary and told her to set up the tables I'd need in the report in blank form. I told her to be ready to take information over the phone as it was called in. As I made the rounds of the subdivisions personally to ver-

ify the information accuracy, I had someone at each location phone my secretary with the data so she could put it directly into the tables.

I was back in the office by four o'clock and had my recommendations added and the report out by four-thirty. I strolled into the division manager's office with it. He couldn't hide his surprise. He asked me what my recommendations were and we talked for a few minutes as he flipped through the report.

As we parted he headed for the president's office with the report. I know damn well he wanted to score his brownie points, too, with a fast delivery like mine. My name is on the report, so it won't hurt me in the front office, either.

The other day one of the schedulers from production control came to me with information that our scrap rate was increasing and that it would eventually show up in increased material costs. I listened attentively but gave no hint of my displeasure at the conditions he had reportedly discovered—or pleasure at his telling me about a hidden condition in the plant.

I looked into the matter myself and confirmed his findings. I called him in, thanked him for his observation, and made him a committee of one to look into the matter.

At work a new financial analyst was hired a few days ago. I had heard some rumors about him and he sounded like a pretty interesting guy. His position in the company is a fairly lofty one, and with good performance it promises to improve. Instead of waiting around to meet him at the copier, I marched up to his office and introduced myself. I never would have done that before taking this program. We had a nice conversation about his background and mine and I found out that he had lived for a time near my home town. After I went back down to my office, I felt very good about what had happened. I felt especially good that

I didn't let his high status in the company deter me from approaching him.

I went to visit my folks for the first time in two years and was alarmed to see that the motel they operate looked so second-rate compared with other choices along the strip. The books showed it, too. A quick survey showed that the internal costs were OK and so were the rooms in terms of furnishings and service. But they needed more business.

I did a quick count of the house on the competitors along the strip and found that their occupancy rates were far better than mom and dad's. I talked my folks into letting me negotiate a loan at the bank for remodeling the exterior of the motel and getting a competitive sign. I also negotiated a reservation exchange franchise for them. I enjoyed doing it. And I got a kick out of having my parents look at me as though I was some kind of tycoon, the way I took charge.

I heard that the top executive of a large local firm was thinking of selling a small subsidiary operation. Instead of procrastinating like I have in the past, I called the executive to get some preliminary information. When he started to stall a few days later, I told him I wanted the information he'd promised by five o'clock that night. Darned if he didn't deliver it personally!

Then I needed a backer, but the one person I thought would be interested and had the money to swing it is considered a "power" in town and is really tough to get to. I tried seven different approaches to reach him by phone, without success—because he didn't know me, I concluded. The eighth time I succeeded with, "Hi, Sue, honey, I've got to speak to Ken immediately." As I suspected, he really liked the concept. I got the biggest part of my capital from him. I'm taking over the business as general manager. I've got a good piece of the ac-

tion, and I'll get a better salary than I've ever earned before. Most amazing of all, it wasn't long ago that when I made a phone call to a stranger I hoped the line would be busy.

I talked to my supervisor and other executives in the firm I work for about my career plans. They all were enthusiastic about me, but like a broken record they said advancement or a significant raise in the near future was out of the question. So I decided to look outside the firm.

I called an old friend of my father who is well known in the personnel field. We had lunch together and discussed my goals and aspirations. He seemed flattered that I'd called him and also seemed to think highly of me. Two days later he reported back that he'd made a lot of phone calls and had firms, names, and numbers for me to call. He said he was confident that I was extremely marketable and asked me to check back with him because he was going to keep looking for other position possibilities in my field.

The project I'm working on is showing great potential and our workload keeps expanding. Another project folded the other day. A good friend of mine from the other project felt this coming weeks ago and said he'd like to transfer into my group. When the announcement became official I went to my boss and expressed interest in three key people, none of whom was the friend in question. I got two of them right away and the third after we went up the line another step.

I called my friend on the phone to break the news that he didn't get the job with me. I felt it was less embarrassing for both of us.

I needed to get some results from our processing lab in one day. This usually proves futile no matter what, because they're always swamped

[199]

and have a supervisor that always "goes by the book."

I decided to deal directly with the technician, but to do that I had to get past the receptionist, who's a real pro at keeping people out. Rather than stress the importance of a quick turnaround (a story she'd heard many times before), I told her that there were technicalities involved that required talking directly with the technician. She let me through.

Handling the technician was easy. He accepted my authority without question. So few people get by the receptionist, he assumed I was somebody special. I told him the job was important and that I needed it the next day. I got what I wanted when I wanted it.

I've worked in a small firm for three years, and every Christmas season there's talk about our office Christmas party, but it never takes place. This year I decided to change all that. I planned out the kind of party I thought the people would like. I chose a convenient time for all personnel. I budgeted out the cost and got the boss's OK on my plans. I assigned responsibility for decorations, food, and gifts. I put the boss on cleanup assignment with me.

I kept the party moving and we had a ball. I know I made points with the boss and everybody else in the firm.

There's an important change in the way I see myself. I have a great deal more confidence in myself, in my work, and in my ability to make things happen the way I want them to. I've learned to recognize success and interpret it as my own.

In the past when I've received good performance appraisals and raises I felt undeserving and beholden to my boss. In my last interview with her I found that I could discuss what I thought my most successful project had been and what areas I thought I could work on. This time I left her office feeling excited about the new projects we discussed—knowing that I make one hell of a contribution to that department.

INSTANT REPLAY

This is the main event. You put all your training together and apply it to your job and to your career to get what you want.

You accustom yourself and others to the "new you" in the workplace. You seek a "big picture" perspective and set your career and job goals accordingly. You aim for performance excellence, personal advantage, and upward mobility. You build an image of strength, respectability, and achievement. You get managerial CLOUT!

The suggested Workouts are:

◆ Redo workouts on the job.

◆ Seek a "big picture" perspective.

Tour your professional territory.

Interact with people in your professional territory.

Count the house.

◆ Establish long-term objectives.

Set career goals.

Set job objectives.

◆ Keep your eye on the goal.

◆ Reassess and redesign your job.

Simplify your job (eliminate rituals, economize time, increase versatility, reduce paperwork).

Avoid isolation.

Do first things first.

Develop support sources.

◆ Take a positive approach to annoyances and problems.

Regard annoyances as challenges.

See problems as opportunities.

- Manage resources.
  Seek alternate uses.
  Arrange resources differently.
  Use imagination in controlling assets.
  Vary the mix of assets.

- Manage operations.
  Make and implement decisions.
  Direct those who work for you.
  Take personal action.
  Delegate.
  Know your subordinates' jobs.
  Influence others.
  Negotiate.

Stay on target.
Get results.
Win endorsement of your actions.

- Demonstrate an upward mobility.
  Identify with superiors.
  Find a mentor.
  Be a mentor.
  Increase your exposure.
  Look like a winner.
  Know your boss's job.
  Surround yourself with competent people.

- Extend your control and influence.

- Actively pursue your career.

ROUND 10:

MANAGING MASTERY

In this final Round you learn how to keep your CLOUT. Just as a prizefighter expects to defend his title, you must expect to defend your position in the organization against those who'd like to see you replaced, either by themselves or others. This means actively maintaining your mastery as well as preventing others from infringing on your territory.

THE CHALLENGE

The challenge of this Round is to stay on top. Your objective is to survive and to strengthen your power position, as well as to get the results you want. Besides meeting the unique responsibilities and problems at the top, you may be called upon to put down threats of takeover by others. You may also need to overcome a subconscious desire to step down in order to avoid the challenge that CLOUT brings.

THE STRATEGY

You keep on top by constantly training and pitting yourself against tough contenders. You continue to practice and refine your skills both in and out of the "ring," until you're able to spontaneously choose the appropriate behavior from your repertoire to meet any situation—and until the attitudes and perspectives necessary for CLOUT become second nature for you. You resist the urge to rest on your laurels or to protect your position by preserving the status quo. You make it a point to look and act like a champion at all times.

THE MOVES

In this Round you initiate change, adapt to reality, take dramatic action, conceal intentions when it's to your advantage, manage reciprocation, attract and hold followers, make your objectives meaningful to others, strive for excellence, think and act creatively, and persist.

WINNING THE ROUND

You know you're winning when you can sustain yourself in the managerial position you've chosen; when you thoroughly enjoy both mastery and the fruits of victory; when attempts to subordinate you become less and less frequent; when you have to search for challenges instead of defend against them. The surest and most gratifying evidence of CLOUT is seeing that what you've done and what you stand for endure in your absence.

THE IMPORTANCE OF MANAGING MASTERY

Positions of prominence at any level in the organization hierarchy are not self-sustaining. This is especially true if you've made it to a top spot. Now more than ever you need to be in control—of yourself, of other people, and of events. Only by effective management of mastery can you expect to retain what you've won, win still more, and keep and enjoy the CLOUT you've worked so hard to get.

AVOIDING TAKEOVER BY OTHERS

You know from your own climb up the hierarchical ladder that the top is also coveted by others. What you have, others seek. Consequently, you need to be able to fend off those who would like to displace you.

Your familiarity with the skills and strategies you employed to make your own ascent helps you recognize and counteract similar moves when other contenders use them against you. Equally important is a realistic awareness of the devious means others may use to unseat you. Whether they play fair or dirty, those who engage in power politics know how the element of surprise lessens risk and increases the likelihood of success. And they know, too, how much better it is to be the surpriser than the surprised:

MANAGING MASTERY

"No offense, Bill, but this is my territory."

Philip L. Lowe, an outside director of U.S. Home Corporation at the time, recalled how chairman of the corporation Charles Rutenberg was displaced.

The night before the annual meeting Rutenberg, several board members, and Guy R. Odom, whom Rutenberg had brought in as chief executive officer less than ninety days earlier, held a convivial business dinner at Rutenberg's home in Florida. "I subsequently dubbed that the Last Supper," said Lowe. "The next morning at the annual meeting, Rutenberg got up and said nice things about Odom, and Odom got up and said nice things about Rutenberg. Then, we convened a board meeting and when the item to reappoint Odom CEO came up, Frederick E. Fisher, Rutenberg's senior vice president and treasurer, made a motion to amend it and name Odom chairman as well. . . . I made a man's-inhumanity-to-man speech. . . . After all Rutenberg helped found the company. . . . There are nicer ways to do things."[1]

Nevertheless, Rutenberg was deposed, and that was the first he knew of it. Not only had all five of his inside directors voted against him, they also proceeded to remove those who had voted for him from all the various directors' committees.[2]

To avoid this kind of surprise and prevent such attacks, you need to bestow trust prudently, keep a constant vigil, and manage information carefully—watching for those who cloud their real intentions with congeniality while keeping a tight lip yourself about your own plans.

MANAGING THE PRESSURE OF RESPONSIBILITY

When you've got CLOUT the buck really does stop with you. The ultimate responsibility for what happens and how it happens is yours.

In other words, you're answerable both for the ends achieved and for the means of achieving them. You're responsible for the values and character of the organization, for important decisions, and for their consequences.

SETTING THE VALUES AND CHARACTER OF THE ORGANIZATION

When you're at the top you guide the character development of your organization. Whether intentionally or simply because of your high position, you emit values and set standards for the people around you.

Some will emulate you because they admire your style and want to be like you. Others, especially people under you in the organization, will take on your values, attitudes, and behavior patterns to try to gain your acceptance or favor. Still others will rationalize that whatever *you* do is all right for them to do.

Whatever the reason, you influence the thoughts and actions of a great many people because of your showcase position. Managing this aspect of mastery puts pressure on you to present a role model which is both acceptable to you and worthy of being copied by others.

The Watergate scandal in the presidential administration of Richard Nixon illustrates how the failure of a leader to set standards of integrity can cause grave consequences.

During the Senate investigation of the break-in at the Democratic National Committee Headquarters and the subsequent cover-up, Senator Howard Baker repeatedly asked, "What did the President know and when did he know it?" From a legal aspect, the what and the when were important. More damning, in terms of executive responsibility, was the fact that Nixon seemed to have set a value climate within the White House Staff and the Committee to Re-elect the President which allowed breaking and entering and bugging. Indications of this came from testimony in the case, the White House tapes, and Nixon's own public deportment throughout the investigation.

Furthermore, many of the people involved in the scandal later attributed their conduct to compliance with the pattern set by higher-ups. In his plea to U.S. District Court Judge John Sirica for a sentence reduction, for example, Nixon's former domestic affairs advisor, John Erlichman, said, "You are effectively rendering your ethical and moral judgments to your superior when you go to work in the White House. . . . In effect, I abdicated my moral judgment and turned it over to someone else."[3]

Nixon's failure to accept the responsibility to maintain the integrity of his high office shook the nation's faith in government, forced his resignation as president, and dragged down innocent and guilty alike as he fell from power.

Whenever you hold a high position in any organization, the many people who see you as an authority figure tend to defer to your judgment. Thus it's all the more urgent that you manage organization character and the climate of means so that you're willing to accept responsibility for your own behavior as well as for those within your sphere of influence.

MAKING IMPORTANT DECISIONS

When you're at the top you're responsible for major decisions which materially affect the course of future events. The burden of their rightness or wrongness as well as the burden of their consequences can't be passed on to others. For some people this realization causes anxiety that results in either bad decisions or the inability to make any decision at all.

This was one of the problems that plagued Anthony Eden when he came into full power as

prime minister of England. As foreign secretary under Winston Churchill, Eden looked and acted the part of the ideal diplomat and British leader. As second in command when Churchill's health failed, he effectively made and carried out decisions in Churchill's name.

When he became prime minister himself and assumed the ultimate responsibility for the government, however, he appeared to break under the pressures of the office. One ill-fated decision took place in October of 1956 when he launched a too-little, too-late, destined-to-fail attempt to seize the Suez Canal which Egypt had nationalized four months earlier. He was roundly criticized by the United Nations and forced to abort the mission. He resigned in broken health the following January.

As long as it was Churchill who held the title and bore the ultimate responsibility of the office, Eden could perform all the duties of the office with distinction and decisiveness. But the total actual responsibility of the office seemed too awesome for Eden to handle.

Managing mastery enables you to make decisions of consequence without freezing at the crucial moment or making irrational choices when you're under pressure.

ACCEPTING CONSEQUENCES

When you're at the top you're obligated to accept full responsibility for the results of your decisions and behavior. That isn't always easy. The ability to honestly accept blame for failure and gracefully accept credit for success varies even among well-known leaders, as the following incidents illustrate:

In 1960, on the eve of summit talks with President Dwight D. Eisenhower, Nikita Khrushchev announced that the Russians had shot down a United States high-altitude reconnaisance plane flying deep inside their borders. Eisenhower denied any deliberate attempt to violate

Soviet air space. Khrushchev's evidence proved overwhelming. The Russians had recovered recognizable pieces of the U-2 plane and captured the pilot, Francis Gary Powers, who confessed to the spying mission. This meant that Eisenhower was either uninformed or a liar. Shortly thereafter he amended his position to admit United States involvement. By this time, however, the summit had been scuttled and Eisenhower had lost a great deal of credibility both at home and abroad.

Less than a year later, the United States covertly underwrote an invasion of Cuba. The landing of the anti-Castro forces at the Bay of Pigs ended up in humiliating defeat. President John F. Kennedy immediately accepted full responsibility for the fiasco. Even though he had only been in office for a few months and was carrying out a plan conceived during Eisenhower's administration, he publicly took the blame. By honestly admitting responsibility for the disaster, he actually gained in popularity with the American people.

Finally, there's the case of Woody Hayes, former Ohio State University football coach who had unusual difficulty dealing gracefully with either success or failure. Here's what sports columnist Jim Murray of the Los Angeles Times *had to say about him when Hayes was fired (after twenty-eight years and a 205–61–10 record) for allegedly hitting a Clemson player who intercepted an Ohio State pass late in the 1978 Gator Bowl game:*

"The first time I ever laid eyes on Woody Hayes was in the locker room after his defeat of USC in the rain in the Rose Bowl in 1955. He promptly assailed the committee for permitting the bands to march on the field, criticized the officials for ineptness, and allowed as how the USC team he just beat would be hard put to finish sixth in his conference, the Big 10. . . .

"The next time I saw Woody was in the [Los Angeles] Coliseum in 1959. USC had just beaten him, 17–0, and a big Trojan tackle,

Dan Ficca, whom Woody had tried to recruit, was taunting him from the corridor. Woody turned around and swung at a couple of nearby newsmen. . . . Woody was consistent. Graceless in victory and graceless in defeat."[4]

Managing the way you express your feelings is an important part of mastery. Real mastery means playing the role of a good loser or a good winner, whether you feel like it or not, especially when you're in the public view.

QUELLING THE FEAR OF SUCCESS

Contradictory as it seems, there is such a thing as fear of success, which makes some people either avoid top spots or back down once they get there.

There are greater expectations from others and changed relationships to deal with when you reach the top. People expect you to maintain your high level of performance. Some go out of their way to criticize you or put you down. The constant exposure to scrutiny and evaluation becomes a burden for some leaders, who then opt for the relative anonymity and ease of a lesser position.

Relationships change, too, as your relative position in the organization changes. Those you worked with may now be working for you. Those you worked for may now see you as a rival. Friendship patterns change as your job makes more demands on your time and throws you into the company of a different set of people.

If you're a woman, you face an additional fear that may deter you from trying for a top spot. Making it as a manager will be seen by many as failing as a "real" woman—one who assumes the traditional role of wife, mother, and helper, not that of successful career woman and boss—for society is slow to accept the idea that women can have a choice or do both.

This "other side" of success causes so much apprehension in some people that they cope by copping out. For that reason, managing the fear of success is as essential to keeping CLOUT as managing fear of failure is to getting it.

WHY PRACTICE SKILLS
AFTER YOU HAVE *CLOUT*

Winning a bout or two—or even making it to the very top—doesn't mean that you can quit training. Just as great athletes work out daily to improve on fundamentals, perfect new strategies, and stay in shape, so must you as a manager keep all the nottims in condition for use on the spur of the moment.

Whether they are on the same team or on the opposite side, the people you deal with in this Round are apt to be winners, too. Playing with or against them brings out the best in you and helps you perfect your skills. In the heat of the contest you learn how tough contenders play the game. You see what it takes to handle tough competition when the stakes are high. You learn the tricks of the trade firsthand from the pros. And you stay at your best by going up against the best time after time, learning to survive in the thick of the contest and learning to enjoy the fight as well as the victory.

Staying in top shape through constant, conscientious practice and refinement of managerial skills, both on and off the job, with all kinds of contenders and in all kinds of circumstances, will enable you to manage CLOUT and keep the upper hand you've won.

THE WORKOUTS

The Workouts in this Round are not directed toward acquiring new skills. Instead they suggest how to apply skills you already have in positions where you have some degree of power. When you apply your skills in these special ways, they boost your authority and add to your credibility and help you keep your CLOUT.

These Workouts are presented in very general terms, not only because everyone's professional role varies considerably, but also because you should be able to make decisions and carry out actions with minimal external direction at this stage of the program.

Contribute Unique Input

Make your presence felt by making unique contributions to the organization. Introduce changes and create unpredictable and unexpected strategies to keep you and your organization on top. Seek challenge, not safety. Remember that survival at the top comes from dynamic, forward thinking and action, not from nursing the status quo.

Reginald H. Jones, chairman and chief executive officer of General Electric, exemplifies this kind of dynamism in both strategy and conduct. Among other things, in 1970 he instigated bold action to divest GE of their losing computer operation to Honeywell, Inc., thereby benefiting both firms. In 1976, he engineered the acquisition of Utah International, Inc. This move gave GE access to Utah International's huge cache of natural resources, particularly coal and uranium, providing them with a good hedge against future inflation and energy shortages. In 1978, his attempt to acquire Cox Broadcasting would expand GE's profitable broadcasting base considerably and give them a good position in the cable TV business.

By actions such as these Jones kept the firm in long-term competitive position. He also kept his own value as an executive high.

Adapt to Realities

Be sensitive and adaptable to changing conditions. Study the environmental climate and external conditions over which you have little control, and adjust your strategies to advantage. Be flexible and match your actions to the times.

The ability to adjust to changing conditions realistically and imaginatively can literally save an organization.

In its early days, Theodore N. Vail guided troubled AT&T toward a "universal" telephone system. At the time neither his firm, the public, nor communications technology could have been adequately served otherwise. Accordingly, he convinced the public and the government that a single firm could do the job better than a multitude of competing firms. At the same time he helped to strengthen public regulation and laid the groundwork for the famous Bell Laboratories to prevent any monopoly stagnation. He also conceived of financing the massive capital requirements through financial securities sold to the small investor who wanted a safe, high-yielding, yet growth-oriented stock.[5]

Today conditions are very different. The rate of technological innovation is practically explosive and standard products and services become obsolete almost overnight. Under the protection of a government-regulated monopoly Bell was hard pressed to survive such a climate. Consequently, John deButts, a more recent chairman of AT&T, engineered a total change in strategy to match the times. He recognized competition as a new fact of life, so he changed the goals from mastering the regulatory process to meeting the needs of the marketplace. To accomplish this new approach he totally revamped the company's structure and broadened its concept of products and services. His new strategy called for meeting the technologically sophisticated and marketing-wise companies in the communication system and computer science fields head-on.

Even though it has both the expertise and capital to compete, without this dramatic shift in strategy AT&T would not be able to make any significant assault on a total market that is destined to change so much that both "telephone" and "telegraph" seem inappropriate to the company's name.[6]

Don't stick with an outmoded fight plan. Different times and different conditions require changes in both strategy and direction.

Conceal Intent

Use ambiguity and secrecy to gain the edge and introduce the element of surprise into your dealings. Don't reveal your intentions or your strategy to adversaries, either in or out of the organization. Realistically recognize the need to sometimes confuse the opposition with misleading action or information in order to plan and implement your strategy and get the results you want.

Nowhere is it more expedient to cloud intent than in the practice of power politics. In fact, when the stakes are high, secrecy may be absolutely essential to accomplishing goals without unnecessary strife and interference.

Jimmy Carter discovered this soon after he became president of the United States. When he ran for office, Carter pledged to strip away the secrecy from the presidency. Once in the White House, however, he repeatedly saw the need to use secrecy as an instrument of power. The extreme secrecy surrounding the normalizing of relations with the People's Republic of China in 1978 is a case in point. On Carter's instructions, only Secretary of State Cyrus Vance and four others were in on it. When members of Congress were consulted on the matter, it was in such an ambiguous manner that the negotiations were not revealed.

Had Carter discussed his intentions ahead of time, dissension from Nationalist Chinese supporters both in and out of government ranks would have made it more difficult to negotiate with mainland China. Furthermore, according to Washington observers, Carter had become "increasingly aware that surprise and drama can be important factors in presidential momentum."[7]

Take Dramatic Action

Take quick, authoritative action when a situation arises that threatens your position, power, or credibility, or when you must restore order in a situation you inherit. Show toughness and determination. Finish what you start. Use the elements of surprise, proper timing, and the force and prestige of your office to help you pull it off.

Both of the two strong adversaries involved in the following illustration used such dramatic tactics.

Early in 1962, President John F. Kennedy put the services and force of his office behind labor-management negotiations in the steel industry in order to get a noninflationary low-raise, no-price-increase accord. In April the United Steel Workers reached an agreement with the steel industry for an all-time low 3 percent productivity wage increase and everyone concerned

assumed that the industry would forgo a price increase in return.

However, on April 10, chairman of U.S. Steel Roger Blough met with President Kennedy and announced a 13½ percent hike in the price of steel, at the same time that he had arranged for the news to be released to the press. Blough's timing caught everyone off guard, including others in the steel industry, most of whom recovered quickly, nevertheless, and raised their prices similarly. Not only did his action demonstrate his strong belief that the government had no business setting steel prices, it also showed that he had no intention of backing down.

Kennedy was both incredulous and outraged and told Blough so. His famous reference to all businessmen as sons-of-bitches worked its way into their conversation.

Then Kennedy went into action. He called David McDonald, president of the United Steelworkers, to let the steelworkers know where he stood. "Dave," he said, "you have been screwed and I have been screwed." He called a press conference and publicly denounced Blough's action. He mustered prestigious people in his administration to contact and put pressure on the steel magnates. He appealed in particular to Joseph L. Block, chairman of Inland Steel, who had not yet raised his price. He instructed the Defense Department not to place orders with firms that had raised their prices. He alerted the Justice Department and FBI to start criminal investigation into price fixing and the FTC to look into unlawful trade practices. He called for a grand jury investigation and suggested that House and Senate committees look into regulatory price and antitrust legislation and consider revoking any favorable tax treatment for steel companies. He had his economic advisor declare that no price increase was necessary in the steel industry. His efforts were successful in getting Inland, Kaiser, and Armco to hold the price line. The rest of the industry folded,

TAKE DRAMATIC ACTION

"Quick! Start the paper work for a fire extinguisher!"

and seventy-two hours after Blough's call on Kennedy, U.S. Steel rescinded its price increase.

Both Blough and Kennedy understood the uses of power. Blough clouded intent. He gave the impression of agreeing without agreeing. By walking into enemy territory to deliver his broadside, he faced the responsibility of his actions squarely.

Although Kennedy had no direct authority over Blough or the steel companies, he didn't like the sting of what he regarded as premeditated deceit. He struck back with every ounce of punch he could throw, giving the appearance of more power than he ever could have delivered. It worked.

Not all managers find themselves involved in heavyweight confrontations such as these. But managers often do find themselves in situations where their authority or credibility is questioned, or where a timely show of strength is called for. Taking quick, forceful action puts everyone on notice that you mean business.

Manage Reciprocation

Be able to accept favors without feeling compelled to return them. Be able, also, to withhold favors that are expected or requested by adversaries, without feeling guilty.

At the same time, don't expect a kindness in return when you give a kindness, especially if the stakes are high. And don't be surprised if someone you've hurt tries to hurt you back out of all proportion to the hurt you inflicted.

Take nothing for granted in the power game. High stakes cause people to act differently from what you might consider "normal." In fact, it's fairly safe to assume that nonreciprocation *is* normal for people used to power play.

In 1939, Ozzie Nelson, who's best remembered for his role in the "Adventures of Ozzie and Harriet" television show, was playing an engagement as bandleader and master of ceremonies in producer Billy Rose's Casa Mañana theater restaurant in New York City. When Rose decided to switch his attention to his Aquacade at the World's Fair in nearby Flushing Meadows, he posted notice that the Casa Mañana show would close in one week. The dancers, showgirls, and some of the biggest names in show business were taken by surprise. Ozzie and his group had a contract that required four weeks' notice of cancellation, however, which he called to the stage manager's attention.

"The next morning," recalled Ozzie, "my phone rang at about eleven o'clock. It was Billy Rose. 'I hope I didn't wake you up, Oz,' he said solicitously. This was the first time he had ever acknowledged that he knew my name. He then went on to explain that he hadn't realized that we had the four-week clause in our contract, but that he had looked it up and I was absolutely correct. 'You've got me over a barrel, Oz,' he went on, 'but if I keep the show open I stand to lose a fortune. All I can do is appeal to your kindness and generosity. Everybody in town says you're a hell of a fine guy. If you could see your way clear to let me off the hook I'd feel indebted to you for the rest of my life.' I could almost hear the violins playing in the background.

"I immediately assured him that it would be fine with me—that we . . . would actually look forward to having a little time off.

"'I can't tell you how much I appreciate this,' said Billy. 'You're a real friend. As I say, I'd love to keep the show open, but I just can't afford it. I'm sure you understand.'

". . . I thought I'd change the subject. 'How are things going at the Aquacade?' [I asked].

"'Terrific,' he answered. 'Just between you and me, I'll make a million dollars on it before the summer is over. And thanks again, Oz,' he added. 'I'll never forget you for this.'

"A couple of hours later I went down to Lindy's Restaurant to get something to eat. There was Billy sitting at his usual table near the window. . . . I said, 'Hi, Billy!' Billy didn't even look up. He just kept right on eating. He did, however, acknowledge my greeting by raising one finger from his fork as he raised it to his mouth, and I must say he did it with flair. He stayed right in rhythm. He didn't miss a beat."[8]*

Needless to say, Ozzie's gesture of consideration saved Rose many thousands of dollars. But since he already had Ozzie's word, he had no further need to extend any social grace. Like the used-car salesman who just sold one of his cars at its posted price, Rose may even have felt a little contempt for Ozzie because he turned out to be such an easy mark.

Attract and Hold Loyal Followers

Establish a dedicated following that identifies with you and your goals more than with the organization and its goals. Nurture their personal allegiance to you by appearing attractive, by displaying competence and confidence, and by maintaining an interesting and challenging work climate.

C. Lester Hogan joined Motorola in 1958 and built a superb organization by attracting good people and using their talents to advantage. He increased Motorola's semiconductor sales from $5 million to $230 million dollars in nine years to make it the leading firm in that industry. In 1968, when he resigned as executive vice-president of Motorola to accept the presidency of ailing Fairchild Camera and Instru-

* From the book *Ozzie* by Ozzie Nelson. © 1973 by Oswald G. Nelson. Published by Prentice-Hall, Inc., Englewood Cliffs, New Jersey 07632. Reprinted by permission of the author and the author's agents, Scott Meredith Literary Agency, Inc., 845 Third Avenue, New York, New York 10022.

ment Corporation, his staff visited him at his home, asking that he take them with him to Fairchild.[9] He ended up by taking seven key people.

Clearly Hogan's staff identified with him, rather than with the organization, and his new job was made easier because he had a dedicated and talented group of followers to help turn Fairchild around.

On the other hand, when Semon Knudsen moved from the executive offices of General Motors to those of the Ford Motor Company, none of his former staff made the transfer with him. As a result, he had no one to protect his flanks or rear. Without protection he was uninformed, misinformed, vulnerable to attack, and virtually sandbagged by insiders who sought the top job. He lasted only nineteen months.

Finally, Marxist historian Roy Medvedev attributes the downfall of Russia's Nikita Khrushchev to his dismissal of a loyal follower, Ivan Serov, as head of the KGB (secret police).

Once the most powerful man in Russia and an influential world figure, Khrushchev was deposed in October 1964 when the Politburo and Central Committee met behind his back while he was vacationing near the Black Sea. They ousted him as premier, as a member of the Presidium, and as first secretary of the Communist party. Even though Serov had proved his loyalty to Khrushchev in earlier Politburo skirmishes, Khrushchev had replaced him with Alexander Shelepin on the advice of Politburo members. It was Shelepin who subsequently lined up the Kremlin security forces behind the anti-Khrushchev plotters. With Serov heading the KGB, that wouldn't have happened.[10]

Make Your Goals Meaningful to Others

Arouse enthusiasm for your goals and inspire loyalty in others. Make your goals meaningful to others by what you do, how you look, and what you say. Speak in terms they can understand. Appeal to a broad audience by expressing universal ideals that a wide variety of people can relate to—or aim your remarks at the special interests of groups with common concerns.

President John F. Kennedy personified charisma so exactly that the term gained unusual popularity during his term in office. His pleasing appearance, spontaneous wit, and easy eloquence contributed greatly to his winning the presidency and holding public confidence and support. His inaugural address, with its compelling lines ". . . ask not what your country can do for you: Ask what you can do for your country," appealed to all segments of his constituency and covered all major concerns of his office.

He was equally appealing to foreign audiences. In France, where his wife charmed the populace with her graceful manner and fluent French, he delighted his audience when he began his address: "I do not think it altogether inappropriate to introduce myself to this audience. I am the man who accompanied Jacqueline Kennedy to Paris—and I've enjoyed it."

In West Germany, in 1963, he endeared himself to the people of Berlin when, after inspecting the Berlin Wall, he spoke to a seething mass of citizens. Shocked by what he'd seen, he told his audience that those who had hopes of compromising with communism should come to Berlin. As the crowd roared its approval, he concluded, "All free men, wherever they may live, are citizens of Berlin, and therefore, as a free man, I take pride in the words 'Ich bin ein Berliner.' "

Although Kennedy's speech consisted of only ten sentences—and half of those were "Let them come to Berlin"—his words and delivery told the West Germans that he understood their concerns. In turn, they accepted him whole-

MAKE YOUR GOALS MEANINGFUL TO OTHERS

"What I mean is . . . like . . . you know . . . it's cool to . . . you know . . . I mean like . . . we oughta . . ."

[212]

heartedly. In fact, he said later, with more concern than smugness, that if he had then told them to march to the wall and tear it down, his listeners probably would have done so.

To make your mastery meaningful to others, develop a system of ideas that represents your personal and professional philosophy. With groups or individuals, in formal or informal contacts, try to put your ideas across with sincerity and clarity. Show that you identify with the concerns of others and try to get them to identify with your goals in return. Apply the light touch when appropriate, to show that you're "human" and have a sense of humor.

Strive for Excellence

Try to do your best. Set for yourself the very highest of professional goals that are within your present and future capabilities. If you can, be the best in your field.

You achieve excellence by setting high performance goals and working long and hard to attain them. This requires practicing skills, overcoming weaknesses and building strengths, and performing with precision. Furthermore, while skills are essential, an insightful, spontaneous inner direction is also necessary.

Excellence in management shows itself in unique approaches, in results, in relationships, in style, and in reputation.

Charles Revson, founder and former chairman of Revlon, Inc., exemplifies a manager who pursued and achieved excellence. He was often described as crude, ruthless, and arbitrary. But when it came to his products or the firm, being best meant everything.[11] *He demanded perfection and quality on all fronts—people, production, packaging, promotion, and products. He inspired people to do more than they thought they were capable of. When he was around you could feel the electricity.*

He produced the best dye markers the navy ever had and Revlon won the Army/Navy "E" award for excellence in production.

But his real passion was cosmetics, and he made his products more appealing through packaging and advertising. His promotion of Fire and Ice, a new line of nail polish, is recognized by the industry as one of the most effective ad campaigns in cosmetic history. He personally spent hours going over engraving proofs.

He pioneered in new product innovations. Among other things, he introduced matching lip and nail colors. His products had to be right. He developed a complete and sophisticated quality control system ahead of others in the industry. As he succinctly put it, "I don't ship shit."[12]

He was equally particular in selecting his successor. He chose outsider Michel B. Bergerac over existing Revlon executives, including his own sons. In three years Bergerac doubled sales and profits, diversified the firm, and increased return on equity from 17 to 20 percent. In choosing him Revson assured that Revlon's name would survive in a changing world.[13]

Excellence is an elusive quality as applied to managers. In pursuit of it you tap the best you have to offer in effort, talent, and skills. You pursue the image you have of yourself at your future best.

Think and Act Creatively

Think beyond the obvious. Look at one thing and try to see another. Put unrelated elements together and create new combinations and situations that give you decided advantage. Make sure that your ideas are sound—socially, economically, and technically.

Thomas Edison, who changed the lives of millions of people with his invention of the electric light, personified this ability.

When Edison became interested in electrical illumination, he went to Ansonia, Connecticut, to see firsthand the Wallace-Farmer 8-horsepower dynamo that supplied current to eight brilliant arc lights of 500 candlepower each. The glare was blinding, capable of lighting a wide area.

Edison was elated. He literally ran back and forth, from lights to instruments to dynamo. He quickly made calculations on the power of the instrument, the lights, the probable loss in transmission—and the amount of coal the system would use.

He was inspired by what he saw—not so much because of what Wallace and Farmer had done, however, but because of what they had not done. He saw immediately what was needed: a means of subdividing the light to milder intensities for use indoors; a system for distributing the electricity similar to the way gas is distributed—from a central power source instead of from a source at each use site; and a system wired to a dynamo in parallel rather than in series so that the lamps could be lighted individually, instead of all turning on and off together.

He also thought in terms of social and commercial implications. He saw in it a product that would be useful to great masses of people, not just a scientific toy. Before he began his experimentation he quantified and costed the raw materials for power, machinery, and wire for a central power station and distribution network of thousands of lighting units. Only after seeing its social and economic feasibility did he tackle the technical problems—the constant-voltage dynamo as a power source, the vacuum bulb to keep air from burning up the filament, the thin carbon filament to offer high resistance so as to glow brightly with low radiation and low current. His planning and confidence were so complete that he attracted none other than J. P. Morgan as a backer in launching the Edison Electric Light Company.[14]

Edison visualized his goal and then worked backward to achieve it. He dealt with the ordinary in extraordinary ways.

Whereas Edison was painstakingly systematic, other creative people appear to simply pop up unexpectedly with original ideas:

Armand Hammer, chairman of Occidental Petroleum, who built a wildcat drilling firm into one of the nation's largest oil and gas companies in a twenty-year span, is noted for a spontaneous, creative quality in his dealings. Here's how one of Hammer's executive assistants describes his approach.

"You'll sit there in his office and feed him all the facts and figures on a situation you think are important. Then he'll lean back and think for a moment and come up with a decision that seems so wild you wonder whether he was even listening to what you told him."[15]
Hammer takes information and uses it so differently that his solution doesn't even seem to be derived from the data given. He solves problems uniquely by thinking loose.

Develop your own creativity by looking at the big picture. See things differently. Count the house.

Persist

When you start something, stick with it. When you make a commitment to a goal, keep it.

Thomas Edison was fond of saying that genius was 1 percent inspiration and 99 percent perspiration. Clearly, he had the proper combination of each to excel in his field. His invention of the electric light illustrates how inspiration contributed to his success. The following incidents illustrate his commitment and determination.

Edison was committed to invention. As a boy, everything he did was aimed at carrying out experiments. He planted a garden and sold vegetables to raise capital for his experiments. He worked as a trainboy to support his experiments. He spent virtually all his earnings as a telegrapher to support his curiosity about electrical devices.

Even after he established himself in business, his contractual work was still only a means of getting funds to furnish his experimental undertakings.

When problems arose, he worked doggedly to solve them. Once, while rushing a new model of stock printer to production to get cash to experiment further, he discovered "bugs" in the printer. He locked himself and his four assistants in the laboratory for sixty hours until they had solved the problem. Legend has it that on his wedding day he went to his laboratory an hour or so after the ceremony to work on some defective stock tickers and didn't return to his bride until midnight.[16]

Define your own goals in a "big picture" framework. Don't restrict yourself by becoming obsessed with one specific end to the exclusion of other important objectives. Realistically choose goals you are capable of achieving.

GENERAL STRATEGY

The groundwork for the Workouts in this Round has been carefully laid in the previous nine Rounds. If you diligently practiced the individual skills as they were offered previously in incremental order, you have acquired all the nottims you need for CLOUT. All that remains is for you to use them constantly to maintain and improve their effectiveness. For like athletic skills, unless you use them, you're apt to lose them.

Continue practicing all you've learned, therefore: initiate change; be curious about people, things, and ideas; seek out and interact with all kinds of people in all kinds of situations; work to get your fair share—or more—and feel good about it; discover how far you're willing and able to go to get what you want, and be realistically aware of how far others will go to get what they want; try to hold your own with the toughest adversaries under the toughest conditions.

Put special emphasis on the nottims that deal with establishing the attitudes and perspectives that maintain mastery: *Look for the big picture. Keep your aspirations high, strive for excellence,* and *think highly of yourself. See defeat as only a temporary setback. Resist external pressures and dependence on others. Welcome challenge. Enjoy action and mastery.*

MORE RULES FOR MANAGING MASTERY

Here are some further suggestions for managing mastery.

1. Establish a high sense of responsibility for yourself and for those who work for you.

2. Rely primarily on your personal influence to direct others, but use the strength of your position, organization, and institution as backups when appropriate.

3. Know what's going on inside and outside your organization. Retain or release information as it serves your purpose.

4. Control the indispensable resource, whether it's talent, knowledge, money, or facilities.

5. Maintain the appearance of cooperation even if you don't intend to cooperate.

6. Obligate others, but don't become obligated.

7. Minimize your dependence on others, but increase others' dependence on you if it serves your purpose.

8. Keep your power intact. Don't let it be leeched away by your subordinates or by the restrictive action of other authorities or their representatives.

9. Set priorities and make decisions and act accordingly.

10. Look like a leader: display confidence, competence, commitment, and mastery.

11. Make alliances when it's to your advantage. Break alliances when they no longer serve your purpose.

12. Maintain your mobility. Be able to move anywhere, anytime, to increase your advantages.

13. Keep options open so you can maneuver freely.

INSTANT REPLAY

Keeping CLOUT is not unlike getting it. To get to the top you work harder and smarter to produce better results than others. To stay there you do more of the same. You continue to perfect your skills until you can choose and apply them easily, appropriately, and spontaneously.

There are pitfalls at the top, and no one is immune to them. However, the means by which you've acquired mastery will help you keep it. The use of Gradualism has given you both competence and confidence and gives you a better chance to thrive at the top. The emphasis on intrinsic incentives and rewards makes you more willing to change, accept responsibility, and live with the outcome of your decisions and actions. The practice of Privacy has shown you how to cloud intent to protect your goals and strategy from direct attack. The breadth of your expanded experience promotes creativity, high standards of performance, and clear thinking in tough transactions.

As your new skills and attitudes are incorporated into your total life style through continual use, choosing the right course of action to maintain and manage mastery becomes second nature. You can cut it. You have CLOUT for keeps.

The suggested Workouts are:

▶ Contribute unique input.

▶ Adapt to realities.

▶ Conceal intent.

▶ Take dramatic action.

▶ Manage reciprocation.

▶ Attract and hold loyal followers.

▶ Make your goals meaningful to others.

▶ Strive for excellence.

▶ Think and act creatively.

▶ Persist.

PERSONALIZING CLOUT:
CHOOSING YOUR OWN STYLE

If you've mastered the nottims, you've got CLOUT. You can cut it. The question still remains: What are you going to do with it? What kinds of objectives will you pursue? What kinds of values will you display? What will you deem "appropriate" action? In other words, how will you personalize your managerial style?

THE DIMENSIONS OF STYLE

Style is set, in part, by the range of skills in your repertoire and by the ease with which you use them. This latter aspect of style might be likened to *savoir-faire*, the subject of the following waggish dialog:

FIRST FRENCHMAN: Savoir-faire *means to act appropriately, even in the most distressing of circumstances.* Par exemple, *suppose a hus-band accidentally comes upon his wife making love to another man. If he bows and says, "Par-donnez-moi, monsieur, please continue,"that's* savoir-faire.

SECOND FRENCHMAN: Oui, *perhaps so, my friend. But to me, if the lover* does indeed *continue, that is* savoir-faire.

FEMALE COMPANION: Non, non! *You are both mistaken.* True savoir-faire *is when the wife says, "Ah, my dearest, you have arrived at last. Come join us. I hope you will pardon us for starting without you."*

Certainly your *savoir-faire*—how polished and sure you are in relationships with others— is the part of style that most people notice first. Far more fundamental to managerial style, however, are your values and purposes, and the balance you strike between them.

[217]

THE IMPORTANCE OF BALANCE

Too much or too little weight placed on either principles or objectives has obvious drawbacks. Cold-blooded, unprincipled scoundrels often leave a trail of human misery behind them, as they totally dedicate themselves to a selfish purpose. Yet history is also full of examples of injustice and inhumanity caused by too rigid devotion to principle—outrages like the medieval Inquisition, the Salem witch burnings of the seventeenth century, and the violence of present-day political terrorists.

CLOUT, by its very nature, predisposes you, as a manager, to dangers at either extreme. The increased confidence and strength of conviction which you now have are apt to make you a strong believer in the rightness of your own moral code and the nobleness of your own objectives. There's a temptation to see either your personal principles or pet objectives as so vitally important that they merge into a single cause—a cause which, in turn, inspires singleminded commitment. While such commitment can drive you to achieve your end, it also can blind you to the importance of maintaining a balance among the essential elements in a situation—ends, means, values, and circumstance.

Fortunately, CLOUT also provides the saving grace—the ability to see the "big picture." The "big picture" perspective enables you to conceptualize and bring into proper relationship these essential elements that contribute to effective managerial action. The way you blend these elements determines your style.

VARIATIONS OF STYLE

All managers with CLOUT are not carbon copies of each other. The "big picture" framework provides plenty of latitude for blending ends, means, values, and circumstance into a unique personal style, as the following examples show.

John D. Rockefeller, founder of Standard Oil, had a burning desire to industrialize America. His goal was to restructure industry to eliminate disorder and waste. To gain his ends he engaged in some outrageous business practices. So intent was he to attain his long-term industrialization goals that he didn't concern himself with immediate consequences of his actions, such as the economic and psychological suffering of those who got in his way.

Yet he taught Sunday School and expressed this often quoted philosophy: "The growth of a large business is merely a survival of the fittest. . . . The American Beauty Rose can be produced in the splendor and fragrance which bring cheer to its beholders only by sacrificing the early buds which grow up around it. This is not an evil tendency in business. It is merely the working-out of a law of nature and a law of God."[1]

Rockefeller built an industrial empire second to none and spent the latter years of his life in philanthropic endeavors.

Rockefeller blended ends, means, values, and circumstances in his own way. What he saw as "big picture," long-term gains made immediate inconveniences and hurt appear inconsequential (or at least, a necessary evil) to him, thereby posing no deterrent to his actions. The benefits to mankind in more jobs, higher living standards, and greater utilization of nature's products in long-term perspective justified to him, at least, stepping on those in his immediate path. His lack of concern for contemporaries actually seemed to derive from his broad interpretation of what God's work is all about.

By contrast, J. C. Penney, the department store executive, was known as the Golden Rule manager. He was driven by a moral fervor to help his contemporaries. He searched for means to make his values into long-term ends. Penney's mode of operation was to train a partner to go out and start another store. That manager would train another person, who, in turn, would repeat the process, and so on. The result was his chain-store system of department stores.

Like Rockefeller, Penney also adjusted his means to accomplish his goal. But Penney's goal was brotherhood, not industrialization. In the long run, his desire to help others resulted in both spiritual and material gain for Penney, as well as for others in the organization. Not only did he establish a system that multiplied the brotherhood effect, he ended up with thousands of manager-partners and a multimillion-dollar empire.

Among other familiar, nonbusiness leaders who displayed varying, distinctive styles are:

The crafty, cruel Ivan the Terrible, czar of Russia and the statesmanlike, philosophical Frederick the Great, king of Prussia; the daring, saloon-wrecking prohibition advocate Carrie Nation and the determined, spiritual founder of Christian Science, Mary Baker Eddy; the oppressive, warring Adolf Hitler, dictator of Germany and the defiant, nonviolent Mahatma Mohandas Gandhi, spiritual and political leader of India; the resourceful, articulate President Franklin D. Roosevelt and the decisive, "give 'em hell" President Harry Truman.

All of these leaders have made their marks on history. They shaped events by their actions. They shaped those around them by their style.

When you have CLOUT you leave your mark on those around you. When you can cut it, people do come trotting after you. Where you take them and how you take them there becomes your responsibility. It is an awesome responsibility and requires some serious thought.

FINDING YOUR PERSONAL STYLE

Here are some questions to help guide your thinking in your search for personal managerial style:

▶ How well and how properly are you serving your own purposes and needs?

▶ How well and how properly are you serving the purposes and needs of those you choose to lead?

▶ How well are you serving the values of your profession, your heritage—particularly those values you wish to preserve and those that nourished your own individual fulfillment?

▶ Are you both drawing from and giving to those people, organizations, and institutions that have significant meaning in your life?

▶ Are your actions derived from a logical perspective which includes both immediate and long-term considerations and consequences?

The answers to these questions will determine your own inviolable top values.

In the early pages of this book we said that taking action tests value limits—and values, in turn, set action limits. Furthermore, coming to grips with this two-way relationship determines managerial style. The concept should be clear to you now. In retrospect you can see how your experiences in the training program provided a testing ground for your values as well as for your skills. No doubt you heard your inner voice warn, "Hold it!" on various occasions. Other times you must have heard it urge, "Go for it!"

From personal, real-life experiences you've gained understanding of what you can do and what you really stand for. You know how your values affect your actions. You've had opportunity to make hard choices and take responsibility for outcomes. You've had occasion to choose realistic goals, view results in proper perspective, deal with inevitable side effects, live with the consequences of actions,

[219]

and realize that you can seldom please everybody.

You've seen that taking action—as a manager must—involves confrontation with options, issues, constituencies, and priorities. You've had a chance to make significant contributions and taste both the challenge and rewards of managerial mastery.

You have what you need to steer a conscious and positive course of action you can live with. You have what it takes to personalize CLOUT.

APPENDIX A:
THE NOTTIMS

BEHAVIORAL SKILLS
USED IN EFFECTIVE MANAGEMENT

MANAGING APPEARANCE

▸ Appears attractive (friendly, understanding, pleasant, flexible, open, trustworthy, optimistic)

▸ Appears credible (competent, knowledgeable, energetic, resourceful, action-oriented, decisive, confident, successful)

▸ Exhibits a driving enthusiasm

▸ Displays ambiguity
Clouds intent
Presents a goal-serving posture
—Appears prestigious (wealthy, powerful)
—Appears ordinary (average, conventional)
—Appears compliant (concerned, conforming, loyal)
—Appears indispensable

MANAGING EXPOSURE

▸ Maintains geographic mobility (moves about freely)
Makes exploring a habit
Seeks new experiences
Seeks new places
Seeks new people

▸ Maintains intellectual mobility
Makes inquiry a habit
Seeks new information
Identifies resources for present and future use
Seeks new perspectives

▸ Maintains high visibility
Draws positive attention to self
Deals directly with groups, formally
Deals directly with groups, informally
Seeks audience with the prestigious
Dares to be distinctive

[221]

- Controls accessibility

  Appears accessible

  Limits own accessibility

  Gets access to others despite barriers

MANAGING ATTITUDES AND PERSPECTIVES

- Keeps aspirations high

- Enjoys mastery

- Thinks highly of self

- Enjoys action

- Welcomes challenge

- Strives for excellence

- Sees defeat as temporary setback, not as failure

- Extends thinking beyond typical boundaries—thinks imaginatively

- Senses and resists external pressures, both subtle and obvious

- Resists dependence on external support

- Abandons the security of habit and sameness

- Visualizes the future in a useful, ordered way

- Looks actively at total environment

- Sees the "big picture"

  Sees how people and things relate

  Puts objectives into "big picture" perspective

  —Keeps end results constantly in mind; avoids being distracted by emotions

  —Tolerates immediate discomforts and inconveniences to achieve long-term satisfactions

  —Resists immediate gains to achieve greater remote gains

  —Ignores the immediate consequences of actions affecting others to achieve "big picture" goals

  —Avoids letting means become ends

  Holds ends and friends in "big picture" perspective

  —Can abandon or disregard friends for ends

—Can make friendships to further ends

—Can terminate ritualistic, unmeaningful friendships

—Can adjust ends to improve relationships

Holds rules and procedures in "big picture" perspective

—Understands rules and uses them to advantage

—Can break or alter rules and procedures to further ends

—Can hold others to conformity

Holds tradition, morality, and social propriety in "big picture" perspective

—Understands propriety and uses it to advantage

—Can abandon "proper" approach when circumstance warrants

—Can subordinate loyalties in favor of commitment to objective

Maintains a flexible concept of justice

—Serves ends, not ego

—Is somewhat pragmatic: what works is what's "right," within self-determined limits

MANAGING CIRCUMSTANCE

- Senses boundaries of situations and defines and shapes them to advantage

- Tries to determine territory and territorial limits; objectives and priorities; strategies, rules, and procedures; means and the general climate of means and values; performance standards and time limits; and membership

- Keeps risks within reason

- Manages information

  Establishes and nurtures sources

  Gathers and assimilates relevant facts

  Processes information perceptively

  Dispenses only needed information to others

- Defines and sets unique, generic, implementable ends (though they may not be disclosed)

[222]

- Manages priorities

  Concentrates on the important

  Delegates, postpones, or ignores less important things

- Fashions strategies

- Seeks analytical and technical help

- Seeks to maintain a continuing advantage

  Arranges new and better combinations of existing elements

  Initiates change

  —Sacrifices certainty for challenge

  —Lives with the consequences of change

  Finds problems

  Spots opportunity

  Discerns and seeks to control the indispensable resources

- Seeks power and influence for their utility

- Seeks responsibility

- Seeks command

- Makes and breaks alliances to further ends

MANAGING ACTION

- Makes single-minded commitment to goals

- Initiates and sustains action for self

- Initiates and sustains action for others

- Commits others to objectives

- Uses unique approach

- Gets results

  Seeks ends, not acceptance

  Finds alternative means

  Gets around obstacles

  Doesn't quit

  Works smart

  Works hard

- Legitimizes actions

- Popularizes actions

- Does the unpredictable and the unexpected

- Acts fast, decisively, and with assurance

- Makes decisions

  Takes action on the choice made

  Lives comfortably with the consequences of decision action

MANAGING TRANSACTIONS

- Nurtures relationships

  Moves in and about people with ease

  Meets and talks to new people with ease

  Builds quick rapport and friendships

  Improves existing relationships

  Sets a positive climate for relationships

  Makes others feel good

  Makes appropriate responses to appeals from others

  —Listens reflectively

  —Avoids moralizing

  Elicits desired response from others

  Terminates conversation with ease and grace

- Maintains independence

  Manages social distance

  Manages emotions

  Is unawed by authority

  Resists conforming

- Manages reciprocation

  Elects whether to accommodate others

  Can obligate others without becoming obligated

  Tolerates getting more and giving less

  Can live with breaking promises

- Influences others

  Establishes an appropriate image

  Persuades others

  Pressures others

  Supplies or withholds information

  Reveals or withholds feelings

  States or withholds opinion

[223]

Offers or withholds support

Gives or withholds rewards

- Delegates duties

Establishes relevant objectives

Establishes standards of performance

Releases personal control

Lives with the resulting consequence

- Develops others

Attracts competent people

Sets learning climate

Dispenses relevant information

Provides unique opportunities

Encourages excellence

Monitors progress

- Directs others

Takes unmistakable command

Makes assertive requests

Accepts responsibility for actions

- Seeks and extends control

Makes and uses contacts and connections

Gathers and assimilates information

Shuns advice when appropriate

Attracts and commits followers

Manages dominance

—Maintains autonomy

—Seeks consensus when expedient

—Interrupts when expedient

—Avoids being interrupted

Seeks and takes power

Takes responsibility

Assesses and tests the power, authority, resources, knowledge, competence, values, patience, loyalty, subservience, and independence of others

Talks to prestigious people with ease

Takes advantage of the competence as well as the incompetence of others

- Negotiates

Learns everything possible about the deal

Learns everything possible about the adversaries

Reads body language that betrays words

Introduces new ways of looking at issues

Welcomes new ideas

Sees ways of integrating benefits to all parties

Disregards saving face

Tests opponents' skill and power early

Pushes for quick settlement when holding the advantage

Seeks cooperation

Compromises in the light of reality

Induces stress when expedient

Maximizes advantage by influencing time, place, circumstance, and issues

Closes deals

Lives comfortably with outcome

- Manages the mode of transaction

Makes informal personal contacts

Makes formal personal contacts

Deals with individual group members

Deals with total group

Sends representatives

Writes messages

Uses telephone often, appropriately, and effectively

APPENDIX B:
NO DOUBT ABOUT CLOUT

To date hundreds of men and women have participated in this training program under our supervision. Included were undergraduate and graduate business administration students, active managers, military officers and personnel, and people who just wanted to increase their coping skills. The program's effectiveness is best proved by the increased capabilities and changed attitudes ascribed to it by those who have participated in the training.

To further substantiate their claims, we undertook an objective before-and-after testing program. Following is a brief summary of the procedure we employed and the significant results obtained.

SUBJECTS

We compared two groups of San Diego State University business administration majors who were enrolled in courses dealing with organizational behavior and interpersonal processes.

The experimental group—those enrolled in the training program—included sixty-six males and twenty-one females. The control group, which followed a more conventional experiential classroom program, was made up of twenty-seven males and ten females.

METHOD

Both groups were exposed to the usual conceptual learning that is appropriate to these kinds of classes. Students in the experimental group, however, spent ten weeks of the semester carrying out the self-administered exercises outlined in the training program, outside the classroom in the real world. To keep extrinsic pressure to a minimum, the point was continually made that grades in no way depended on compliance.

Students in the control group did classroom experiential exercises of a more conventional nature—role playing, games, simulations, individual and group coaching and practice, case dramatization, and other forms of small-group classroom experimentation.

A battery of six tests, camouflaged with meaningless titles, was administered to both groups at the beginning of the semester and again at the end of the semester.

The tests used were:

The Rathus Assertiveness Schedule

Measures assertiveness—the extent to which people insist on what is rightfully theirs in a forthright yet nonaggressive manner.[1]

The Rotter I/E Control Test

Measures the locus of control—the extent to which people are controlled by their own inner strengths or guided by external forces.[2]

The Coopersmith (adjusted by Bennett) Self-esteem Test

Measures the degree of self-assurance and self-worth people display.[3]

The Mach V Test

Measures the degree of Machiavellian tendency people possess. High Machiavellians display an ability *both* to conform *and* to deviate from convention to gain personal advantage. They display an ability *both* to establish *and* to use human relationships to advantage. They have an ability to stay on course and avoid being sidetracked by emotion.[4]

The Mitton Leadership Profile

Measures the tendency toward either an administrative or an entrepreneurial style.[5]

RESULTS

The hypothesis of the experiment was that those following the training program outlined in this book would increase their managerial ability, as reflected in the test scores. The results bore this out. The experimental group changed as follows:

▶ *Higher assertion*—as indicated by higher scores on Rathus.

▶ *Greater internal strength*—as indicated by lower scores on Rotter.

▶ *Higher self-esteem*—as indicated by higher scores on Coopersmith.

▶ *Higher Machiavellianism*—as indicated by higher scores on Mach V.

▶ *Increased entrepreneurial style*—as indicated by lower scores on Mitton.

In each test set the shift in characteristics measured in the experimental group was statistically significant. No changes of statistical significance took place in the control group.*

Although there were no significant differences between male and female subjects in initial test scores, women in the experimental group tended to increase their self-esteem more than men by the conclusion of the experiment.†

CONCLUSIONS

The experiment indicates that the training method described in this book is superior to the traditional method of in-class experiential training in changing people as measured by these tests.

The evidence indicates that significant changes in attitudes and perspectives do take place after exposure to the training. This is perhaps even more meaningful in view of the short training time (ten weeks) made necessary by the class format and semester time limitations. We feel that even better results are obtained when participants proceed entirely at their own pace.

Further proof of the program's effectiveness comes from the testimonials of the participants, who report that they can do things they've never done before—with satisfaction and self-assurance—to get results they want.

---

* The null hypothesis was tested using matched-pairs t-test. For the experimental group the null hypothesis was rejected for each test ($p < .001$), and all mean differences were in the hypothesized direction. For the control group there was no significant change for each test ($p > .05$).

† Significant at the .005 level.

CHAPTER NOTES

CHAPTER 1

[1] *Hombre* (Beverly Hills, Calif.: Hombré Productions, Twentieth Century-Fox Film Corporation, 1967). Adapted from Elmore Leonard, *Hombre* (Westminster, Md.: Ballantine Books, 1974).

CHAPTER 4

[1] Max Ways, "Hall of Fame of Business Leadership," *Fortune,* January 1975, pp. 64–72.

CHAPTER 7

[1] Kaiser Industries Corporation, *The Kaiser Story* (Oakland, Calif., 1968).

[2] "On the Move: To the New Generation of Skateboarders, Frank Nasworthy is Mr. Wheels," *People,* July 5, 1976, pp. 32–35.

CHAPTER 8

[1] "Mary Tyler Moore Show," © 1976 by MTM Enterprises, Inc. (Studio City, Calif.).

CHAPTER 10

[1] Robert Hessen, *Steel Titan: The Life of Charles H. Schwab* (New York: Oxford University Press, 1975), pp. 13–21.

[2] Quoted in "The Corporate Woman: Up the Ladder, Finally," *Business Week,* November 24, 1975, pp. 58–68.

[3] Jon Jecker and David Landy, "Liking a Person as a Function of Doing Him a Favor," *Human Relations* 22 (1969): 371–78.

CHAPTER 11

[1] Thomas Moriarty, "A Nation of Willing Victims," *Psychology Today,* April 1975, pp. 43–50.

[2] Quoted in "The Wooden Style," *Time,* February 12, 1973, p. 67.

[3] *Ibid.,* p. 66.

[4] Quoted in J. W. Weiner, "ITT: Can Profits Be Programmed?" *Dun's Review,* November 1965, pp. 39–41, 103–4.

[5] "Clubby World of ITT," *Time,* March 27, 1972, p. 86.

[6] Michael H. Hart, *The 100: A Ranking of the Most Influential Persons in History* (New York: Hart Publishing Co., 1978).

CHAPTER 12

[1] For an interesting discussion on group decisions and group influence, see Irving Janis, *Victims of Groupthink* (Boston: Houghton Mifflin, 1972).

[2] Quoted in Alexander Stuart, "Citizen Connally: The Businessman You Never Knew," *Fortune,* July 31, 1978, p. 91.

[3] *Ibid.,* p. 88.

CHAPTER 13

[1] J. Mel Hickerson, *Ernie Breech: The Story of His Remarkable Career at General Motors, Ford, and TWA* (New York: Meredith Press, 1968), pp. 64–69.

[2] Ruth Brandon, *A Capitalist Romance: Singer & the Sewing Machine* (Philadelphia: Lippincott, 1977).

CHAPTER 14

[1] Louis Krarr, "Roy Ash Is Having Fun at Addressogrief-Multigrief," *Fortune,* February 27, 1978, p. 48.

[2] *Ibid.,* p. 47.

[3] Allen Nevins, *Ford: The Times, the Man, the Company* (New York: Scribner's, 1954), pp. 72–76.

[4] *Ibid.,* pp. 568–87.

[5] Quoted in "Where Being Nice to Workers Didn't Work," *Business Week,* January 20, 1973, p. 98. © 1973 by McGraw-Hill, Inc. All Rights Reserved.

[6] John Brooks, *Once in Golconda* (New York: Harper & Row, 1969), p. 265.

[7] Quoted in "Irvine: Taking an Unexpected Route to Reduce Its Huge Debt," *Business Week,* April 10, 1978, p. 107.

[8] *Ibid.*

[9] Quoted in Arthur M. Louis, "John deButt's Long March from Trainee to Chairman," *Fortune,* December 1976, p. 124.

[10] Quoted in Robert Hessen, *Steel Titan: The Life of Charles M. Schwab* (New York: Oxford University Press, 1975), p. 179.

[11] *Ibid.,* pp. 178–79.

[12] "The Way I Make My Numbers Is for You Guys to Make Your Numbers," excerpted from *Forbes,* February 15, 1972, p. 26.

[13] "Why Northwest Airlines Is No. 1 in Profits," *Business Week,* February 16, 1976, pp. 78–80; "Tough Truckline," *Wall Street Journal,* April 12, 1977, p. 1.

[14] Quoted in "Everyone Who Makes It Has a Mentor," *Harvard Business Review,* July-August, 1978, p. 97.

[15] Quoted in Louis, "John deButts's Long March," p. 131.

[16] *Ibid.*

[17] *Ibid.,* p. 133.

[18] Quoted in "Women Finally Get Mentors of Their Own," *Business Week,* October 23, 1978, p. 74.

[19] *Ibid.*

[20] Quoted in "Up the Ladder, Finally," *Business Week,* November 24, 1975, p. 62.

[21] *Ibid.,* p. 64.

CHAPTER 15

[1] Quoted in Harold Seneker, "Machiavelli, Meet U.S. Home," *Forbes,* November 27, 1978, p. 124.

[2] *Ibid.,* pp. 122–24.

[3] Quoted in *Los Angeles Times,* October 5, 1977, part 1, pp. 1, 22.

[4] Jim Murray, "Attila of Football," *Los Angeles Times,* January 3, 1979, part 3, p. 1. Copyright © 1979, Los Angeles Times. Reprinted with permission.

[5] "Laureates from Two Centuries," *Fortune,* January 1975, p. 70.

[6] "Behind AT&T's Change at the Top," *BusinessWeek,* November 6, 1978, pp. 114–15.

[7] Hugh Sidey, "The Presidency: The Virtue of Secrecy," *Time,* January 1, 1979, p. 61.

[8] Ozzie Nelson, *Ozzie* (Englewood Cliffs, N.J.: Prentice-Hall, 1973), pp. 144–46.

[9] "The Fight that Fairchild Won," *BusinessWeek,* October 5, 1968, pp. 106–13.

[10] Dan Fischer, "Khrushchev Couldn't Hold Back Tears," *Los Angeles Times,* December 18, 1978, part 1, pp. 1, 9.

[11] Andrew Tobias, *Fire and Ice* (New York: William Morrow, 1977).

[12] *Ibid.,* p. 59.

[13] "Revlon without Revson," *Forbes,* June 26, 1978, pp. 42–47.

[14] Mathew Josephson, *Edison* (New York: McGraw-Hill, 1959), pp. 178–89.

[15] Quoted in "Gut Decision Making," *Forbes,* June 1, 1968, p. 25.

[16] Josephson, *Edison,* p. 99.

CHAPTER 16

[1] Quoted in William James Ghent, *Our Benevolent Feudalism* (New York: Macmillan, 1902), p. 29.

APPENDIX B

[1] Spencer A. Rathus, "A 30-Item Schedule for Assessing Assertive Behavior," *Behavior Therapy* 4, no. 3 (May 1973): 398–406.

[2] Julian B. Rotter, "Generalized Expectancies for Internal versus External Control of Reinforcement," *Psychological Monographs: General and Applied* 80, no. 1, whole no. 609 (1966).

[3] Stanley Coopersmith, *The Antecedents of Self-esteem* (San Francisco: W. H. Freeman, 1967), pp. 265–66; L. A. Bennett, D. E. Sorensen, and H. Forshay, "The Application of Self-esteem Measures in a Correctional Setting," *Journal of Research in Crime and Delinquency* 8, no. 1 (1971): 1–9.

[4] Richard Christie, Florence R. Geis, et al., *Studies in Machiavellianism* (New York: Academic Press, 1970), pp. 22–25.

[5] Daryl G. Mitton, "Dimensions of Leadership Style," *Management of Personnel Quarterly* (Winter 1971): 9–12.

INDEX